Complete British Animals

Paul Sterry

Collins

HarperCollins*Publishers* Ltd.
77–85 Fulham Palace Road
London W6 8JB

The Collins website address is:
www.collins.co.uk

Collins is a registered trademark of
HarperCollins*Publishers* Ltd.

First published in 2005

A catalogue record for this book is available from the British Library.

ISBN 0 00 720137 0

Acknowledgements
I would like to thank Andrew Cleave MBE for his assistance and encouragement with this project,
and for allowing me to have access to Bramley Frith Environmental Education Centre, where many
of the photographs were taken.

Edited and designed by D & N Publishing
Lambourn Woodlands, Hungerford, Berkshire.

Colour reproduction by Nature Photographers Ltd.

Printed in Hong Kong by Printing Express Ltd.

CONTENTS

INTRODUCTION TO BRITISH ANIMALS

The word 'animal' can mean different things to different people. In a scientific context, it is used to describe all living organisms other than plants and fungi. But in more general use it is often employed in a rather arbitrary, catch-all sense simply to embrace whatever creatures the speaker has in mind. Given this potential for ambiguity it is important to clarify at the outset what the word means in the context of this book: *Complete British Animals* covers the vertebrate groups of mammals, reptiles and amphibians.

On the face of it, Britain and Ireland are not promising destinations for the prospective animal enthusiast. The land mass covered by the region is comparatively small and fragmented, and this alone might be expected to have a bearing on the extent of our mammal, amphibian and reptile fauna. Furthermore, geographical isolation from mainland Europe since the end of the last Ice Age has meant that many terrestrial animals have been unable to colonise of their own accord. However, despite these shortcomings, a wealth of animal life can still be found in the region and some species that do occur here do so at higher densities than in adjacent areas of mainland Europe. Underpinning this diversity is the rich array of habitats to be found in Britain and Ireland, the product of our region's topography, geology and history of land use. Good fortune, in the form of the Gulf Stream, dictates a mild and comparatively equitable climate for much of the time. And the sea itself contributes to the diversity of animal life, too: seals live around our shores and the open oceans harbour cetaceans, although it has to be said that comparatively few of them venture close to land. And we must not forget humankind's contribution – unfortunately largely negative – in the form of the introduction of alien species (frequently unwelcome when seen with hindsight) and the persecution and extinction of many native animals.

It is probably fair to say that mammals, reptiles and amphibians have traditionally always been poor relations to birds in terms of their popularity among people with a general interest in natural history. In the case of mammals this is, to a degree, understandable, because many species are either secretive, nocturnal or both, hampering people's ability to observe, and hence enjoy, them. In the case of reptiles and amphibians, they tend to be easily visible for just a few brief weeks or months of the year.

The study of the region's animals may not always be easy but it certainly has its rewards, and budding animal observers soon begin to relish the challenge for its own sake. Given a year or so, anyone with the smallest amount of determination and a willingness to travel can easily observe the majority of British and Irish animal species. With some creatures it is simply a matter of knowing where and when to look, while for others a degree of fieldcraft or prior knowledge is helpful. *Complete British Animals* aims to provide the reader with a thorough grounding in the identification, biology and behaviour of British animals. But with fieldcraft in mind, the book also seeks to provide tips and guidelines to make observation easier and more rewarding. Simply observing animals in the wild can be fun in itself. But many people will want to take things further, and *Complete British Animals* aims to help in this regard.

THE REGION COVERED BY THIS BOOK

The region covered by this book comprises the whole of mainland England, Wales, Scotland and Ireland, as well as offshore islands including the Shetlands, Orkneys, Hebrides, Isle of Man and the Scilly Isles. In addition, I have also included the Channel Islands in this book because their proximity to, and ecological affinities with, northern France makes a valuable contribution to our wildlife. Lastly, the seas surrounding our islands are also included in the geographical extent of this book because of their obvious significance to seals, whales and dolphins. Although many of the latter two groups spend much of their lives out of sight of land, they are just as much a part of our wildlife heritage as terrestrial species and, with the rise in popularity of pelagic trips, they are now accessible to the 21st-century animal-watcher.

THE CHOICE OF SPECIES

All regularly occurring native and alien terrestrial species that live in the wild in Britain and Ireland are included in *Complete British Animals*. In the case of cetaceans, both those of seasonal and year-round occurrence are featured. Furthermore, for completeness sake I have included animals with domesticated cousins that exist as feral populations in the wild today, or those whose ancestors roamed our region wild and free in the distant past.

HOW TO USE THIS BOOK

This book has been designed so that the text and photographs for each species are on facing pages. Labels state clearly the identity and, if appropriate, the age and sex of each species shown.

By and large, the order in which the species appear in the main section of the book roughly follows the standard systematic classification of mammals, reptiles and amphibians, which is the system that is adopted by most other field guides. However, in a few instances I have tinkered with the standard running order to allow, for example, unrelated species with habits in common (for example, seals and cetaceans) to be grouped together.

SPECIES DESCRIPTIONS

At the start of each species description the most commonly used and current English name is given. This is followed by the scientific name of the animal in question, which comprises the species' genus name first, followed by its specific name. In a few instances, reference is made, either in the species heading or the main body of the text, to a further subdivision – subspecies – where this is pertinent. There then follows some measure of the species' size. In most instances the length is given, but for bats wingspan is provided and with deer shoulder height is the given dimension.

The text has been written in as concise a manner as possible. To avoid potential ambiguities in species descriptions, the adult and juvenile appearances are described first, including any differences between the appearance of the sexes. Information is then given about the voice of the animal.

HABITAT AND STATUS

Many of our animals are habitat-specific and so information is provided about their preferences and predilections. Not only does this help narrow down the field for observers trying to identify a mystery mammal, reptile or amphibian, but it can also be used as a pointer if it is desired to seek out actively a particular species. I have also provided some details about the distribution and status of each species in the region. Where the information is available, a rough indication of population numbers is given. The figures are necessarily very rough estimates – many animals are difficult to survey with any great accuracy, and in all cases populations (especially those of small mammals) fluctuate from year to year, and from season to season. So, treat these figures as guides, and not as definitive population figures.

HABITS AND NATURAL HISTORY

Mammals, reptiles and amphibians lead complex and interesting lives, and as a reflection of this I have included as much information as possible about their habits and natural history. Details are provided about diet, day-to-day social life and behaviour, breeding and, if appropriate, territoriality.

OBSERVATION TIPS

For each species I have provided information that should help the animal-watcher pinpoint the species in question, or at least improve the chances of discovery or observation. In some cases, tips are provided that will help distinguish the animal from any superficially similar cousins.

MAPS AND CALENDAR BARS

The maps show the distribution and occurrence of each species in the region. Species that have incredibly precise habitat requirements will have well-defined boundaries to their presence or absence in the region. However, for most animals things are not so clear-cut and their occurrence does not end abruptly. To reflect this, a graded fading of colour to white (absence) is used. With maps for terrestrial species, the sea area is grey.

Key to terrestrial animal maps
■ Areas where quite common and widespread.
■ Areas where scarce but still widespread.

Key to marine mammals occurring year-round
■ Areas where observed on a regular basis.
■ Areas where scarce.
■ Areas where rare.
■ Areas from which the species is absent.

Key to marine mammals occurring seasonally
■ Areas of regular occurrence.
■ Areas from which the species is absent.

The maps represent the current ranges of animals in the region in general terms. Please bear in mind that, given the size of the maps, small and isolated populations will not necessarily be featured. Furthermore, the ranges of some marine species in particular change from year to year.

Alongside the maps can be seen a calendar bar, giving further information about the species in question. Where appropriate, three colours have been used to colour the months of the year. They denote the following: ▆ = period of general activity; ▆ = breeding season (when the species is generally active as well); ▆ = hibernation. In the case of mammals, the breeding season is taken to cover the period of gestation to the point where the young are weaned (periods of delayed implantation or delayed fertilisation are not included); with reptiles, the breeding season covers the period from the point of fertilisation of the eggs to their hatching; in the case of amphibians, the breeding season is taken to cover the period from fertilisation of the eggs to metamorphosis of the larvae to adults.

PHOTOGRAPHS

Great care has gone into the selection of photographs for this book and in many cases the images have been taken specifically for this project. Preference was given to photographs that serve both to illustrate key identification features and to emphasise the beauty of the animal in question. Wherever possible I have tried to avoid the rigid constraints of previous photographic guides, adopting instead contemporary approaches to design that make full use of computer software.

For each species, the right-hand page has an appropriate habitat as a backdrop, on which is overlayed a photograph of the animal in question in its most typical form. Additional inset photographs, both on this page and on the text page, depict other interesting aspects of the species; these include close-ups of different parts of the body, tracks, droppings and skulls.

GLOSSARY

Adult – a full-grown and sexually mature animal that is capable of breeding.

Amplexus – the mating embrace adopted by paired frogs and toads where the male grasps the female with his front legs. This strategy ensures the success of external fertilisation and reduces the risk of competition from competing males.

Arboreal – tree-dwelling.

Blow – the spout of a whale as air is expelled from the lungs via the nostrils.

Calcar – a hardened, rodlike structure arising from the ankle of a bat and used to provide support to the edge of the tail membrane in flight.

Carnivore – an animal that feeds on meat and whose teeth, digestive system and behaviour are adapted to this lifestyle.

Caudal – relating to the tail.

Cloaca – the point where the digestive, urinary and reproductive tracts meet and their contents are expelled via a single opening.

Crepuscular – active at dusk.

Cryptic – camouflage markings that allow an animal to blend in with its surroundings. The term can also be applied to an animal's way of life.

Delayed implantation – the process in mammals where attachment of the early embryonic stage to the wall of the uterus is delayed; comparatively few mammals adopt this strategy and the length of the delay varies according to the species concerned.

Echolocation – the method by which a bat perceives its surroundings, involving the interpretation of reflected high-frequency sound, the source of the sound being the bat itself.

Diurnal – active during the daylight hours.

Dorsal – relating to the upper surface of an animal.

Feral – a previously domesticated animal that now lives in the wild.

Gestation – the period spent by a developing mammalian embryo and infant in the mother's uterus.

Herbivore – an animal that feeds on plant material.

Hibernation – a state of winter dormancy in which the animal in question's activity, body temperature and energy requirements are greatly reduced.

Hybrid – an animal with parents of different species.

Insectivore – strictly speaking, an animal that feeds exclusively on insects, although the term is often used to embrace those with a wider diet that includes other invertebrates.

Invertebrate – an animal without a backbone.

Juvenile – a sexually immature animal.

Lactation – the production of milk from mammary glands, employed by mammals to feed their infants.

Latrine – a localised spot where certain mammal species deposit faeces on a regular, and cumulative, basis.

Metamorphosis – the process whereby the larval stage of an amphibian (a tadpole) is transformed, morphologically, into an adult.

Nocturnal – active after dark.

Peduncle – the basal stalk from which deer antlers grow.

Predator – an animal that hunts and kills live prey.

Prehensile – capable of gripping; used in the context, for example, of a Harvest Mouse's tail.

Refection – the process where the (relatively undigested) product of food's first passage through the digestive system is consumed again in order to extract more nutritional value and, in some cases, water; seen, for example, in shrews and lagomorphs.

Species – a group of genetically similar individuals, members of which can reproduce with one another and produce viable offspring. Typically, members of different species cannot interbreed and produce viable offspring, although some members of the amphibian world challenge the concept.

Spermatophore – a packet of sperm, produced by male newts and transferred to females to ensure fertilisation of the eggs.

Subspecies – a geographically isolated population of individuals of a given species that possess morphological characters and an external appearance different from populations elsewhere in the species' range.

Tadpole – the larval stage of an amphibian.

Tragus – a projection of skin seen at the front of the ears of bats.

Ventral – referring to the under surface of the body of an animal.

Vertebrate – an animal with a backbone.

CLASSIFICATION

Over the centuries, successive generations of natural historians and scientists have examined and explored the natural world. Gradually, the relationships between species have been teased out, understood and defined, and the resulting hierarchy is referred to as 'classification'. A brief summary of this may help the reader gain a better understanding of the relationships between the animal species covered by this book.

Within the overall scheme of things, members of the animal kingdom are assigned to a number of *phyla* (singular *phylum*), this term being applied to the most important categories of related animals. The phylum to which all creatures with a vertebral column belong is called Chordata (the chordates). Animals that lack this feature are called invertebrates and are placed in a spectrum of additional phyla that include protozoans (single-celled animals), coelenterates (jellyfish and their allies), annelids (earthworms, leeches and their relatives), arthropods (insects, crustaceans and spiders), molluscs (snails and their relatives) and echinoderms (sea-urchins, starfish and their allies).

The most significant members of the chordate group are those that possess a vertebral column made of bone or cartilage; they are placed in a subdivision – subphylum Vertebrata – commonly called the vertebrates, within which there are five further categories or classes. *Complete British Animals* deals with three of these: amphibians, reptiles and mammals; fishes and birds, the two remaining vertebrate classes, are covered by companion volumes. Classes are then further divided into groups called orders that contain smaller divisions, each of which is called a family. Each family will contain a number of genera (singular genus), members of which (species) share the same genus name (the first part of an animal's scientific name) while having different specific names (the second part of such). A combination of the two means that every animal, indeed every named living organism, has its own unique scientific name.

For Britain and Ireland, amphibians are divided into two orders: the Urodela (or Caudata) (newts); and the Anura (frogs and toads). Our reptile fauna comprises three orders: Sauria (lizards); Serpentia (snakes); and Chelonia (turtles and terrapins). Mammals are the most diverse of the three classes covered by *Complete British Animals*. In the context of Britain and Ireland, the group embraces 10 classes: Insectivora (shrews and Mole); Chiroptera (bats); Lagomorpha (hares and Rabbit); Rodentia (mice, voles and rats); Cetacea (whales and dolphins); Carnivora (Fox, Wildcat and mustelids); Pinnipedia (seals); Perissodactyla (horses); Artiodactyla (deer, cattle, goats and sheep); and Diprodontia (Red-necked Wallaby).

BASIC BIOLOGY

There are obvious and striking morphological differences between amphibians, reptiles and mammals, and these features make members of each group readily separable from one another at a glance. However, beyond the superficial, there are in addition fundamental differences in the biology of the three groups. As a consequence, while some mammals, reptiles and amphibians may have diets and habitats in common, they all lead radically different lives and are adapted to survive and reproduce in completely different ways.

AMPHIBIANS

You only have to pick up a frog or toad to discover that it has a rather soft and supple skin. In common with other amphibians the dermis lacks the cornified (hardened) layer seen in reptiles, and this means that the animals are, to a degree, more vulnerable to damage caused by predators or the rigours of day-to-day life. More significantly, perhaps, water loss occurs more rapidly in amphibians than in reptiles, and as a consequence most are tied to water, or at least to damp environments. Desiccation is combated by the secretion of mucus, but on the plus side the soft skin and proximity of blood vessels below the surface allow oxygen to be absorbed directly into the body. The colour of the skin can also be modified to match the amphibian's surroundings, a useful ploy when it comes to avoiding detection by predators. The skin is shed or 'sloughed' periodically; typically, its owner then eats it.

Amphibians cannot generate internal body heat in the same way that birds and mammals do. Consequently, in biological terms they are classed as 'ectothermic' animals, and more popularly thought of as cold-blooded. A more satisfactory way of describing their thermoregulation would be to say that the environment around them determines their body temperature. However, amphibian behaviour ensures that they avoid excessive heat and cold, and so their relationship with their environment is far from passive.

The dependency of amphibians on water goes beyond the need simply to avoid desiccation because, among native British and Irish species at least, reproduction takes place in the aquatic environment. Although each species may be unique in terms of its favoured habitat, courtship behaviour and the appearance of its young stages, the development stages of all amphibians conform to the same basic plan. For the enthusiastic student of natural history, the amphibian life-cycle has one distinct advantage over those of its relatives. Unlike reptiles and mammals, where development occurs inside an opaque shell, or within the body of the mother, in amphibians all the large-scale changes are clearly visible to the naked eye. I have chosen to illustrate the amphibian reproductive cycle using the Common Frog because it is familiar to most naturalists.

As is the case with other amphibians, layers of jelly surround the egg of a Common Frog. These swell on contact with water to produce a protective, transparent bubble through which oxygen can pass and waste products can diffuse into the water. Inside, the developing embryo is nourished by a yolk sac and it soon comes to resemble a dark 'comma'. The length of time spent in the egg is influenced by water temperature, but generally after a couple of weeks a tiny tadpole, with stubby external gills, hatches. Feeding on a diet of grazed algae and detritus, the tadpole grows, the external gills become resorbed and the tail size increases, allowing it to become free-swimming. External legs then appear – the hind pair followed by the front pair – and the diet begins to incorporate more animal material. As larval development reaches its final stages, the tail shrinks and is absorbed, while the body shape itself metamorphoses into something resembling a miniature adult frog. By the time the transformed tadpole leaves the water (usually 3–4 months after spawning) the tail has all but disappeared and froglets really do resemble miniature adults, albeit ones with proportionately large heads.

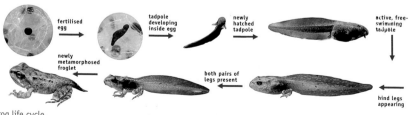

fertilised egg

tadpole developing inside egg

newly hatched tadpole

active, free-swimming tadpole

newly metamorphosed froglet

both pairs of legs present

hind legs appearing

Frog life cycle.

REPTILES

The tough, and in parts hardened, outer layer of a reptile's skin is a distinctive feature of the group as a whole. With snakes and lizards, it takes the form of plates or 'scales'. The fact that the scales overlap, and are embedded in less hardened skin, affords these reptiles a considerable degree of body flexibility and, in many cases, allows speedy movement. Lizards, or at least those with external legs, use them to run at speed, while legless lizards and snakes employ muscular, S-shaped movements of the body to achieve forward propulsion; the ventral scales gain purchase on the ground and the body is flexible enough to allow them to move relative to one another. In turtles and terrapins, much of the body is enclosed by an inflexible shell comprising horny plates that abut one another; the neck and limbs, which are more flexible, protrude through openings in the shell.

Having a tough layer of skin provides reptiles with a degree of protection from predators and from physical damage. It also helps reduce water loss and, as a consequence, many species are able to survive well away from water and in comparatively dry habitats. Snakes and lizards periodically shed or 'slough' the outer layer of skin.

Like their amphibian cousins, almost all reptiles are ectothermic creatures, unable to generate their own body heat. However, to use the term 'cold-blooded' would be misleading because they are extremely adept, in behavioural terms, at gaining the optimum amount of heat from their surroundings; they make use of radiated heat from the sun and heat absorbed from the ground they are resting on. On a summer's day, a reptile's blood is likely to be decidedly warm! The downside of being dependent upon external sources of heat is that British reptiles have to hibernate during the winter months. The exception to the ectothermic rule in reptiles is the Leatherback Turtle, which can generate its own body heat and whose immense body size allows for heat retention. This unique feature explains why it is able to swim in the chilly seas of the North Atlantic.

The developmental stages of reptiles occur inside an egg with an opaque shell; in some species (such as the Grass Snake, shown here) the eggs are deposited in the ground, while in a few reptiles they develop inside the body of the mother. Consequently, it is impossible for the average naturalist to follow the developmental stages, and they must be satisfied by the knowledge that what emerges from the egg is a miniature version of an adult, perfect in every detail.

MAMMALS

In terms of their ability to make the most of the environment in which they live, the most fundamental advantage that mammals have over reptiles and amphibians is their ability to generate body heat and maintain a more or less constant internal temperature by a complex regime of thermoregulation. Consequently, they are, to a degree, independent of whatever the weather can throw at them and, seen as a whole, the spectrum of mammal species is able to exploit almost all terrestrial and aquatic habitats partly as a consequence of being warm-blooded. In land-based mammals at least, the presence of hair is another defining character and one that is inextricably linked to the regulation of heat loss; as a result, many species have thicker coats in winter than in summer.

In all mammals, fertilisation is internal and, with the exception of marsupials, the embryo and developing infant is nourished via a placenta, which is implanted at an early stage. Young placental mammals are born with varying degrees

Young mammals, such as this Grey Seal pup, suckle milk from their mothers as their main source of nutrition in the early stages of life.

of independence and maturity depending on the species involved – baby mice are blind and naked, while a newborn deer is capable of standing on its legs within an hour or so.

THE ORIGINS OF BRITISH SPECIES

Terrestrial animal species that occur naturally in Britain and Ireland colonised the region in the wake of the last Ice Age, some 10,000 years ago, before rising sea levels flooded the land bridges that linked what we now call mainland Europe to Britain, and Britain to Ireland. Since that time, humankind has been responsible for some significant extinctions in our region – Brown Bear, Wolf, Reindeer and Beaver to name but four. There have also been a number of alien introductions, both accidental and deliberate, to the region – Brown and Black Rats, Grey Squirrel, American Mink and Muntjac, for example – and people have also been responsible (irresponsible might be a better way of putting it) for relocating native species to parts of our region where previously they did not occur; the introduction of Hedgehogs to certain offshore islands is a case in point.

HABITATS FOR ANIMALS

A combination of geology, geography and historical land use has conspired to create a wealth of different habitats in Britain and Ireland, and we are indeed fortunate to live in an area that boasts such a diverse array. By and large, British and Irish habitats are fragmented. However, the mosaic effect created by the juxtaposition of several different habitats does mean that a surprising diversity of animal life can sometimes be found in a comparatively small area.

Although a few animals are rather catholic in their choice of habitat, naturalists soon come to realise that the majority have much more specific needs. Their behaviour, feeding requirements, and indeed structure, have evolved to suit special niches in particular habitats. However, although a species may be habitat-specific, it does not follow that it will be found in *all* examples of this habitat throughout the region. Climatic factors can have a profound effect on a species' range, influencing, for example, the ability of an animal to feed, or more profoundly, to survive extreme weather. And, of course, humans must be factored into the equation too: extermination of certain animals at the local level is almost commonplace.

Fundamentally, the character of any given habitat is influenced, and in some cases, determined, by the geography and geology of the area, and this manifests itself in botanical composition. However, humans continue to play a part in the appearance of the landscape and this is the single most significant factor affecting the majority of wildlife-rich sites today. Only some of our coastal habitats and a few remote areas of the highest mountaintops can truly be said to have escaped human interference over the last few centuries.

It would be a mistake to view all human influence as being to the detriment of wildlife diversity, and indeed some habitats, such as heathland, owe their very existence to the clearance of trees from the land. As an example of a positive contemporary role, woodland management carried out in a traditional manner can exert a beneficial influence on plant and animal diversity. Indeed, active land management is an integral part of the day-to-day work undertaken on almost all nature reserves.

For some naturalists, studying the distinctions between our different habitats may seem a rather abstract pursuit, and one that lacks relevance to their everyday activities. However, it really is worth spending time familiarising yourself with their basic characters and differences for more practical reasons. Developing an understanding of the habitat in which an animal lives will help you appreciate more fully the life of the creature in question, and help set it in the context of the environment as a whole. From a more practical point of view, by being able to recognise a habitat at a glance means you will save yourself a lot of time and effort when it comes to pinning down localised species. Habitat preferences are also a useful clue to the identity of certain animals.

The following pages detail all of our most characteristic and distinctive habitats. Within each habitat section there is information about their character and vegetation, along with their significance to mammals, reptiles and amphibians, and the key species for which they are best known.

WOODLAND

Although the forests that once cloaked Britain and Ireland have long since gone, many parts of England, Wales and Scotland still harbour pockets of woodland; some of these are large enough to retain a wilderness feel and a characteristic array of forest plants and animals. Ireland fares less well in terms of woodland and consequently its tally of forest animals is less impressive.

Deciduous woodlands are found throughout most of the region and are (or would be, if allowed to flourish) the dominant natural forest type everywhere except in parts of Scotland where, locally, evergreen conifers predominate. As their name suggests, deciduous trees shed their leaves in autumn and grow a new set the following spring. The seasonality seen in deciduous woodland is among the most marked and easily observed of any habitat in the region.

Almost all woodland in the region has been, and still is, influenced in some way by humans. This can take the form of simple disturbance by walkers at one end of the spectrum or clear-felling at the other.

The human influence is not always harmful to wildlife, however, and sympathetic coppicing of Hazel, for example, is seen as a vital element in the strategy for Hazel Dormouse conservation.

Within their overall ranges, Bank Voles, Wood Mice and Grey Squirrels are generally common and widespread, while Yellow-necked Mice and Hazel Dormice occur locally, mainly in the south. Moles are often surprisingly numerous woodland residents, given suitable soil conditions, while Common and Pygmy Shrews favour woodland clearings and marginal scrub. Although not exclusively woodland dwellers, Brown Hares and Rabbits often reside where the boundaries abut open country, and in similar locations Foxes and Badgers sometimes excavate their underground retreats. Depending on the region, one or more deer species usually occupies deciduous woodland, although in many areas they are excluded by disturbance caused by humans and their dogs. Deciduous woodlands are also home to a significant proportion of our bat species: they find winter and summer retreats in tree holes and crevices, and food in the form of night-flying insects. Deciduous woodland is not a classic habitat for reptiles and amphibians. Having said that, however, Common Frogs, Common Toads and newts are likely to occur in the vicinity of woodland ponds outside the breeding season and, where the woodland in question is open and sited on sandy soil, Adders may occur along the woodland rides.

Coniferous woodlands do exist as a native habitat in the region but are restricted to a few relict pockets of Caledonian pine forest in the Highlands of Scotland. Seen anywhere else in Britain and Ireland, conifers (mainly alien species) will either have been planted or will have seeded themselves from nearby mature plantations. Around half the woodland cover in the region today consists of conifer plantations.

Unlike deciduous trees, conifers are, with the exception of a few species, evergreen and keep their leaves throughout the year. Instead of having broad, often rounded leaves, they have narrow ones called needles. Their flowers and seeds are borne in structures called cones, and the shape of the trees themselves is often conical in outline.

Areas of native Caledonian pine forest in Scotland support an interesting range of species: Wildcats are more or less restricted to this terrain; and Pine Martens and Red Squirrels are probably at their most numerous in these forests, although mature conifer plantations further south do support these species. Generally speaking, plantation conifer woodland supports a limited biodiversity compared to its native, deciduous counterpart. Many general woodland mammals may occur, but invariably their numbers are low.

HEDGEROWS AND SCRUB

Once so much a feature of the British countryside, hedgerows have suffered a dramatic decline in recent decades, grubbed out by farmers keen to expand arable field sizes, or, more insidiously, wrecked – both in terms of appearance and in their value to wildlife – by inappropriate cutting regimes. While many landowners remain indifferent to the plight of this valuable wildlife resource, there does appear to be something of a resurgence in interest in hedgerows in the countryside at large: their value, both in wildlife terms, and as stock-proof barriers and windbreaks, is again appreciated by many.

The extent of scrub in the landscape has also diminished in recent times. Although difficult to define in strict habitat terms, most people would understand the word to mean a loose assemblage of tangled, medium-sized shrubs and bushes interspersed with patches of spreading plants such as Bramble and areas of grassland. Scrub is frequently despised

by landowners – sometimes even by naturalists too – but its value to many species formerly considered so common and widespread as not to merit conservation attention should not be underestimated.

Hedgerows usually comprise the species, and acquire the character of, any woodland edge in the vicinity. Scrub, too, reflects the botanical composition of the surrounding area although, because it is essentially a colonising habitat and not an established one, the dominant bushes and shrubs tend to be those that are fastest growing.

Both habitats are often favoured by species otherwise associated with woodland margins. Bank Voles, Wood Mice, and Common and Pygmy Shrews all occur, and Stoats and Weasels take their toll of these small mammals. Although hard to detect, Harvest Mice are sometimes present and Rabbits excavate sizeable warrens, often partly sheltered by a bramble patch or dense shrub.

GRASSLAND AND FARMLAND

Full of wildflowers and native grass species, a good grassy meadow is a delight to anyone with an eye for colour and an interest in natural history. Unfortunately, prime sites are comparatively few and far between these days, either lost to the plough or having been 'improved' for grazing by farmers, who seed them with fast-growing, typically non-native grass species and apply selective herbicides to kill 'competing' plants. When this happens, grassland loses much of its value to wildlife.

In the context of Britain and Ireland, grassland is essentially a manmade habitat, having arisen as a result of woodland clearance for grazing in centuries past. If a site is to be maintained as grassland, continued grazing or cutting is needed to ensure that scrub regeneration does not occur. In the past, the way in which grassland was managed had the beneficial side effect – from a naturalists' perspective – of increasing wildlife diversity. Under modern 'efficient' farming regimes the reverse is the case.

Arable fields also fall loosely into the category of grasslands – crop species such as wheat, barley and oats are grasses after all. However, where modern farming methods are employed, biodiversity is minimal – in general, the aim is to grow a monoculture crop, free from pests and competing plants; the use of chemicals has helped farmers achieve this aim extremely effectively. From a wildlife perspective, the problem is that many of the so-called pests (and non-target invertebrates, many of which are also killed of course) are food for insectivores such as shrews and bats, while 'weed' seeds are important in the diet of small rodents. Certainly when it comes to most native small and medium-sized mammals, farmed land yields very little for them to eat. There are a few species that have actually benefited from modern farming, or at least are not deterred by it, Rabbits and Brown Rats (both introduced species) among them.

When it comes to animal watching, Brown Hares (and Irish Mountain Hares in Ireland) are still easy to see in some parts of the region and, especially during the winter months, small parties of deer will venture out of cover at dawn and dusk to feed. Where they are not killed or discouraged, Moles can be common, even on farmland, so long as the soil remains in a fit state to support earthworms. Unimproved grassland will support flourishing Field Vole populations (they are much scarcer on heavily grazed or ploughed farmland) and, where the cutting regime is appropriate, Harvest Mice may occur; the latter species has all but disappeared from intensively farmed land.

HEATHLAND

Heathlands are home to a number of fascinating animals – reptiles in particular – some of which are rare and almost unique to this habitat. Heathlands are under considerable threat today and are the subject of much attention from conservation bodies. In terms of their significance to wildlife, the most important examples of the habitat are found in southern England, with the majority of sites concentrated in Surrey, Hampshire and Dorset. However, additional isolated examples of heathland can be found further afield, in south Devon and Suffolk, for example, and in coastal districts of Cornwall and Pembrokeshire. This fragmented distribution adds to the problems that beset the habitat: 'island' populations of plants and animals have little chance of receiving genetic input from other sites and are vulnerable to local extinctions.

Heathland owes it existence to humans and came about following forest clearance on acid, sandy soils. Regimes of grazing, cutting and periodic burning in the past have helped maintain the habitat, and continued management is needed to ensure an appropriate balance between scrub encroachment and the maintenance of an open habitat. Ironically, humans are also the biggest threat to the habitat today: uncontrolled fires cause irreparable damage, while the destruction of heathland for housing developments obviously means the permanent loss of this unique habitat.

The habitat's name is clearly derived from the presence, and often dominance, of members of the heath family of plants, all of which flourish on acid soils. For the ultimate visual display, visit an area of heathland in August and September when these plants are in full bloom. However, in order to get the best views of the habitat's reptile residents, a visit in early spring is recommended. Adders and Common Lizards are perhaps the most widespread and easily observed species. Grass Snakes and Slow-worms also occur more sparingly and, in a few privileged locations in the south, Sand Lizards and Smooth Snakes complete the full reptile complement.

UPLANDS

Together with more remote stretches of coastline, upland areas are perhaps the only parts of Britain and Ireland to retain a sense of isolation for the visitor. Many of these areas appear wild and untamed, although in reality this is often just an illusion and few areas can be said to be truly pristine.

In centuries gone by, all but the highest peaks would have been wooded. Clearance of trees removed the natural woodland and subsequent, often excessive, grazing by sheep prevented regeneration. In general terms, moorland (grass or heather) is the dominant habitat in upland areas, although the characteristic plants and appearance vary considerably from region to region, and are profoundly influenced by soil type and climate. In a few areas, mountains dominate the landscape, sometimes rising to altitudes above the level at which trees would grow if they were allowed to do so; these areas harbour unique communities of plants and animals.

In the Scottish Highlands, and to a lesser degree elsewhere in the region, Red Deer are a frequent sight in upland areas, although they tend to descend to lower levels during the winter months. Mountain Hares live up to their name and are well adapted to the seemingly hostile environment, and on the lower slopes, especially on grassy moors, Field Voles can be common. A range of other small mammals (and predators such as Stoats and Foxes) also occurs in upland regions, although the range of species that occur, and their abundance, diminishes with increasing altitude.

Where small mammal populations are healthy there is a good chance that Adders will be present. Common Frogs and Palmate Newts are also widespread, both sometimes occurring in seemingly bleak and inhospitable terrains.

COASTAL HABITATS AND THE OPEN SEA

In habitat terms the coastline is arguably Britain's crowning glory. Although development has marred considerable stretches of the coast, particularly in southern England, those areas that remain unspoilt there, and elsewhere in Britain and Ireland, are rich in wildlife. In general, coastal habitats are not the most productive places for the mammal, reptile and amphibian enthusiast, but there are, nevertheless, a number of highlights.

In a few locations around the region, estuaries and saltmarshes support colonies of Common Seals, which may also be found hauled out at low tide on nearby sandy beaches; they are very locally common

(particularly in the Wash). In the northwest of their range, Natterjack Toads breed in pools at the highest reaches of certain saltmarshes and, in northwest England, a few select established dunes are home to colonies of Sand Lizards.

The rocky shore is a superb destination for the keen student of marine biology, and the intertidal zone simply teems with life. For the mammal enthusiast there is less on offer, but in the north and west in particular, Grey Seals sometimes haul out on the rocks at low tide and Otters hunt for fish and sea urchins along the shoreline. On the Isles of Scilly, the Lesser White-toothed Shrew can sometimes be seen foraging for invertebrates along the strandline.

Cliffs offer the visitor breathtaking scenery and a sense of untamed nature, owing to the minimal impact humans have had on this landscape. Rocky coastline, particularly in the north and west of the region, often supports populations of Grey Seals, whose moaning calls announce their presence. Many grassy cliffs harbour huge colonies of Rabbits, and Wild Goats and Soay Sheep are found in a few locations, the latter mainly on islands. A few exposed headlands offer opportunities for cetacean watching, although the majority of sightings occur out of sight of land.

The open sea is the domain of the region's whale and dolphin species, although of course a few – Harbour Porpoise, Bottlenose Dolphin, Risso's Dolphin and Long-finned Pilot Whale in particular – do venture into inshore waters.

FRESH WATER

For many naturalists, freshwater habitats have the same magnetic appeal as the coast. Sites range in size from small ponds and streams to large lakes and river systems, and few people have to travel far to visit one or more of these habitats.

If the water body in question is relatively clean and unpolluted, and supports a rich diversity of plant and invertebrate life, then Water Shrews may occur. Where emergent and marginal vegetation is particularly lush, Water Voles sometimes survive, although habitat destruction and the depredations of American Mink have exterminated them from much of their former range. In contrast, Otters are now returning to streams and rivers from which they have been absent for decades.

During the daytime, probably the easiest waterside mammal to observe these days is the Brown Rat. After dark, several species of bat take advantage of the night-flying insects that flourish in the vicinity of unpolluted streams, rivers and lakes.

Fresh water is the domain of amphibians and all our species must return there to breed. The still, or at least extremely slow-flowing, water of ponds and lakes is favoured. Although some water bodies harbour all our common native amphibian species during the breeding season, over time one or two tend to dominate, with factors such as water chemistry and the inclination of the pond in question to freeze in winter, or dry up in summer, influencing matters. Wherever there are frogs, toads and newts in abundance, you are likely to find Grass Snakes, too, since all are important in the diet of this most amphibious of our reptiles.

THE URBAN ENVIRONMENT

For the majority of people in Britain, who live in towns and cities, the urban environment is the one with which they are most familiar. It is encountered on a day-to-day basis, with trips to the countryside relegated to weekend visits or holiday excursions. It would be a mistake, however, to assume that the urban environment is without its wildlife interest. Several mammal species are extremely adaptable and have successfully colonised this seemingly unpromising habitat, and garden ponds are a valuable refuge for many amphibians.

Many features associated with our buildings and gardens mimic particular niches in natural habitats. So, mature gardens with hedgerows and shrubs resemble woodland margins and harbour elements of this habitat's small mammal fauna – Wood Mice and sometimes Common and Pygmy Shrews are fairly widespread. These days, you would be forgiven for thinking that Hedgehogs are entirely restricted to built-up areas and, where they are not persecuted, Foxes sometimes occur in urban habitats at densities that exceed those in the countryside at large. From a Pipistrelle Bat's point of view, buildings resemble manmade cliffs, with their roof spaces doubling as artificial caves, and unsurprisingly these sites are popular for roosting and hibernation. And then there is the ubiquitous Brown Rat, which thrives thanks to the wasteful way that we live our lives.

Lastly, we should not forget the domestic cat: the pampered lifestyle that many pets lead does nothing to diminish their innate drive to kill and their negative impact on wildlife is truly monumental.

ANIMAL WATCHER'S CALENDAR

As a naturalist in Britain and Ireland you will soon discover that animal behaviour, and the ability to see certain species, varies considerably throughout the year. To help readers get a feel for the rhythm of nature, and to get the most from the region's mammals, reptiles and amphibians, the following animal watcher's calendar details some of the highlights.

JANUARY

The dead of winter is a challenging time of year for wildlife generally, with temperatures at their seasonal low and food in short supply. Some animals avoid the problem by hibernating and, in January, all of our reptiles and amphibians will be tucked away in some sheltered or underground refuge.

Apart from bats, Hedgehogs and dormice, our mammal species remain active throughout the winter, although Badgers and Grey Squirrels in particular are less likely to forage for food if the weather is particularly inclement. However, for the naturalist, a fresh fall of snow at this time of year can prove to be a bit of a blessing: tracks, trails and signs become easy to discern.

Beloved of television sound departments (and frequently used in an inappropriate seasonal context) the nocturnal cries of Foxes (mostly vixens) are heard mainly in January. Female Foxes are only in oestrus for three weeks each year (in mid-winter) and are capable of conception for just three days in that period. So the need to attract a mate is self-evident. During the hours of daylight, deer are often relatively easy to locate in January, even in deciduous woodland because of the absence of leaf cover.

FEBRUARY

Often the coldest month of the year, February can be marked by the arrival of cold northerly and easterly winds that sometimes bring with them heavy falls of snow. Snug in its winter nest, located perhaps among a tangle of tree roots, the Hazel Dormouse is, to a degree, protected from the worst of the weather. All our bat species hibernate, too, although they will occasionally emerge on mild winter nights to drink and, insects permitting, feed.

Our native reptiles will also still be in a state of hibernation. However, visit a few chosen locations on the south coast of England and, within its restricted range, the alien Wall Lizard is often seen basking in February when there is a bit of warmth in the sun.

British mammals invariably have thicker coats during the winter months than they do in summer. In most cases, the coloration remains broadly similar throughout the year but two species in particular show marked seasonal differences, at least in parts of their range. In northern Britain, Stoats acquire a largely white coat of ermine in winter, and a similar colour is seen in Scottish Mountain

The nocturnal mating activities of Foxes are often indicated at this time of year by the eerie scream of the vixen.

Wall Lizards are skilled at optimising the amount of heat they obtain from the environment: they select sunny spots that are shaded from the wind for basking, flatten their bodies to increase the exposed surface area, orientate according to the changing direction of the sun and frequently shift position so that their ventral surfaces can absorb heat from warmed rock surfaces.

⊙ So-called 'mad March hares' sometimes engage in bouts of boxing. Although it might seem reasonable to assume that the opponents are rival males, in reality the pair usually comprises an unreceptive female warding off the unwelcome attentions of a male.

⊙ In particularly good ponds, seething masses of frogs and spawn can be seen in March with barely any amphibian-free surface water visible.

Hares. In both species, this is an adaptation that allows them to blend in with snowy surroundings. A downside to this strategy becomes apparent if the weather turns mild: Mountain Hares and ermine-clad Stoats are stuck with the colour until they moult in spring, so in the absence of snow they stand out like sore thumbs.

MARCH

With the appearance of buds and catkins on the trees, there is a feeling of spring in the air, although a cold snap can quickly shatter this illusion. Nevertheless, many of our animal species sense the changes that accompany the increasing day length and March marks the start of the breeding season for many creatures.

Visit an area of open countryside and you may be privileged to witness the antics of Brown Hares. Small groups of animals often gather together and, because they are preoccupied with the business of courtship and mating, they tend to be almost oblivious to the gaze of human onlookers.

A rise in air temperature triggers Common Frogs to emerge from hibernation, and if there is an accompanying rise in water temperature then courtship and mating will ensue. Although the most frantic activity takes place after dark (and can be witnessed by torchlight) there is still plenty to see during the day. Mating pairs in amplexus embrace can be seen in the shallows and clumps of frogspawn are usually easily visible. March is the peak month for spawning frogs across much of the region, although in the far southwest it occurs much earlier and in the north it can be delayed by up to a month.

APRIL

Leaves and flowers burst into life and there is a significant increase in the number of insects around, both as larval and adult stages. Many animals time their breeding season to coincide with this availability of food and even those that do not will be feeding for all their worth.

Although there is a degree of overlap, Common Toads tend to make their appearance onto the freshwater scene a few weeks later than do Common Frogs and early April is a prime time to look for them. Sit quietly beside a favoured pond and you will notice that loitering males adorn the margins, eagerly awaiting the arrival of females for mating.

For some mammals, the reproductive cycle may also only be getting underway, but most female Badgers will have given birth to their cubs in late January or early February, in their underground setts. However, it is not until April that the cubs make their appearance above ground; by sensitive preparation this charming annual event can be witnessed by careful observers.

Badger cubs are keen to explore the world around them when the adults permit, and typically are encouraged to venture above ground for the first time in April. All the activity takes place from dusk until dawn, so do not expect to see any signs of life around the sett during the daytime.

MAY

Away from the Highlands of Scotland, nighttime air temperatures in May seldom dip low enough to cause a frost. Many small mammals will have produced at least their first brood of the year by now and all our terrestrial reptiles will be out and about.

With the exception of Muntjac (which do not have a defined breeding season as such) May is the key month in which the females of most deer species give birth. In all cases, the young are extremely well camouflaged, and although they are capable of walking and running from an early age their usual response is to crouch, camouflaged among the vegetation. If you discover one, do not be tempted to approach too closely.

On warm, sunny mornings in May, lizards are often inclined to sunbathe in order to raise their body temperature and hence their metabolic rate. The easiest of our three native species to observe is the legless Slow-worm, and you should look for it resting on bare patches of ground on south-facing grass- or scrub-covered slopes. On dull days, animals can sometimes be found resting under discarded manmade objects such as corrugated iron or roofing felt.

Infant deer, in this case the fawn of a Roe Deer, merit a high 'ahh' rating among the general public and only the most detached of observers can fail to be moved by the sight of one.

JUNE

In wildlife terms, June is an extremely productive month and, these days, the sunniest periods of the year often occur at this time. Plant and insect life in particular proliferate and in turn mammals, reptiles and amphibians find plenty to feed on.

Invertebrate life is usually at its most plentiful in early summer, and the abundance of moths and other night-flying representatives of insect groups, such as beetles and flies, are eagerly eaten by bats.

June is one of the most pleasant and rewarding times of year to go seal-watching. Both Common and Grey Seals can be found along stretches of the north Norfolk coast, and animals can be seen hauled out and basking at certain states of the tide; in some locations seals can be seen from a distance, on foot, but the best sites are accessible only by boat.

So long as you do not push your luck, hauled-out seals can often be viewed at surprisingly close quarters. At this time of year you should see adult animals and rather scruffy young animals (born the previous autumn) moulting their juvenile coats.

JULY

The summer months are a prime time for the naturalist as animal life proliferates. Adult amphibians are usually comparatively hard to find at this time of year since most will have left their breeding ponds and lakes and moved to terrestrial habitats, their habits becoming essentially nocturnal. If it is a warm summer then temperatures are likely to be too hot for reptiles to bask in the middle

The Brown Long-eared Bat is one of the most distinctive and easily recognised of its kind in the region, and the almost comically long ears can even be discerned in flight. The species sometimes hunts for insects close to outside lights where these are located near dense, shrubby vegetation or trees.

ⓒ When they leave the pond in which they were spawned, young Common Frogs often still have a residual tail. However, over the next few days this will be absorbed back into the body and they will come to resemble miniature versions of their parents.

ⓢ From the moment they hatch, Grass Snakes are active predators. The sensitive tongue 'tastes' airborne smells, including the scent of prey animals, and these are processed by special organs inside the mouth to gain an olfactory picture of the world around them.

of the day, but an early morning or late afternoon search is often productive. Young mammals can be relatively easy to observe in July, however, because many will not yet perceive humans as a threat.

As the month progresses, occasional heavy downpours of rain are a feature and, in addition to replenishing the drying water table, this often acts as a trigger to encourage young froglets to leave their natal ponds. Their departure means that they are no longer a concentrated source of food for predators. Nevertheless, they are still preyed upon by numerous creatures, the Grass Snake among them. Their small size means that even recently hatched reptiles can include them in their diet.

AUGUST

The nights are beginning to draw in noticeably by August and the seasons are on the turn. Fruits, nuts and seeds are beginning to form and ripen on the trees and shrubs, and their appearance will not have

gone unnoticed by woodland and hedgerow mammals. Almost all amphibians, adults and young, will have abandoned water by now and reptiles will be taking advantage of the relative abundance of prey.

Most small rodent species in the region are, to a large extent, nocturnal in their habits. But none more so than the Hazel Dormouse, individuals of which you will never see during the daylight hours. After dark, however, they forage actively in the tree canopy, searching for developing nuts and insects. August is the month in which most female Dormice produce their young and it is a classic time for those studying these adorable creatures to discover them in specially provided nest boxes.

The Humpback Whale is the most 'playful' of the great whales at the surface and so identification of the species is relatively straightforward. Although still rare, several are seen each year off northern and western coasts, mainly in summer and early autumn.

August is a good month in which to look for cetaceans. If conditions are calm then sightings can sometimes be obtained from prominent headlands, mainly in the west of the region. However, ferry crossings and specially organised pelagic trips are more likely to yield sightings of larger, offshore species.

SEPTEMBER

In most years, September is the month in which fruits, berries and nuts appear in prodigious quantities in areas of hedgerow, scrub and woodland. Although still active, our terrestrial reptiles will be fattening up on their preferred prey in readiness for hibernation and taking advantage of the remaining warmth offered by the sun's rays.

Small rodents take advantage of this seasonal supply: Hazel Dormice put on weight in preparation for the rigours of hibernation, while some other species cache food that is surplus to their immediate requirements. And it is not just animals with a primarily vegetarian diet that take advantage of this bounty: omnivores such as Badgers will forage for fallen fruit and nuts, and even Foxes (usually thought of as strict carnivores) will feast on blackberries given the opportunity.

The breeding season may be over for most animals, but for some – seals in particular – it is just beginning. Visit parts of the Lincolnshire coast, or walk the cliffs of Pembrokeshire, for example, and you stand a reasonable chance of seeing a newly born Grey Seal pup. Its mother will mate again within a few weeks of giving birth, implantation being delayed until late winter.

ⓒ Wood Mice forage for food on the woodland floor throughout the year, but the greatest rewards are to be found in the autumn months. A keen sense of smell allows them to find fallen hazelnuts, berries and fruits, some of which are stored rather than eaten.

ⓓ Appealing eyes ensure that there are few more adorable sights than a Grey Seal pup in its white, infant coat. Baby seals look helpless, and indeed they are vulnerable to predators and the ravages of the sea. Consequently, survival is greatest among pups that are born on inaccessible and sheltered beaches.

OCTOBER

Many of us associate October with misty mornings and dew-soaked vegetation. In addition to conjuring up a visual image, however, October also has auditory connotations: it is the prime time to hear the evocative sound of rutting deer. Red Deer are the noisiest of our species to engage in this autumn ritual and, because the preoccupied animals have generally got other things on their minds, they are usually relatively easy to observe.

Although the precise timing varies from year to year, many of our animal species that hibernate will retire to their winter retreats sometime in October. This is certainly true of most of our bats, although in mild autumns when insects are still on the wing, they may remain active for a while longer. Creatures such as the Hedgehog are more set in their ways and by the end of the month only those individuals that have failed to achieve their necessary pre-hibernation weight (youngsters born late in the season) are likely to be active still.

NOVEMBER

Although the month may start off mild, the increasing frequency and severity of frosty nights serves as a reminder that winter is just around the corner. Food becomes harder to find for many of our animals and all those that hibernate will have done so by now. Those mammals that remain active throughout the winter months will have acquired a thick winter coat to help keep them warm.

⊙ The rather vulgar belching bark of a Red Deer stag marks the annual rut and is an announcement to rival males, and potential mates, that he means business.

DECEMBER

The first severe gale of winter is normally all it takes for most deciduous trees to lose any remaining leaves, and so by early December bare branches and trunks will dominate the woodland skyline. However, from the naturalist's point of view, it does mean that increased light levels make observation of deer and other sizeable woodland mammals easier. Given the harshness of the weather, and the lack of available food, it is easy to see why certain species choose to hibernate.

The coast is often battered by severe weather at this time of year, and although this is not conducive to watching marine mammals as such, it does afford rather grisly opportunities for the examination of beached dead animals and their bony remains.

⊙ Heavy downpours of rain at this time of year ensure that in many areas the ground becomes saturated or even waterlogged. This is a cue for Brown Rats to abandon many waterside locations in favour of drier sites, often those associated with farms and human habitation.

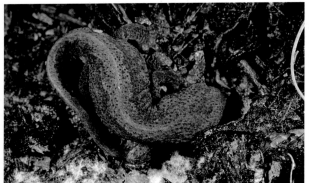

ⓒ Hibernating newts are sometimes discovered hiding underneath fallen logs. No attempt should be made to wake or warm them, and the animal's cover should be restored as soon as possible.

CONSERVATION ISSUES

Complete British Animals is primarily a field guide, but to live up to the implications of the title some of the problems faced by the region's mammals, reptiles and amphibians must be addressed. Great Britain still harbours a wealth of natural history and retains large tracts of land full of wildlife interest. But even (or perhaps *particularly*) in my lifetime, many native animal species have declined catastrophically as a result of human activity. Factors influencing their demise include habitat loss or degradation, the consequent direct or indirect reduction in available food, and in some cases direct persecution by humans.

As elsewhere in the world, at the root of the problems faced by our environment is the scale of the human population, its quest for economic improvement in its many guises, and recent technological advances that have made many of these aspirations more achievable. The problems manifest themselves in issues such as pollution, the swallowing of land for housing, industry and road projects, and, last but certainly not least, modern farming and fishery practices. Whatever the causes, the result has been fragmentation and degradation of wildlife-rich habitats, an overall decline in biodiversity, and local extinctions of certain species.

In ecological terms, mammals, reptiles and amphibians are located high in the food chain. As a result, the plight of many species is indicative of the problems that beset the habitats in which they live; as such they can be seen as conservation indicators. However, it is a mistake to view these animals in isolation and outside the context of the environment as a whole. Consequently, even though your fundamental interest in wildlife may be confined to a small group of species, as a responsible naturalist you should concern yourself with environmental matters generally in addition to your own chosen field.

WHAT IS CONSERVATION?

Broadly speaking, the essential aim of conservation is to preserve, or in some cases to restore, the maximum naturally occurring biodiversity that any given area can support in terms of *native* species – fundamental is the need to distinguish between native and alien plants and animals. Conservation measures have to be tailored to suit the particular habitat or landscape in question and cannot be made without an appreciation of ecology. Particularly pertinent is the concept of *habitat succession*, whereby a succession of increasingly stable plant communities leads eventually to the formation of a *climax community*. To illustrate this process, picture a newly formed freshwater pond. Left to its own devices, marginal vegetation will soon encroach and the area of open water gradually diminish. Eventually, enough substrate will gather for colonising willows to put down roots. Over a period of years, more substantial trees are able to grow, as the ground becomes drier, leading eventually to the formation of mature deciduous woodland; in this example, the woodland is the climax community.

In the context of Britain and Ireland, many of the habitats that we value so highly in wildlife terms are intermediates in the chain of succession (grassland, heathland and many freshwater habitats, for example); unless land management is carried out they lose their essential character, and often the key species for which they are important as well. In addition, active measures sometimes have to be taken to redress the consequences of people's previous actions. In Britain and Ireland, conservation seldom means setting the land aside and doing nothing.

WHO IS TO BLAME?

Ultimately, of course, as voters and consumers in society, we all share some of the responsibility for environmental damage. But this does not alter the fact that the causal agents often act outside the sphere of influence of the individual, and certainly not on their behalf.

Because of its economic power, one of the most immediate threats to our wildlife comes from commerce. A few businesses do genuinely have an interest in nature conservation, but it is probably fair to say that, for most, environmental issues are very much secondary to their primary economic goals. Although the ways in which commercial interests affect our wildlife and habitats are sometimes blindingly obvious – just think of oil spills and other forms of pollution – the effects are not always immediately apparent. Many industries consume natural products, or items that are themselves composed of natural products, typically depleting the earth's resources in a destructive, rather than a sustainable, way. In such instances, economic growth can only mean an increase in the pressure on the environment.

And then, of course, there is farming, although strictly speaking this should be treated as a branch of commerce: farming is a business, after all. Without doubt the greatest impact on British and Irish terrestrial wildlife in the last 50 years has come as a result of changes in agricultural land use and the modernisation of farming practices, some of which have been driven by governmental directives. In addition there are market forces at work, namely the stranglehold that some supermarket chains have on the economics of farming, underpinned by the public's insatiable demand for cheap, convenient food.

Since humans arrived in the region, agriculture has always been an agent of change in the landscape and has helped shape the landscape. And, in part, it is as a consequence of the resulting mosaic of man-influenced habitats that our region has such potential for biodiversity. Until as recently as the 1930s perhaps, the way in which the land was farmed, and the slow pace of change, ensured that even land in production accommodated a surprising diversity of wildlife. Nowadays, however, 'efficient' farming methods, and the profligate use of chemicals, means that where farms adopt modern practices this is no

There is not much scope for native wildlife on this patch of 'rural' England.

longer the case. While it is an over-simplification to view farming *per se* as bad, most modern agricultural practices are a little short of a disaster for the biodiversity of native wildlife.

Thankfully there are still parts of Britain and Ireland where the pace of agricultural change has been slow. In many northern and upland districts, for example, traditional hay meadows are still a feature of the landscape and, even where the land is farmed more intensively in the lowlands, some farmers leave margins for wildlife (often, it has to be said, because of financial incentives or sporting interests). Nevertheless, landowners still exist who are at best indifferent, or at worst gleefully antagonistic, towards conservation; for them, any interest in wildlife in the broadest sense is seemingly restricted to species that can be exploited, or which are perceived to impinge on their livelihood.

Problems affecting our environment are not restricted to the land by any means. The chronic low-level pollution and catastrophic oil spills that blight our seas, not to mention the industrial-scale exploitation of offshore fish stocks, are no less disastrous just because we cannot observe the effects with our own eyes. Aspects of marine conservation are discussed in more detail on p.25.

BRITISH ANIMALS AND CONSERVATION

Of the groups covered by *Complete British Animals*, reptiles and amphibians arguably arouse the least contention, particularly when it comes to people with no interest in conservation. By contrast, however, the way in which we, as a society, relate to mammals polarises people's opinions, probably because many creatures impinge on our lives in tangible ways. There are issues and dilemmas associated with almost every species. Some people refuse to look at the cases individually and see the problem in overall terms as being one of town versus country. Others perceive it as a clash of interests, involving people whose primary relationship with the countryside involves wanting to kill things on one side, and those who cherish the natural environment without the need to exploit it on the other. These stereotypes are emotive and seldom entirely accurate: most people's relationship with the countryside is, to say the least, ambiguous and their attitudes to wildlife selective. Clouding the issues are a variety of considerations: for example, a significant proportion of those who live in the countryside (including some farmers it has to be said) do not approve of hunting; and there are plenty of urban dwellers who kill things in the countryside as a recreational pursuit. And, of course, sociological and political factors sway many people's attitudes. As food for thought, the following brief selection of topics is worthy of consideration by anyone interested in conservation.

Introduced Species Over the millennia that humans have occupied Britain and Ireland, a number of species introductions have occurred to the region, some deliberate, others accidental. The majority of animals now kept in domestication arrived in this way. In addition, a significant number of alien species now live wild in the region as a consequence of accidental liberation, escapes from captivity or deliberate release. By and large, with hindsight, these additions to our native fauna are seen as being unwelcome.

The Rabbit was originally brought to Britain and Ireland as a source of meat and fur. Inevitably animals escaped into the countryside and today they are present in their millions. Because mammalian predators of Rabbits, such as Stoats, Foxes and Badgers, are not looked upon favourably in farming areas, as it stands today, humans are the Rabbit's most significant predator.

Grey Squirrels come from North America and were first introduced to Britain in 1876. Since then, colonisation of the region by the species has been remarkable and its spread is generally linked to the decline in range and numbers of the native Red Squirrel. The control of Grey Squirrel numbers is now seen as a vital element in the conservation of its cousin. In addition, it often has a profound impact on hazelnut production and therefore its presence in lowland deciduous woodland has implications for Dormouse conservation. Grey Squirrels also have a significant economic impact on forestry and as a consequence of this, more than anything, it is illegal to release or relocate the species. In the absence of arboreal mammalian predators in lowland Britain, humans are the Grey Squirrel's most significant enemy.

When it comes to myxomatosis in Rabbits, conservation, animal welfare concerns and pragmatism collide. Few people would actually wish such a grisly end on any animal. But without the disease, numbers would undoubtedly be higher than they already are today, which would be bad news for farmers, and in some instances for conservationists too.

American Mink are not native to Britain and Europe and were brought to the region to be farmed for their fur. Inevitably, some escaped from captivity, taking up residence along waterways. To make matters worse, misguided people motivated by welfare concerns actually liberated farmed animals in some instances. As a direct consequence of Mink depredation, numbers of many species of waterside nesting birds and Water Voles have declined and local extinctions have occurred. Whatever your feelings about the fur trade and caging animals, the only valid option when it comes to American Mink in Britain and Ireland is to kill them. There is an irony to the fact that, today, conservationists undertake much of this killing. On a slightly positive note, the return of Otters to many lowland rivers may help the problem. Otters, which feed primarily on fish, appear to exclude American Mink from their territories. So that's good news if you are a Little Grebe or Water Vole, but how will people with commercial fishing interests respond to the reappearance of the Otter I wonder?

The problem of alien introductions is not restricted to species brought to Britain from other parts of the world, and the relocation of an animal from one part of our region to another where it is not native can have similarly devastating environmental consequences. Take the case of the Hedgehog, arguably one of the most popular of all British mammals. Seen in the context of most people's lives it is indeed an adorable addition to the average garden. Elsewhere, the story is less clear-cut.

Hedgehogs are often described as insectivores but in reality they are omnivorous. Unsurprisingly, they will eat almost any invertebrate and, if the opportunity arises, they will also consume the young and eggs of birds. Ground-nesting species of birds seldom attempt to breed in the average garden, and so most people are unaware of the Hedgehog's predilections but, in the countryside at large, occasions do arise when nests are raided. However, in the context of mainland Britain, where Hedgehogs are native, their ecological impact on native ground-nesting birds (this includes Grey Partridge, Woodcock and duck species) can

The American Mink was the final nail in the coffin for many Water Vole populations already badly affected by habitat destruction and degradation. In order for scenes such as this not to be a thing of the past, Mink have to be killed.

be seen as part of the natural order, amongst other things because there are predators, such as Badgers, to keep the Hedgehogs themselves in check. However, those with shooting interests often view them in a harsher light, particularly in relation to the Pheasant (an alien species), which in many areas is encouraged to live at densities far above those observed in parts of Asia where the species originates. Gamekeepers have little compunction about killing Hedgehogs, which may go some way to explaining the species' relative scarcity away from urban and suburban areas.

For conservationists, the Hedgehog is a dilemma and one that forces all of us to examine the role of sentimentality in our attitudes towards wildlife. Again we return to the question of ground-nesting birds, but in this particular instance ones which, for obvious reasons, specifically choose to breed on remote islands that lack ground predators.

Until the early 1970s, the Uist islands in the Outer Hebrides supported large numbers of breeding waders and populations of some species were of international importance. In addition, the islands also hosted some of the last nesting Corncrakes in Britain. Then, in 1974, four Hedgehogs were released on South Uist. Now they have spread along the island chain and their population is estimated at 5,000. Wader numbers have halved in the last 20 years or so, their eggs and young succumbing to the predatory habits of the Hedgehogs.

The problem highlights the need to look at conservation dilemmas dispassionately and how judgements about wildlife management should be made on rational, scientific grounds. In the case of the Uists, the obvious solution is to remove the alien Hedgehogs and, indeed, this is what Scottish National Heritage has been doing since 2003. Relocation proved to be too expensive and the policy is to kill Hebridean Hedgehogs by lethal injection. Predictably, perhaps, there was an outcry from some members of the public

Foolishly, the Hedgehog has been introduced to many offshore islands in addition to the Uists. This individual, foraging for invertebrates on the seashore, was photographed on St Mary's in the Isles of Scilly.

but the culling programme went ahead nevertheless: 253 were killed in 2004, and 185 were 'rescued' by interested parties although whether the problem was simply shifted somewhere else is unclear.

The issue of Hedgehogs on the Uists serves to remind us of the folly of introducing species to regions, or countries, from which they were previously absent. It also illustrates a woeful lack of understanding of basic ecology among some members of the public, and just how sentimentality can cloud the judgement when the relative merits of conserving or destroying species need to be weighed up objectively. Would the same reaction have been evoked had the problem been one of rats and not Hedgehogs? Most people's response would be a resounding 'no' and, assuming that to be the case, it is useful to consider the situation on Lundy. Until recently, introduced Brown and Black Rats were found on this tiny island in the Bristol Channel, and it served as one of the last refuges for the latter species in Britain. Rats of both species are implicated in the decline of burrow- and ground-nesting seabirds, something that has been observed on Lundy. So a decision was made to attempt rodent eradication. This provoked objections from some parties who wanted to *conserve* the Black Rat, because, in the context of Britain, it is on the verge of extinction (it is abundant worldwide). Nevertheless, the extermination attempt went ahead and both rat species appear to be extinct on Lundy.

But what about officially sanctioned reintroductions I hear you ask? In some instances, there is a case to be made for introducing endangered species to sites from which they are absent but *only* where there is good scientific evidence to support the assertion that they occurred there in the past. Sand Lizards and Dormice are examples of some of the animal species involved. Before such programmes can take place, a number of national and international scientific criteria have to be satisfied, and official reintroductions are not undertaken on a whim.

DEER MANAGEMENT

In the absence of natural predators, such as the Wolf, Brown Bear and European Lynx (all now extinct in our region), healthy adult deer have few natural enemies. Because of the impact that their grazing and browsing (the various species feed in subtly different ways) has upon vegetation, a need to control their numbers is perceived by many landowners and those with financial interests to protect in the countryside. In ecological terms, what this means is that people are unwilling to allow deer numbers to rise to the carrying capacity of the environment. There is a conservation angle too: the adverse effect that deer have on the regeneration of coppiced woodland in the lowlands and pine forest regeneration in the Scottish Highlands is seen as significant. As a consequence, deer shooting is a widespread activity across the region.

It is worth bearing in mind that only Red and Roe Deer are actually native to our region. So should the remaining species be treated in a manner similar to other alien introductions such as the Rabbit and Grey Squirrel? Rightly or wrongly, this is certainly the case when it comes to the diminutive Muntjac. But how should we react to the introduced Chinese Water Deer? Although the British population

Is prevention better than cure? On a small scale, block-and-mesh fencing (usually associated with industrial sites) is effective at preventing access to areas of newly coppiced woodland by Fallow and Roe Deer; in such circumstances it is an alternative to culling.

is tiny, it is thought to be the equivalent of around 10 per cent of the entire world population remaining in its native land. Could there be an argument for making it a special case, or is that just double standards at work?

Whether or not deer culling is necessary, the fact is that shooting takes place, and on a scale that many people are unaware of. The stated intention is often to act, in the absence of natural predators, in a regulatory manner on the population for the benefit of the species, as well as the landowner. Whether or not this is always the case is questionable. It presupposes a detailed knowledge (scientific rather than anecdotal) of population numbers and trends. In many instances, the numbers shot are influenced not in ecological terms by the carrying capacity of the environment but by the perceived economic damage they are doing to crops or woodland; or, of course, by how much shooting interests are willing to pay to kill deer. Certainly if one of the intentions is to re-create the actions of natural selection, then trophy hunting (a not unimportant element in deer hunting) would appear to be at variance with this intention since a probable outcome is that *death*, not survival, of the fittest is achieved.

BATS

Bat numbers have declined in recent decades, markedly so in some species, catastrophically in others. A number of factors are likely to be at work, including the reduction in available food (night-flying insects) and disturbance and destruction of sites for summer roosting and winter hibernation. In recognition of their plight, all bat species are protected by law, and reckless endangerment, let alone destruction, could, in theory, result in imprisonment or a hefty fine. Whether or not the law has any impact on the most significant factors adversely affecting bats is debatable.

Females of many species of bats congregate in maternity roosts with their young during the summer months, and hollow trees are often favoured. Unsurprisingly, tree surgery undertaken at this time of year can have a devastating impact on bats, as indeed it can at other times of the year too (some species hibernate in tree hollows). This particular Daubenton's Bat's mother was chain-sawed in half, inside the nursery roost it occupied, by contractors working on behalf of Hart District Council in Hampshire; more than 50 other bats were in occupancy at the time of the destruction. The incident was reported to, and investigated by, the police; at the time of writing, no prosecution had taken place.

CATS

When it comes to conservation, the cat is a problem species in many respects. On one hand, there is the native Wildcat (*Felis sylvestris grampia*), a scarce and protected animal with a restricted distribution in the Scottish Highlands. On the other hand, there is its domesticated cousin (*F. s. catus*), an abundant and widespread pet that frequently occurs as a feral animal as well.

The close relationship between the two is obvious from their scientific names, but our attitudes towards them are often ambiguously different. Conservationists regard the Wildcat with delight but look upon domestic cats with horror because of the impact they have on native wildlife. The fact that domestic cats kill things is not in itself the main issue, but their sheer numbers in the region is – an estimated 6 million occur in Britain alone and, as a result of being fed by their owners, they are able to occur at densities that are infinity higher than could be supported in nature. Pampering and a diet of tinned food do nothing to curb their predatory instincts, and birds and small mammals (even bats and small predators, such as Weasels) suffer the consequences. Furthermore, domestic cats roam far more widely than many of their owners appreciate. I know of an isolated Water Vole colony, at least a mile from the nearest habitation, which was exterminated by a cat that was identifiable as a pet. And their attentions are not confined to warm-blooded animals – Slow-worm colonies are quickly wiped out when new rural housing developments bring with them the inevitable quota of these predators.

MARINE MAMMALS

Many people naively think of whaling as a thing of the past, a historical anachronism relegated to an era where people's unenlightened greed drove them to exploit natural resources to the limit of commercial viability. Sadly, this is not the case. Although whaling (or what is conventionally understood by the term) does not occur in British and Irish waters, it does take place in neighbouring seas and affects species that occur in our region. Visit almost any marine- or cetacean-related website to find out which nations are still killing whales.

Lest we, in Britain and Ireland, develop too sanctimonious an attitude to whaling, it is important to examine our own role in the continuing plight of marine mammals, both in our own seas and further afield. If you eat marine fish, other than ones you have caught yourself on a rod and line perhaps, then there is a real chance that you are contributing to their plight, not to mention that of the marine environment as a whole. There is the obvious point to make that the industrial scale of modern fisheries is, quite literally, removing fish from the mouths of those whale, dolphin and seal species that depend on this source of food for their lives (not just their livelihoods). But there are other issues: conventional trawlers kill thousands of dolphins and porpoises each year, these deaths euphemistically referred to as *by-catch*; the recent trend towards pair-trawling for Sea Bass is proving to be an even more efficient way of killing dolphins; long-lines set to catch tuna in a so-called dolphin-friendly manner still manage to catch certain cetacean species, not to mention large numbers of albatrosses.

Even fish farming (notably for salmon) has serious adverse consequences for the marine environment. Localised pollution (waste food and faeces) is an obvious problem but, in addition, seals are shot to prevent them eating the fish (as they are elsewhere by those with fishing interests), although, in theory at least, seasonal and geographical restrictions apply to this practice. Furthermore, salmon are often fed on fishmeal derived from deep-sea fish stocks that are being plundered to the point of extinction. All so that supermarket shelves can be stocked with cheap salmon for the public to buy. Cheap maybe, but at what cost to the marine environment?

So is there such a thing as fish fit for consumption by anyone with an environmental conscience? Visit the Marine Conservation Society's website (www.fishonline.org) to find out.

Thousands of Harbour Porpoises are killed each year in British and Irish waters alone; they are part of the so-called by-catch of the fishing industry. If you purchase and eat marine fish, you may well be helping to fund their destruction.

FOXES

Few mammals typify the divide between urban residents and the farming community more clearly than the Fox: both the animal itself, and what it has come to symbolise for the pro- and anti-hunting lobbies, are guaranteed to cause pulses to race. Many people enjoy feeding and watching Foxes in their gardens but, by contrast, they are widely reviled and persecuted in the countryside at large.

That Foxes have an essentially carnivorous diet is not in dispute and, if there is a chance of a meal, they will tackle anything from a grasshopper or beetle to birds the size of a Pheasant and mammals such as Brown Rats and Rabbits. Like all native predators, they are an integral part of the countryside at large, and in stable environments (where the balance of nature is not upset by humans) they play a vital role in natural selection by ensuring the survival of the fittest: weak, sickly and elderly prey animals are selected in preference to fit, healthy individuals simply because they are easier to catch. So is there a need to control Fox numbers? In simple ecological terms, no. As with other predators, in a stable environment the species' population dynamics and mortality will be controlled by a number of natural factors including food availability, disease and available territory; as a sign of the times, road deaths have an increasingly significant impact on fox numbers. Complex hormonal and behavioural controls also exist in Foxes that restrict the breeding potential of subordinate animals in stable territories. Disrupt these biological controls, by disturbing territories or removing dominant animals for example, and these inhibiting forces disappear.

The perceived need to control Foxes arises where humans, and in some cases localised natural conditions, skew the balance, presenting Foxes with a concentration of prey that is easy to catch. It is little wonder that Foxes take an interest in Pheasants, particularly since in some areas, and at certain times of year, they are present in extraordinary numbers: an estimated 15 million of these alien birds are reared in pens and released in Britain each autumn for the purposes of being shot. If a Fox is able to gain access to a rearing pen then the confined birds present an irresistible target and many more are likely to be killed than can be consumed. This response to a freely available abundance of prey is not unique to the Fox by any means, and indeed there are plenty of instances where human parallels can be drawn.

The depredations of Foxes are also well documented among ground-nesting seabirds such as terns and gulls, which breed colonially. Given the choice, most species would nest on inaccessible islands, but nowadays they are often obliged to occupy suboptimal (mainland) sites thanks to the actions of humans elsewhere. There is also a risk involved with nesting on manmade islands in lagoons because Foxes are not deterred by a short swim. On dark, windy nights, when the birds cannot escape, havoc can be wreaked in the space of just an hour or so if a Fox gains access to a colony. Predictably, conservation organisations try their utmost to exclude Foxes (and other predators) from these sensitive sites and control measures are utilised that do involve killing them.

So, in certain circumstances there are similarities between the way in which conservationists and those with shooting interests deal with Foxes. The differences lie in the motives of the people undertaking the control. In the case of seabird colonies, a judgement will have been made on scientific grounds that the need for conserving nationally scarce nesting species (typically endangered by the actions of humans elsewhere) outweighs the welfare of the common and widespread Fox. In the case of pheasant shooting, the aim is to promote an alien species at the expense of a native predator, and to safeguard economic interests.

In the context of economic interests in the countryside, the desire to control Foxes is perhaps understandable, if not justifiable on ecological grounds. Fox hunting, with horse and hound, is an altogether different issue. The fact that this pastime has been elevated from countryside pursuit to rural tradition clearly has more to do with sociological factors than it does with ecological ones.

BADGERS

Its iconic stripy face is an emblem for nature conservation and most people get a real thrill from seeing a Badger in the wild or, indeed, from just knowing that the species is part of the British and Irish fauna. But talk to members of the farming community (on whose land most Badgers live) and few people have a good word to say for them. For some farmers, it would seem, the only good Badger is a dead one.

Over the years Badgers have been accused of a variety of agricultural misdemeanours, from damaging crops and eroding banks to killing ground-nesting birds. To the extent that these can be regarded as crimes then the Badger is guilty, because the ecological niche that it has evolved to fill is that of a foraging, omnivorous excavator, albeit one whose main dietary component is earthworms. However, the most recent deed for which Badgers stand accused is more serious, at least from an agricultural viewpoint, namely that they are responsible for the presence and spread of bovine tuberculosis (bTB) in cattle. Look at the facts in a detached way though and it is not obvious that there is a case to answer or that the punishment meted out is justified.

Bovine tuberculosis is a chronic, contagious disease of cattle caused by the bacterium *Mycobacterium bovis*. It is related to, but not the same as, human TB (caused by *M. tuberculosis*) and it is also recorded in certain wild animals, and occasionally in humans as well. The main means by which animals contract the disease is droplet infection, that is the inhalation of airborne bacteria liberated by coughing and sneezing; the proximity of infected and uninfected animals to one another has a bearing on the rate of infection, as does the health of those uninfected animals that inhale bTB bacteria. A secondary means of contracting the disease is through oral ingestion. In its dormant state, human TB can persist in the soil for many months and it does not seem unreasonable to assume that the same is true of bTB.

Once rife in the British and Irish national herds, bTB was virtually eradicated from most areas by the mid-20th century by a policy of tuberculin skin testing and the slaughter of infected animals. However, bTB persisted in the West Country and in parts of Ireland, and today it is showing signs of spreading to other regions, or rather, isolated cases have occurred outside known hotspots for the disease. For an individual farm, bTB can have a significant impact on productivity (milk and meat) and hence livelihood, although it has to be said the farmers are compensated financially, to a degree, for slaughtered cattle.

Much of the 'evidence' relating to the cause and spread of bTB is circumstantial, inconclusive or contradictory but, some would say for reasons of political expediency, Badgers, rather than cattle themselves, have been singled out as the main culprit. So the theory goes, they act as a reservoir for the disease and are agents of reinfection and dispersal. That some Badgers are bTB carriers is not in dispute. But there again, so are many other wild-living animals, deer and Brown Rats included.

The first Badger infected with bTB was recorded in 1971. Carrier Badgers are found only in areas where diseased cattle have been recorded and post-mortem results suggest that only around 20 per cent of Badgers in infected areas actually harbour the disease. How Badgers are supposed to infect cattle in the wild has not been satisfactorily explained, and it is extremely hard, under experimental conditions, for one Badger to infect another. Conversely, cross-infection in cattle kept in close confinement manifestly does take place. Despite the lack of convincing evidence, over the last couple of decades tens of thousands of Badgers have been killed by government agencies. The slaughter has failed to have an impact on the incidence of bTB.

Looking at the issue from an epidemiological perspective it seems likely that cattle contract the disease from other cattle and that Badgers acquire the disease from infected cattle, not vice versa. Looking further afield, it is perhaps worth noting that bTB is a global disease and not unique to Britain and Ireland; it is prevalent in large parts of the world where Badgers do not occur.

Human TB has been studied extensively and it may be useful to consider aspects of its epidemiology when pondering how best to deal with bTB. Human TB thrives in situations where people live in crowded, often damp conditions that aid airborne transmission of the disease through coughing and sneezing, and subsequent inhalation; individuals whose immune systems have been challenged (often by their diet) are most at risk. If you care to make comparisons with the cattle form of the disease then the confined conditions under which some animals live (not to mention the somewhat peculiar diet – for a herbivore – that they may be fed) may have a bearing on things. Statutory guidelines on cattle husbandry regarding disease mitigation, in line with policies relating to human habitation, would probably benefit all concerned.

Interestingly, the recent rise in bTB incidence has come in the wake of the foot and mouth epidemic, the spread, extent and duration of which was exacerbated by the transportation of infected cattle around the region. For the period of the outbreak, tests for bTB were suspended and cattle were kept in confinement; therefore, it does not seem unreasonable to assume that cases of bTB infection went undetected. Combine this with the fact that, even today, cattle do not have to receive tuberculin tests before they are transported and a possible explanation emerges for the sudden appearance of the disease in far-flung and novel locations after restrictions on animal movements were lifted. Indeed, in some cases of novel outbreak, this means of infection has been demonstrated. The explanation is more plausible, some would say, than Badgers abandoning their normally rather sedentary habits and running, in some cases, hundreds of miles before depositing infected faeces, or sneezing on healthy cattle, and infecting them.

Until recently, the standard approach by governmental bodies to any outbreak of bTB was to slaughter the infected cattle, quarantine the farm in question and attempt to kill any Badgers in the vicinity. More recently, an attempt (the so-called 'Krebs trial') has been made to determine the links between Badgers and bTB by quantitative study. In a 'scientific' manner it aims to make comparisons on cattle infection rates between data collected from areas where Badgers are not killed, locations where Badgers are culled in response to bTB outbreaks (reactive culling trial sites) and sites where local Badger eradication has taken place (proactive culling trial sites). Many conservation bodies regarded aspects of the trial's methodology and implementation to be flawed, and hence any conclusions subsequently drawn from the results to be of dubious value. But in any case the reactive culling aspect of the trial had to be suspended when a 27 per cent *rise* in the incidence of bTB in cattle was observed in areas where this action was taking place; proactive culling continues.

Setting aside the reasons why bTB persists in certain areas, and is spread to new ones, a more rational approach would be to tackle the problem from the cattle perspective. Currently, the majority of governmental fundings associated with bTB are directed towards Badgers. Certainly this distorts attempts to explore alternative approaches to finding a solution, which might include the following: improving the efficacy of the current tuberculin skin test; increasing the frequency of its use; introducing a policy of health certification prior to cattle movement; and, above all, the development of a bovine vaccine. And of course a vaccine for Badgers and other forms of wildlife would be nice too.

Over the last two decades, a succession of statutory bodies responsible for agriculture has come and gone. Despite an absence of incontrovertible scientific evidence to back up their actions, each has focused on Badgers as the primary agents responsible for bTB rather than address the problem in a more holistic manner. A cynic might say that the Badger makes a convenient, and silent, scapegoat.

Of course, from a conservation perspective, the spectre on the horizon is the possibility that scientifically robust experiments might some day actually convince the government of the day that there is a genuine link between Badgers and the spread of bTB. What then? The logical consequence, for the government at least, would be to implement widespread eradication of Badgers. Indeed, if some elements of the farming press are to be believed then the case is already proven and nothing short of a mass extermination programme will satisfy them. For anyone with a concern for native wildlife, this prospect is appalling, and the message it would send to the farming community (in regard both to Badgers and other forms of wildlife) hardly bears thinking about. Alarmingly, there is already circumstantial evidence to indicate that a few landowners have made up their minds and are taking matters into their own hands.

If the unthinkable did happen then it can only be hoped that public outrage would force the issue and oblige alternative methods of bTB control to be explored. If that failed, surely it would be harder than it currently is to reconcile extermination policies with the Badger's protected status. Perhaps statutory bodies commanded with the task of nature conservation, currently distinctly mute on the subject, would then express an opinion? Or maybe the 80 per cent of Badgers killed at cattle-infected locations, which turn out to be healthy animals, have already forfeited the limited legal protection granted to them?

ⓒ The gradual and insidious urbanisation of the countryside is a major threat to the natural environment.

ⓒ A motorway is an insurmountable obstacle for most animals, and a death trap for others.

URBANISATION OF THE COUNTRYSIDE

One of the most significant threats to rural land comes from new housing developments, which occur in response to the (largely unchallenged) declared need for more houses, particularly in the south of England. The most obvious effect of 'greenfield' housing development is that it destroys for ever the patch of countryside on which it is built. This gradual erosion of the landscape is bad enough in farmed areas, but where the land in question has some significance in biodiversity terms the consequences for conservation can be catastrophic. But the effects are felt further afield as well. The demand for water inevitably leads to increased

abstraction, which in turn impacts on the water table and river levels. And new estates have to be supplied with new or widened access roads, with all the destruction that entails. It is perhaps with a hint of irony that developers often name the roads on new housing estates after habitats and flora destroyed in their making: 'Woodland Close', 'Meadow View' and 'Hawthorn Rise' are just three I have noticed in recent years.

And then there is modern society's love affair with the internal combustion engine. Setting aside the obvious polluting side effects of cars and lorries, roads themselves occupy significant areas of land and although roadside verges sometimes teem with wildlife this is little compensation for what has been lost. They also present major obstacles to many animals. Those species that are unwilling or unable to cross them (Dormice, for example) have isolation imposed on them while those that cross them run the risk of being killed. However, how many of us would be willing to give up our cars to save wildlife? Not many I suspect.

It is ironic that road-death surveys represent probably the best way of monitoring the return of the Polecat to many of its former haunts in lowland England.

WHAT CAN BE DONE TO ASSIST CONSERVATION?

Can we rely on Government to act as guardians of our native habitats and biodiversity? Probably not. Whatever party is in power, economic matters, be they housing-, farming-, fishing- or industry-related, ultimately always seem to be given priority over environmental issues and it is probably naïve to expect otherwise. If you are in any doubt, just think of the number of times in recent years when schemes to widen existing roads or create new ones have been allowed to destroy Sites of Special Scientific Interest, sites that supposedly have some legal protection. Furthermore, rightly or wrongly, there is a generally held perception among amateur conservationists that the powers of statutory bodies responsible for the task of promoting nature conservation are being eroded along with their willingness to tackle controversial issues head-on.

Often there is little that individual conservationists can do on their own, unless they happen to be large landowners. Short of remaining a lone voice in the wilderness, the best option is to become a member of a society or group that is able to speak with a louder voice. A list of conservation organisations can be found at the back of the book.

Probably the most effective step that can be taken to safeguard our terrestrial environment is to remove as much land as possible from the threat of development or intensive agriculture by ownership. Buying land on a piecemeal basis and establishing small nature reserves is one way, but a far more effective option is to donate money to the likes of one of the county Wildlife Trusts, specifically for the purchase of land. But the job does not stop there. Nature reserves invariably need managing and, again, this is where you can help: join the ranks of conservation volunteers and help out.

Of course, there are a few positive steps that individuals can take to improve things on a smaller scale and to minimise their own impact on the environment. For example, grow your own food if you have the space. If that is not feasible then buy organically grown food wherever possible, ideally obtaining as much as you can from local sources (including farmers' markets) where you can either see what is going on at the farm in question or talk to the producer. But be prepared to pay a premium for the privilege of encouraging environmentally friendly farmers. Nobody in their right mind would suggest that this is going to change the way that Britain and Ireland are farmed in the short term, but every little helps, as they say. And if you eat marine fish, which for most people cannot be sourced locally, consider the environmental consequences associated with catching, or farming, what you intend to eat.

Away from the food front, you can oppose all large-scale developments in the countryside on principle, be they roads or proposed housing schemes; once land has been built upon, it is lost for ever and can never be replaced. Closer to home, you can turn your garden into your own private nature reserve and guidelines for creating a wildlife-friendly garden can be found on p.192.

For all my concerns about conservation in Britain and Ireland, all is not doom and gloom. An increasing number of people appreciate the need for active conservation measures, and a small army of motivated and informed naturalists and conservationists has evolved in recent decades. An excellent network of nature reserves exists along with study groups and lobbying pressure groups. Long may all of these interested parties continue their good work, and be sure to become one of them yourself.

HEDGEHOG *Erinaceus europaeus*
TOTAL LENGTH 23–27cm; WEIGHT 50–120g

A distinctive mammal that is unique among British species on account of its body coating of protective spines. The Hedgehog is a familiar resident of many gardens and despite its nocturnal habits it is encountered relatively frequently. Sadly, it is often seen as a road casualty as well. **ADULT** has a coating of several thousand spines (which are modified hairs) on the back. These are typically sleeked back when the animal is foraging, but are erectile and are particularly effective as a deterrent to predators when the animal rolls into a defensive ball. The head and the underparts are covered in coarse hairs. Note the relatively short external ears and the muzzle-shaped head that ends in a sensitive nose. The legs are relatively short but they can transport the animal at surprising bursts of speed when the urge takes it. **JUVENILE** is born blind and naked but soon acquires a coating of relatively stout whitish spines. After about 3 weeks it resembles a miniature adult. **VOICE** – Hedgehogs utter a piercing pig-like squeal when distressed. Various grunts and snorts are heard when animals are courting or feeding. HABITAT AND STATUS – The Hedgehog is widespread in the region but, at the local level, its precise distribution is rather patchy. It favours areas that boast a mosaic of grassy and scrub habitats. Meadows with neighbouring hedgerows and woodlands are sometimes good for the species but by far the highest densities occur in gardens and parks. A number of factors may be at work influencing this suburban bias, which, on the face of it, might seem rather unlikely. Often quoted is the correlation between the presence of Badgers and the absence of Hedgehogs, the inference being that because the former is able to kill and eat the

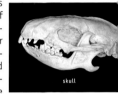

skull

latter it is able to cause local extinctions and prevent recolonisation. However, at the anecdotal level, I know plenty of areas that seemingly look suitable for Hedgehogs, but from which both they and Badgers are absent and have been as long as I can remember. So there may be other factors at work here. In farmland areas where invertebrates are controlled by pesticides a simple paucity of food may be an underlying factor. Then, of course, there is the spectre of pesticide accumulation and resultant poisoning to consider. Furthermore, Hedgehogs were formerly widely killed by gamekeepers on account of their predilection for the eggs and chicks of ground-nesting birds; the extent to which such controls are practised may have declined in recent years but it is still a factor affecting Hedgehog numbers. Controversially, a few misguided people have released Hedgehogs to several offshore islands, including the Scilly Isles, the Uists and North Ronaldsay, where previously they did not occur. On the latter 2 sites in particular they are wreaking havoc on populations of ground-nesting wading birds, with the result that the only option to safeguard the breeding birds (populations of which are of national importance) is to kill or remove the Hedgehogs from these islands (*see* p.22 for further discussion). HABITS AND NATURAL HISTORY – Hedgehogs are strictly nocturnal and forage on the ground for invertebrates such as earthworms and beetles. Despite their seemingly unwieldy appearance they can climb with surprising agility and can even swim, albeit reluctantly. When alarmed or disturbed, the typical defence is to roll into a ball, the spines forming a seamless coating. Hedgehogs hibernate and typically remain dormant in protected or underground nests from late October to early April. Mating occurs after emergence from hibernation and litters of 4–5 young are born from spring to early autumn. Young that are born late in the season stand little chance of surviving hibernation because there will be insufficient time for them to achieve a large enough body weight to see them through the winter. Adult Hedgehogs are notorious for being plagued with an abundance of fleas and ticks. OBSERVATION TIPS – Hedgehogs are relatively easy to observe in most lowland towns and villages in Britain; they are even surprisingly common in mature parts of cities such as London. Look for sausage-shaped droppings deposited on your lawn; these often contain visible signs of the animal's diet including shiny beetle wing-cases. Saucers of cat food or bread and milk will often attract Hedgehogs, as will the construction of protected nesting and hibernation sites.

5-day-old babies

ticks

dropping

HEDGEHOG
⌃ ABOVE **Defensive posture**
⌄ BELOW **Mother with young**

MOLE *Talpa europaea*

BODY LENGTH 11–15cm; TAIL LENGTH 3–4cm; WEIGHT 70–130g

An unmistakable subterranean mammal that has a cylindrical body covered in black fur. Moles are seldom seen above ground but signs of their presence in the form of molehills are a familiar sight in the countryside. **ADULT** is ideally suited to life underground. The cylindrical body allows easy passage through tunnels and the velvety fur will lay in any direction, so the Mole is not hindered if it moves backwards or forwards. The front feet, which are broad, spade-like and armed with sharp claws, are the perfect tools for digging. The eyes are tiny and almost completely hidden by fur, and external ears are absent. The tail is furry and is often held erect and the head is elongated into a sensitive snout, which the Mole uses to detect its prey. **JUVENILE** is born naked and blind. Fur begins to appear at around 2 weeks of age and thereafter they resemble miniature adults. **VOICE** – Moles occasionally utter shrill screams but are otherwise silent. HABITAT AND STATUS – Favoured habitats include meadows and grassland, arable fields and woodland, the common factor being well-drained, invertebrate-rich soil. Waterlogged and stony ground is avoided, for obvious reasons, and Moles are scarce in acidic soils where prey animals, particularly earthworms, are scarce or absent. The Mole is extremely widespread in mainland England, Wales and Scotland and it is probably one of the commonest of all our mammals, although precise numbers are difficult to assess. It is absent from Ireland. HABITS AND NATURAL HISTORY – Moles live an almost exclusively underground life in a network of tunnels. Deeper, permanent tunnels are patrolled regularly in search of soil invertebrates – earthworms are by far the most important prey – that may have fallen in; semi-permanent runs near the surface are explored for surface-dwelling creatures. Molehills are essentially spoil heaps from tunnel excavations. At the heart of a Mole's territory is an underground sleeping chamber, in which a nest of grass and leaves is constructed. The female gives birth once a year (usually 3 or 4 young in a litter), typically in late spring. The young are born naked and blind, and they are weaned after 5–6 weeks. Moles have got something of a bad reputation among certain members of the farming and gardening communities on account of the perceived unsightly appearance of molehills and disruption caused by surface tunnels. Both parties conveniently overlook the untold benefits to soil aeration, and hence the contribution to soil health generally, performed by Moles. Fortunately, many people, myself included, choose to tolerate the presence of Moles in the garden, despite their occasional incursions into the flowerbed or vegetable patch, in the knowledge that this will encourage a fascinating member of our native mammal fauna, and one that both aerates the soils and kills unwelcome soil invertebrates such as Cockchafer larvae and leatherjackets. Besides which, when potted up, the fine tilth of molehill soil makes an excellent growing medium for seeds and seedlings! OBSERVATION TIPS – Being almost exclusively subterranean, Moles are always going to be difficult to observe. Males sometimes venture above ground in spring, presumably in search of female territories, and at such times they are occasionally seen running, at surprising speed, across roads. During periods of summer drought, or winter flooding, animals will occasionally be forced to the surface too. If you wait motionless in a field in which Moles are known to occur you can sometimes detect their movements through surface tunnels by the trail of quivering grass stems as the animal pushes the roots aside beneath the ground.

earthworm

front paw

skull

MOLE
⌃ ABOVE **adult**
⌄ BELOW **molehill**

COMMON SHREW *Sorex araneus*

BODY LENGTH 5.5–8.5cm; TAIL LENGTH 3.5–5.5cm; WEIGHT 6–12g

As its common name suggests, this is a widespread and numerous species in most parts of mainland Britain. Like its cousins, the Common Shrew leads a frenetic life, its search for invertebrate food seemingly never ending. **ADULT** has fur that is dense enough to give the coat a velvety appearance; the upper parts are dark brown while the flanks are paler buffish brown, the colour grading to greyish white on the underparts. The head extends to a pointed snout, the tip of which is armed with long, bristly whiskers. Note the tiny, beady eyes and rather small external ears. The teeth have reddish tips but these can only really be appreciated in dead specimens. The tail is essentially naked and, when compared to body length, is relatively shorter than in a Pygmy Shrew. The feet are rather large for an animal of this size and the front pair is sometimes used to manipulate prey when feeding. **JUVENILE** is similar to an adult but smaller; the tail is covered with short hairs. **VOICE** – Utters high-pitched twittering squeaks when feeding and shrill screams during aggressive encounters; these sounds are faintly audible to people with good hearing and can be picked up by bat-detectors.

HABITAT AND STATUS – Common Shrews are widespread and common throughout much of mainland Britain and several tens of millions are probably present in the region as a whole. The species does not occur in Ireland, and is not found on the Scilly Isles, Shetland, Orkney and the Outer Hebrides. Common Shrews occur in a wide range of habitats and locations, including hedgerows, grassland, woodland margins and mature gardens, the common factors being the presence of plenty of ground cover and an abundance of invertebrate prey. HABITS AND NATURAL HISTORY – Although Common Shrews are classed as insectivores, in reality they take a wider range of invertebrates than just insects, including spiders, woodlice, slugs and snails; occasionally they are said to eat carrion. Apart from brief rest periods (every hour or so) of a few min-

refection

utes, they are active throughout the 24-hour period, foraging both at ground level (in leaf litter and ground vegetation) as well as in burrows. Their eyesight is rather poor so instead they rely upon their keen senses of touch, hearing and smell to find their way around and locate food. Their high metabolic rate demands that they feed almost constantly and indeed they will die if they go without food for much more than an hour. Common Shrews lead solitary, territorial lives and defend their home ranges aggressively against intruders of their own kind, except where courtship and mating are concerned. One or 2 litters (containing on average 6 young) are born, mainly between May and August. At birth the babies are blind and naked, but they develop rapidly and are weaned at around 3 weeks old. Like its cousins, the Common Shrew could almost be said to be an annual species, an unusual concept among mammals. By late summer it is most unusual to encounter an adult animal, the implication being that, with the breeding season complete, those that have not succumbed to predation have simply died of the shrew equivalent of exhaustion or 'old age'. Indeed, anecdotal evidence supports this contention: during the summer months, it is not unusual to come across dead shrews lying in the open, seemingly without a mark on them to indicate the cause of death. OBSERVATION TIPS – Common Shrews are difficult to observe other than by chance, partly because they spend a significant proportion of their time underground. If you have good hearing you might be able to detect their shrill calls in the undergrowth; with a stealthy approach, you can occasionally pinpoint the animal and get a close view. Common Shrews are sometimes discovered by turn-

skull

ing over boards or sheets of corrugated iron lying on the ground in grassland. However, observations will be brief because the animal will quickly scuttle off into cover. NOTE – The almost indistinguishable **Millet's Shrew** (*S. coronatus*) occurs only on Jersey, where the Common Shrew is absent; it is thought to have been introduced. Its habits and habitat preferences are the same as for Common Shrew.

COMMON SHREW
⌃ ABOVE **adult** ⌄ BELOW **adult**

PYGMY SHREW *Sorex minutus*

BODY LENGTH 4–6cm; TAIL LENGTH 3–4.5cm; WEIGHT 3–7g

The Pygmy Shrew is our smallest land mammal, and weighs even less than the diminutive Harvest Mouse. It has a high metabolic rate that demands of it a frenetic lifestyle, and consequently it is constantly on the move in search of food. **ADULT** has a coat of dense fur that is uniformly dark brown on the upper parts and flanks, while the underparts are contrastingly pale grey-ish white. As with other shrews, the head is elongated into a pointed snout that is armed with long, sensitive bristles; the eyes are small and beady and the external ears are partly hidden by fur. The tail is proportion-ately long compared to the body length and is covered with fine hairs. The tips of the teeth are red but this can only be appreciated in dead specimens. **JUVENILE** resembles a minia-ture adult. **VOICE** – Utters high-pitched squeaks when foraging for food; these are inaudible to most people but can be picked up by a bat-detector. HABITAT AND STATUS – The Pygmy Shrew is an extremely widespread species in the region and is found throughout most of mainland Britain and Ireland. It also occurs on many islands (in some instances it may have been introduced) although it is absent from the Scilly Isles, the Channel Isles and from Shetland. The species is found in a wide range of habi-tats including deciduous woodland margins, hedgerows, meadows, heathland and moors, the common factor being the presence of dense ground cover and an abundance of invertebrate food. It is impos-sible to put an accurate figure on the population size but it is likely to number in the millions across the region as a whole. HABITS AND NATURAL HISTORY – Pygmy Shrews are on the go for much of their brief lives, pausing now and again for a few minutes' rest before resuming their quest for food; they

adult feeding

are active both by day and at night, and throughout the year. Typically they forage in leaf litter and at ground level in vegetation, and are less inclined than Common Shrews to venture underground. However, they are seemingly adept at climbing because, not infrequently, they are discovered in Dor-mouse and bird boxes attached to trees and sited a couple of metres from the ground. Prey items include a wide range of invertebrates, including snails, slugs, spiders, woodlice and beetles. Females give birth in spring and early summer. There can be 2 litters a year, each containing 5–7 young; at birth the babies are blind and naked but at just 3 weeks old they are weaned. Like its Common cousin, the Pygmy Shrew is essentially an annual species; a few animals may live for 13 or 14 months, but most adults die within a year of being born, mortality being high during the summer months. OBSERVATION TIPS – Because of their small size and the fact that they lead unobtrusive lives, Pygmy Shrews are rather difficult to observe in the wild. If you have good hearing, or better still access to a bat-detector, you should be able to identify the species' presence in a given area. With luck you may then be able to watch an animal, albeit briefly, as it scuttles through the undergrowth.

PYGMY SHREW
ⓐ ABOVE **adult feeding** ⓑ BELOW **adult**

WATER SHREW *Neomys fodiens*

BODY LENGTH 6.5–9.5cm; TAIL LENGTH 5–8cm; WEIGHT 10–20g

As shrews go, this is a distinctive species and when seen well it looks strikingly bi-coloured. As its common name suggests, the Water Shrew has a distinct preference for aquatic habitats. **ADULT** has a dense coating of fur. The blackish upper parts and flanks usually contrast markedly with the whitish underparts and typically there is a clear demarcation between the 2 areas of colour; uniformly dark animals occur occasionally. In water, the fur traps a layer of air that gives a submerged animal a silvery appearance. The head is armed with sensitive bristles for detecting prey and the eyes are small and beady. Fringes of hairs on the tail, and on the proportionately large hind feet, assist swimming. The teeth are red-tipped but this can only be appreciated in dead specimens. **JUVENILE** is similar to an adult but smaller. **VOICE** – Utters a range of high-pitched squeaks during social encounters, and these can be detected by people with good hearing. HABITAT AND STATUS – Water Shrews are widespread across mainland Britain, although they are least numerous in the far north of Scotland and are absent from most islands. They are typically associated with freshwater habitats: slow-flowing and well-vegetated streams, along with watercress beds, are strongholds for the species. For Water Shrews to thrive, however, the water must be unpolluted (or as unpolluted as water can be in Britain today) and relatively undisturbed so that an abundance of aquatic and marginal invertebrates thrives there. Water Shrews are also encountered, less frequently, in more strictly terrestrial habitats such as hedgerows and meadows.

HABITS AND NATURAL HISTORY – Water Shrews forage for food, off and on, throughout the 24-hour period, although they are most consistently active after dark. At times they hunt along the margins and in the shallows of water bodies, but they are not averse to diving in search of prey, including the aquatic larvae and nymphs of insects, molluscs, crustaceans and worms; they will even tackle small fish and amphibians and have venomous saliva that presumably helps subdue some of their prey. Water Shrews excavate burrows and use established, well-trodden runways through the waterside vegetation. In particularly good habitats for the species (notably watercress beds and chalk streams) individual territories may overlap. During the summer months, Water Shrews are occasionally encountered well away from water, sometimes in completely inappropriate terrain. These seemingly 'lost' individuals are presumably ones that have been obliged to abandon aquatic habitats as they dry up. Females give birth in spring and early summer; there may be 1 or 2 litters a season, each containing 6 or more young. The babies are blind and naked at birth but are weaned at around 4 weeks of age. The average lifespan for a Water Shrew is just over a year. OBSERVATION TIPS – Water Shrews are reckoned to be more nocturnal than most of their cousins. Ironically, however, given the right location and a bit of luck, they are often the easiest shrew species to see at close quarters. Observers can sometimes sit quietly beside a chalk stream or watercress bed and watch animals swimming by or foraging along the margins. When submerged they are easy to spot and identify – look for an animated silvery bubble moving along the stream bed.

WATER SHREW
ABOVE adult

LESSER WHITE-TOOTHED SHREW *Crocidura suaveolens*

BODY LENGTH 5–8cm; TAIL LENGTH 2.5–4cm; WEIGHT 3.5–6g

A tiny and highly active shrew with an extremely restricted distribution in the region. **ADULT** has dense fur that is grey-brown in colour; the upper parts and flanks are rather dark but they grade to greyish white on the underparts. The head is extended to form a pointed muzzle, armed with sensitive, bristle-like whiskers; the eyes are small and beady while the external ears are relatively large and not hidden by fur. Note the bristle-covered tail. The teeth, including the tips, are white. **JUVENILE** is similar to an adult but smaller. **VOICE** – Utters shrill squeaks that are audible to people with good hearing. HABITAT AND STATUS – The Lesser White-toothed Shrew is widespread in southern Europe, its range extending up the west coast of France to southern Brittany. With its European range in mind, it is not surprising, therefore, to find its occurrence within our region is entirely southerly: it is found only on the Scilly Isles, and on Jersey and Sark in the Channel Islands. Suggestions have been made that in all of its British locations the species is an ancient introduction. The Lesser White-toothed Shrew occurs in a wide range of habitats that offer plenty of ground cover and abundant invertebrate life: bracken-covered banks, heathland and grassy areas are all favoured and it also forages on the seashore strandline. HABITS AND NATURAL HISTORY – Like all its cousins, this species is active for much of the day and night, pausing only occasionally for a rest. It feeds on a wide range of terrestrial invertebrates; on the seashore, it will take Sandhoppers and other related crustaceans. Given the mild climates experienced by the islands on which the Lesser White-toothed Shrew occurs, it is perhaps not surprising that the breeding season extends from spring to autumn, allowing 3 or 4 litters (each containing half a dozen or so young) to be produced. OBSERVATION TIPS – Lesser White-toothed Shrews can sometimes be seen moving through low vegetation but, on the Scilly Isles in particular, they are perhaps easiest to see on the seashore. This is not because they are necessarily more common in this habitat than elsewhere, but because it is more open, making observation easier. Even somewhere as relatively disturbed as Porthcressa Beach has produced sightings.

GREATER WHITE-TOOTHED SHREW *Crocidura russula*

BODY LENGTH 5–8.5cm; TAIL LENGTH 2.5–4.5cm; WEIGHT 10–14g

Extremely similar to, but marginally larger than, the Lesser White-toothed Shrew although, since the two will never be encountered side by side, the difference is rather academic. Because the distribution of our two *Crocidura* shrews does not overlap, a knowledge of their ranges provides the only realistic chance of accurate field identification. There are subtle differences between the teeth of the two species but separation on these grounds is best left to the experts. **ADULT** has dense fur that is grey-brown in colour; the upper parts and flanks are rather dark but they grade to greyish white on the underparts. The head is extended to form a pointed muzzle, armed with sensitive, bristle-like whiskers; the eyes are small but the external ears are relatively large and not hidden by fur. Note the bristle-covered tail. The teeth, including the tips, are white. **JUVENILE** is similar to an adult but smaller. **VOICE** – Utters shrill squeaks. HABITAT AND STATUS – The Greater White-toothed Shrew favours a wide range of habitats with plenty of ground cover, including hedgerows, woodland margins and grassy areas. It is widespread in mainland western Europe but in our region it is restricted to the Channel Islands of Guernsey, Alderney and Sark. HABITS AND NATURAL HISTORY – Like other shrew species, the Greater White-toothed Shrew is active throughout most of the 24-hour period, only pausing for brief moments to rest. Litters of 4 or 5 young can be produced at almost any time of the year, except the dead of winter. The babies are blind and naked at birth, but are weaned after just 3 weeks. OBSERVATION TIPS – If you have good hearing, listen for the Greater White-toothed Shrew's shrill calls, which may allow you to pinpoint the animal responsible. It can sometimes be discovered by quickly turning over boards or sheets of corrugated iron lying in grassy places.

LESSER WHITE-TOOTHED SHREW
⌄ adult

GREATER WHITE-TOOTHED SHREW
⌄ adult

GREATER HORSESHOE BAT *Rhinolophus ferrumequinum*

BODY AND TAIL LENGTH 9–11cm; WINGSPAN 30–35cm; WEIGHT 15–30g

A large and impressive species. The Greater Horseshoe Bat has a bizarre and distinctive facial appearance. **ADULT** is covered in rather soft, fluffy greyish-brown fur that is palest on the underparts and flushed rusty brown on the back. The nostrils are surrounded by a fleshy noseleaf that, when viewed head-on, is horseshoe-shaped; seen from the side fleshy projections are visible. These structures are associated with echolocation – in *Rhinolophus* bats, the signals are emitted via the nose, with the mouth shut. The ears, which lack a tragus, are broad and greyish brown. The wings are darker greyish brown.

JUVENILE is similar to an adult but it lacks the reddish-brown flush on the back. **VOICE** – Sometimes utters squeaking calls at roosts. Echolocation is in the 80–83kHz range. HABITAT AND STATUS – Just a few thousand Greater Horseshoe Bats survive today, living in the southwest of England and Wales. During the summer, the species roosts in cellars and roofs. In winter, they hibernate in caves, mines and cellars. They feed over meadows and in woodland clearings, hunting for insects up to the size of Cockchafers. HABITS AND NATURAL HISTORY – On mild nights Greater Horseshoe Bats typically emerge from their roosts an hour or so after sunset and feed throughout much of the night; the wingbeats are relatively slow. Hibernation occurs from October to April although bats emerge on mild winter nights to feed and drink. Hibernating bats shroud themselves in their wings. Mating occurs mainly in the autumn but, due to delayed fertilisation, the young are not born until early summer in the following year. Females with young gather in nursery colonies, often numbering several hundred individuals. Each female can produce just 1 baby a year and the young become independent at 2 months. OBSERVATION TIPS – At known sites, Greater Horseshoe Bats can sometimes be observed leaving their roosts at twilight. Please note, however, that like all bats, this species is protected by law and must not be disturbed in any way.

LESSER HORSESHOE BAT *Rhinolophus hipposideros*

BODY AND TAIL LENGTH 6–7.5cm; WINGSPAN 19.5–25cm; WEIGHT 6–9g

A medium-sized bat that is superficially similar to, but appreciably smaller than, its Greater cousin; both share the same facial appearance. **ADULT** has relatively long, fluffy fur that is greyish brown on the upper parts and greyish white below. Viewed from the front, the nostrils are surrounded by a fleshy, horseshoe-shaped noseleaf. The ears, which lack a tragus, are rather broad; both the ears and the wings are greyish brown.

JUVENILE is similar to an adult but the fur is greyer. **VOICE** – audible chattering squeaks can sometimes be heard at nursery colonies. Echolocation takes place in the 105–115kHz range. HABITAT AND STATUS – The species favours open woodlands and hedgerows. Summer roosting takes place communally in roofs and cellars; caves and mines are typical hibernation sites. The Lesser Horseshoe Bat is now restricted to southwest England, Wales and west Ireland and the population is estimated at over 15,000 individuals. HABITS AND NATURAL HISTORY – During the summer, Lesser Horseshoe Bats emerge at dusk and feed throughout the night. Compared to its Greater cousin, the wingbeats are more rapid. Hibernation occurs from October to April, the bats shrouding themselves in their wings. Mating occurs mainly in autumn but, due to delayed fertilisation, the young are not born until early summer in the following year. Lesser Horseshoe Bats are generally more solitary than their Greater cousins. However, females that have recently given birth, or that are just about to, gather in nursery colonies. Each female can produce just 1 baby a year; this is weaned after a month or so and becomes independent a few weeks later. OBSERVATION TIPS – If you are in the vicinity of a known summer roost, you might be lucky enough to see the bats emerge while there is still a glimmer of light left in the evening sky.

GREATER HORSESHOE BAT

LESSER HORSESHOE BAT

DAUBENTON'S BAT *Myotis daubentonii*
BODY AND TAIL LENGTH 7.5–9.5cm; WINGSPAN 25–27cm; WEIGHT 8–15g

A medium-sized bat that is often associated with water. Compared to some of its cousins it has relatively small ears and the tragus in the ear is also proportionately small. **ADULT** has silky fur that is yellow-brown above and greyish white below, the division between the two colours being relatively well defined. In profile, the head is rather rounded. The feet are disproportionately large, the calcar is long and the tail membrane is joined to the base of the toes. **JUVENILE** is darker and greyer than an adult, with a dark spot on the chin. **VOICE** – Echolocation calls are typically in the 45–55kHz range and so are essentially inaudible to the human ear, although people with good hearing can apparently hear various clicks and chirps. HABITAT AND STATUS – Daubenton's Bat is typically observed feeding over the still waters of ponds, lakes, canals and slow-flowing rivers. Often these habitats have wooded margins and the bats will sometimes forage in nearby clearings or over waterside grassland. The species is widespread across mainland Britain and Ireland; it is least numerous in the far north and in upland districts. More than 100,000 individuals are thought to be present in the region as a whole. HABITS AND NATURAL HISTORY – During the summer months, Daubenton's Bats emerge from their daytime roosts roughly 30–60 minutes after sunset and feed throughout most of the night. The wingbeats are relatively slow and they usually fly low over water when feeding; this allows them to grab insects that are close to, or actually on, the water surface, using their feet or tail membrane, without interrupting their flight. Caddisflies, mayflies, and midges and other night-flying Diptera are important in the diet. During the summer months, Daubenton's Bats roost, often communally, in the vicinity of water – usually in buildings, among brickwork under bridges, or in tree holes. Hibernation takes place from October to April, and caves, mines and undisturbed tunnels are favoured. Mating takes place from autumn to spring but implantation is delayed. Hence the young (1 per female) are born in early summer. OBSERVATION TIPS – Visit almost any suitable area of fresh water after dark and you stand a chance of seeing Daubenton's Bats. Bats will sometimes patrol the same stretch of water at regular intervals if the feeding is good, so if you train a torch on a favoured spot one should eventually fly through the beam.

NATTERER'S BAT *Myotis nattereri*
BODY AND TAIL LENGTH 8–9.5cm; WINGSPAN 25–30cm; WEIGHT 6–12g

A medium-sized bat. Compared to its cousins, the ears are noticeably large and the tragus is proportionately long. **ADULT** has medium-length fluffy fur that is yellowish brown on the upper parts and greyish white below. The face is almost bald and reddish in colour. In profile, the head appears rather elongated, creating an almost dog-like muzzle appearance. The wings are broad and the calcar reaches half the length of the tail membrane. **JUVENILE** is similar to the adult. **VOICE** – Echolocation calls are uttered across a broad range (35–80kHz). People with good hearing can hear high-pitched calls without the aid of a bat detector. HABITAT AND STATUS – Natterer's Bats favour light woodland, farmland, hedgerows and grassland. The species is widespread, absent only from the far north and from most Scottish islands. Around 100,000 individuals may be present in the region as a whole. HABITS AND NATURAL HISTORY – During the summer months, Natterer's Bats emerge from roosts an hour or so after sunset and continue to forage, off and on, throughout the night. Thanks to their rather broad wings, their wingbeats are relatively slow and they are capable of hovering momentarily. Nightflying insects, such as moths, beetles and bugs, feature heavily in their diet. During the summer, they roost in tree holes, buildings and under bridges; they will also use woodland bat boxes. Sites such as undisturbed canal tunnels and mines are favoured for hibernation, which occurs from October to April. Mating takes place at any time from autumn to spring but, thanks to delayed implantation, the young (1 per female) are not born until early summer. OBSERVATION TIPS – Mature parks and open woodland are particularly good for this species. If you stand beneath a mature tree and stare skywards, you may see the silhouette of a foraging bat.

DAUBENTON'S BAT

NATTERER'S BAT

BRANDT'S BAT *Myotis brandtii*

BODY AND TAIL LENGTH 7–9.5cm; WINGSPAN 21–25cm; WEIGHT 5–9g

A rather small and comparatively little-known species. Brandt's is very similar in appearance to the Whiskered Bat, from which it was only distinguished as a separate species as recently as 1970. Although subtle differences in external features exist between the two, separation in the field is problematic and frequently impossible. Certain identification is achieved only by examining the dentition. **ADULT** has relatively long, fluffy fur that is rich yellowish brown on the upper parts and greyish white underneath. The ears, which are dark brown, are relatively shorter than those of the Whiskered Bat (although they still look long when seen in isolation). The tragus is relatively shorter than in the Whiskered, and it has a convex posterior margin. The wings are dark brown and rather narrow. **JUVENILE** is similar to an adult but darker overall. **VOICE** – Utters twittering squeaks when alarmed. Echolocation occurs in the 40–80kHz range. HABITAT AND STATUS – Brandt's Bat favours open woodland and, although the species' full range is perhaps imprecisely known, it is certainly widespread in Wales and the west and north of England. HABITS AND NATURAL HISTORY – Although feeding activity is mainly nocturnal, Brandt's Bat can often be seen flying at dusk and occasionally it emerges from its roost in the late afternoon. The flight is rapid, although it also glides for short periods. Moths, flies and other insects are caught on the wing and feeding is often concentrated in the vicinity of woodland streams and ponds. In summer, Brandt's Bats often roost in buildings, roofs and bat boxes; in winter, hibernation occurs in tunnels, caves, tree holes and cellars. The young (1 per female) are born in early summer, females gathering in nursery roosts. The young become fully independent of their mothers after a couple of months. OBSERVATION TIPS – A summer visit to a wooded stream in Wales in the early evening should yield sightings of this species. As night falls, however, it may prove impossible to distinguish this species from other similarly sized bats that occur in the region.

WHISKERED BAT *Myotis mystacinus*

BODY AND TAIL LENGTH 6.5–9cm; WINGSPAN 19–23cm; WEIGHT 4–8g

Superficially similar to Brandt's Bat but typically marginally smaller in all respects. Although examining the dentition is the only foolproof means of distinguishing the two, a few external features exist that can help pinpoint the identity of an individual. **ADULT** has rather long, fluffy fur that is typically dark brown on the upper parts and greyish below. The ears are dark brown and the tragus is relatively longer than in the Whiskered Bat, with a straight (not convex) posterior margin. The wings are dark brown and rather narrow. **JUVENILE** is similar to an adult. **VOICE** – Utters high-pitched squeaks if disturbed. Echolocation occurs in the 40–80kHz range. HABITAT AND STATUS – Whiskered Bats favour open woodland and park grassland, often feeding over meadows or in the vicinity of water. They can sometimes be found in mature gardens in rural locations. The species has a scattered distribution in England and Wales and also occurs in Ireland, mainly in the south and west. HABITS AND NATURAL HISTORY – Whiskered Bats are less likely than Brandt's to emerge before dusk and are more exclusively nocturnal in their feeding habits. Their flight is rapid, the precise path constantly changing; however, they often patrol regular routes. In summer, they roost in buildings, tree holes and bat boxes; in winter, hibernation occurs in caves, mines and tunnels. Females give birth to a single young each year and often congregate in nursery roosts. Babies are born in early summer; mating will have occurred the previous autumn but fertilisation is delayed until spring. The young become fully independent of their mothers after a couple of months. OBSERVATION TIPS – Whiskered Bats can sometimes be seen emerging from rural outbuildings at dusk. In mature gardens and parks, they are occasionally illuminated in flight by outside lighting, to which moths and other insects are attracted.

BRANDT'S BAT

WHISKERED BAT

BECHSTEIN'S BAT *Myotis bechsteinii*

BODY AND TAIL LENGTH 8–10cm; WINGSPAN 25–30cm; WEIGHT 8–13g

A medium-sized and relatively long-eared bat, and one of the region's rarest and most endangered species. **ADULT** has rather long, fluffy fur that is reddish brown above and greyish white below. The bare face is pinkish red and the ears are proportionately long and broad, with 9 transverse folds visible; the tragus is long, narrow and pointed. The wings are dark brown and rather broad, with the membrane joined to the base of the feet. **JUVENILE** is similar to an adult but paler overall. **VOICE** – Echolocation mainly in the 50–60kHz range. HABITAT AND STATUS – Bechstein's Bat is associated mainly with deciduous woodland. Its distribution is patchy in the region, and it has been recorded from southern England and south Wales. It is difficult to assess the exact status of the species but it is likely that not many more than 1,000 individuals survive today in the region as a whole. HABITS AND NATURAL HISTORY – Bechstein's Bat has a rather delicate, almost fluttering flight, and is adept at catching flying moths and other small, nocturnal insects. Tree holes are used as roosting sites throughout the year, hibernation taking place there during the winter; in summer, bat boxes are sometimes occupied by this species. Mating occurs in the autumn but delayed fertilisation means that the young (1 per female) are not born until early summer the following year. Females occupy nursery roosts while pregnant and caring for their babies. OBSERVATION TIPS – Bechstein's Bat is such a rare species in the region that you are unlikely to discover one by chance. If you do, however, it should be reported immediately to your local bat group or Wildlife Trust because this species needs all the help it can get.

SEROTINE *Eptesicus serotinus*

BODY AND TAIL LENGTH 10.5–13.5cm; WINGSPAN 33–38cm; WEIGHT 17–35g

A large and impressive bat that is often associated with buildings and human habitation. **ADULT** has sleek fur that is dark brown on the upper parts and yellowish brown below. The nose and face are rather dark, as are the ears, which are broadly oval and bear 5 transverse folds; the tragus is sickle-shaped (curved in a forward direction) and roughly one-third the length of the ear. The wings are long, rather broad and dark. **JUVENILE** is similar to, but typically even darker than, an adult. **VOICE** – Utters shrill squeaks at roost sites. Echolocation occurs mainly in the 25–30kHz range. HABITAT AND STATUS – The Serotine Bat is associated with open woodland, parks and even mature gardens, often in the vicinity of rural human habitation. The species is fairly widespread in southern England and south Wales although the counties of Dorset and Sussex represent its strongholds in the region. It is likely that more than 10,000 individuals occur in the region as a whole. HABITS AND NATURAL HISTORY – Foraging flights typically start shortly after sunset, the wingbeats being rather slow and fluttering. Insects up to the size of Cockchafers and hawkmoths feature in the diet of the Serotine Bat. Buildings, barns and outhouses are favoured roosting and hibernation sites. Mating occurs in the autumn, but delayed fertilisation means that the young (1 per female) are not born until early summer the following year. Females occupy nursery roosts while pregnant and caring for their babies, which become independent after a couple of months. OBSERVATION TIPS – Because Serotine Bats emerge from their roosts to feed while there is still a glimmer of light in the evening sky, reasonable views can sometimes be obtained. A roost site can usually be identified by the presence of droppings outside the entrance, and by the occasional outburst of noisy squeaks from its residents inside. It goes without saying that such sites must not be disturbed in any way.

BECHSTEIN'S BAT

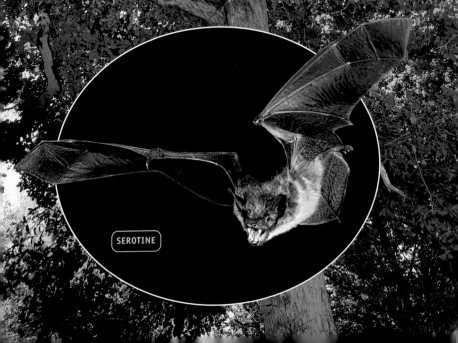

SEROTINE

NOCTULE *Nyctalus noctula*

BODY AND TAIL LENGTH 10–14cm; WINGSPAN 35–45cm; WEIGHT 20–40g

The largest bat in the region and an impressive animal by anyone's standards. The Noctule is also one of the most likely species to be encountered at dawn and dusk. **ADULT** has rather short fur that is golden brown overall, darkest on the back and paler below. The face is blackish brown, as are the ears, which are relatively large and broadly oval to triangular; the tragus is mushroom-shaped. The wings are long and rather narrow. **JUVENILE** is similar to an adult but much darker overall. **VOICE** – Loud clicks are uttered by flying bats and noisy 'yickering' calls can sometimes be heard from daytime roosts. Echolocation occurs in the 20–45kHz range. HABITAT AND STATUS – The Noctule favours open areas such as marshes, meadows and large woodland clearings, but it also occurs in mature suburban gardens and parks. The species is widespread, though seldom particularly numerous, in England and Wales. Although numbers have declined in recent decades, several tens of thousands of individuals are probably still found in the region as a whole. HABITS AND NATURAL HISTORY – Noctules take to the wing at dusk, sometimes while it is still light enough just about to make out the rich orange-brown colour of the fur. They forage, off and on, throughout the night and are sometimes still on the wing at dawn; flying insects up to the size of Cockchafers and hawkmoths are taken. Tree holes are favoured roost sites and bat boxes are sometimes used in summer. Hibernation takes place from November to April and deep tree holes and crevices are favoured. Noctules mate in the autumn but because of delayed fertilisation the young (1, occasionally 2, per female) are not born until the following summer; the young are fully independent after a couple of months. In spring and summer females occupy nursery roosts and the young often reside in a crèche. In summer and autumn males are solitary, territorial and reside in mating roosts, which are visited by females. OBSERVATION TIPS – Because of its size, the Noctule is relatively easy to see well and identify. Look for splattered droppings and urine around the entrance hole to the roost site.

LEISLER'S BAT *Nyctalus leisleri*

BODY AND TAIL LENGTH 8–11.5cm; WINGSPAN 30–35cm; WEIGHT 10–20g

A medium-sized bat that is superficially similar to, but appreciably smaller than, a Noctule. Leisler's Bat is an active, open-country species. **ADULT** has rather long fur that is dark brown on the upper parts and lighter buffish brown below. The face is blackish, as are the ears, which are broadly oval to triangular, with 4–5 transverse folds; the tragus is mushroom-shaped. The wings are dark and relatively narrow. **JUVENILE** is similar to an adult but typically darker. **VOICE** – Utters shrill calls in flight. Echolocation occurs in the 15–45kHz range. HABITAT AND STATUS – Leisler's Bat feeds over marshes, meadows and in open woodland. The species is widespread and fairly common in Ireland but its distribution elsewhere in the region is rather patchy. Several thousand individuals are probably present in the region as a whole. HABITS AND NATURAL HISTORY – Leisler's Bats take to the wing just as it is getting dark; maximum feeding activity is usually concentrated just after dusk and just before dawn. The flight is fast and the wingbeats are rapid. Tree holes and roof spaces are favoured roost sites and bat boxes are sometimes used in summer. Hibernation takes place from November to March and deep tree holes and crevices are used. Leisler's Bats mate in the autumn but because of delayed fertilisation the young (typically 1 per female, but twins are not unknown) are not born until the following summer; the young are fully independent after a couple of months. In spring and summer females occupy nursery roosts and the young often reside in a crèche. In summer and autumn males are solitary, territorial and reside in mating roosts, which are visited by females. OBSERVATION TIPS – Ireland, the species' stronghold, is the place to be if you want to see a Leisler's Bat although scattered colonies can be found in central southern England as well. If you want to encourage the species then put up bat boxes; viewed from a safe distance, the bats can be seen emerging from them at dusk.

NOCTULE

LEISLER'S BAT

COMMON PIPISTRELLE *Pipistrellus pipistrellus*

BODY AND TAIL LENGTH 6–8.5cm; WINGSPAN 18–24cm; WEIGHT 3.5–8.5g

Our smallest, most numerous and widespread bat. **ADULT** has sleek, fluffy fur that is typically rich orange-brown above and buffish brown below. The face is blackish, as are the ears, which are broadly oval to triangular with 4–5 transverse folds on the outer edge; the tragus is club-shaped and slightly curved. The wings are dark brown. **JUVENILE** is similar to an adult but typically darker and less rufous. **VOICE** – People with good hearing can sometimes detect high-pitched contact calls. Echolocation calls peak at around 45kHz. HABITAT AND STATUS – The Common Pipistrelle is widespread and many hundreds of thousands of individuals are thought to be present in the region as a whole. It occurs in rural wetlands and woodlands, as well as mature gardens and parks in towns and villages. HABITS AND NATURAL HISTORY – Common Pipistrelles emerge from their roosts half an hour or so after sunset and feed off and on throughout the night. Their flight is fluttery, the bats constantly changing direction as they locate prey. Roof spaces in modern houses appear to be the roost sites of choice. Female Common Pipistrelles are colonial during the summer months, giving birth (usually 1 young per female) in the summer months. Males are solitary and territorial in summer and autumn, with females visiting their chosen roosts. Common Pipistrelles hibernate, off and on, from November to March, in mixed-sex colonies. OBSERVATION TIPS – Watch for this species hawking for insects around lighting in the garden. They are found in houses built as recently as the 1970s and 1980s. NOTE – **Nathusius' Pipistrelle** (*P. nathusii*) is occasionally detected by bat workers. It is superficially similar to the Common Pipistrelle but is marginally larger, has a relatively longer thumb and hairs are present on the upper surface of the tail membrane. It favours more rural habitats than its Common cousin.

NATHUSIUS' PIPISTRELLE

SOPRANO PIPISTRELLE *Pipistrellus pygmaeus*

BODY AND TAIL LENGTH 6–8.5cm; WINGSPAN 18–24cm; WEIGHT 3.5–8.5g

Essentially identical in appearance to the Common Pipistrelle and indistinguishable in the field without the aid of a bat-detector: the two species echolocate at discretely different frequencies. **ADULT** is similar to an adult Common Pipistrelle (*see above*). **JUVENILE** is similar to a juvenile Common Pipistrelle (*see above*). **VOICE** – Utters high-pitched contact calls that people with good hearing can detect. Echolocation peaks at a frequency of around 55kHz – higher than the Common Pipistrelle, hence soprano. HABITAT AND STATUS – Only recently has the Soprano Pipistrelle been recognised as a species in its own right, distinct from the Common Pipistrelle with which it was once lumped. Consequently there is little precise information available to determine its true distribution and abundance although it seems to be as widespread as its cousin, and relatively numerous too. HABITS AND NATURAL HISTORY – Similar to the Common Pipistrelle although it favours more rural habitats. OBSERVATION TIPS – Without the aid of a bat-detector, operated by an experienced bat worker, identification is impossible.

BARBASTELLE *Barbastella barbastellus*

BODY AND TAIL LENGTH 8.5–11cm; WINGSPAN 25–29cm; WEIGHT 7–13g

A medium-sized and extremely rare bat in the region. **ADULT** has long, glossy fur that is blackish brown, darkest on the back and palest on the belly. The face is blackish and has a rather squashed, pug-like appearance. The ears are dark and broadly triangular; they meet in the middle of the forehead and have a rather long, triangular tragus. The wings are dark, broad and pointed. **JUVENILE** is similar to an adult. **VOICE** – Typically silent within the range of human hearing. HABITAT AND STATUS – The Barbastelle favours undisturbed wooded areas and will sometimes visit mature rural gardens. It is restricted mainly to southern England and south Wales. HABITS AND NATURAL HISTORY – Barbastelles sometimes emerge from their roosts half an hour or so before sunset. They feed, off and on, throughout the night. Tree holes, caves and roofs in old buildings are used for summer roosts and trees and caves are used for hibernation. OBSERVATION TIPS – This species sometimes feeds while flying low over the water.

COMMON PIPISTRELLE

BARBASTELLE

BROWN LONG-EARED BAT *Plecotus auritus*
BODY AND TAIL LENGTH 7–10.5cm; WINGSPAN 24–28cm; WEIGHT 6–12g
A widespread and distinctive bat. **ADULT** has fluffy, long fur that is buffish brown above and buffish white below. The ears are the species' most distinctive features and are extremely long, almost comically so. They are pinkish brown and have numerous transverse folds; note the long, narrow and pointed tragus that appears translucent pink for much of its length. The face is rather uniformly pinkish brown and the wings are brown. **JUVENILE** is similar to an adult but appears greyer overall, creating potential for confusion with a Grey Long-eared Bat. **VOICE** – Utters various chirping squeaks when alarmed. Echolocation peaks in the 30–40kHz range. HABITAT AND STATUS – The Brown Long-eared Bat favours a wide range of wooded habitats, being found in parks, mature gardens and hedgerows as well as deciduous and mixed woodland. It is widespread throughout mainland areas as far north as southern Scotland and is reckoned to be our second most-numerous bat after the Common Pipistrelle; more than 100,000 individuals may be present in the region as a whole. HABITS AND NATURAL HISTORY – Brown Long-eared Bats typically emerge from their roosts after dark and feed, off and on, for much of the night. Summer roost sites include tree holes and roof spaces; bat boxes are often occupied. Hibernation takes place from November to April and roof spaces, cellars and caves are preferred. Brown Long-eared Bats have a rather slow flight with fluttering wingbeats. They feed mainly on moths, some of which are taken on the wing; they also glean prey from foliage. Babies are born in early summer (typically 1 per female), the bats occupying nursery roosts; the young become independent after 6 weeks. OBSERVATION TIPS – Shine a torch into a tree canopy, or along a hedgerow, and with luck you should see Brown Long-eared Bats diving into the foliage to glean insects. The species' long-eared appearance make it almost unmistakable.

adult in flight

daytime roost

droppings

GREY LONG-EARED BAT *Plecotus austriacus*
BODY AND TAIL LENGTH 8–11cm; WINGSPAN 26–30cm; WEIGHT 7–14g
Superficially very similar to a Brown Long-eared Bat but separable with care using external features, notably the colour of the fur. **ADULT** has long, fluffy fur that is dark grey above and greyish white below. The face is dark (particularly between the eyes), giving the species something of 'highwayman's mask' appearance. The ears are extremely long (a shade longer even than in the Brown Long-eared Bat) and the tragus is grey, not translucent pink. The wings are dark grey-brown. **JUVENILE** is similar to an adult. **VOICE** – Utters various chirping squeaks when alarmed. Echolocation occurs mainly in the 35–40kHz range. HABITAT AND STATUS – Being intolerant of cold winters, the Grey Long-eared Bat has a southerly distribution in Europe; southern England is the northwestern limit of its range. Most records come from Devon, Dorset, Hampshire and Sussex; it also occurs on the Channel Islands. It is likely that several hundred individuals are present in the region at any one time, although it is impossible to gauge the population size with any accuracy. Grey Long-eared Bats are usually associated with mature gardens in towns and villages. HABITS AND NATURAL HISTORY – The Grey Long-eared Bat emerges from its roost after dark and forages throughout the night. The flight is rather slow and fluttering; it will hover occasionally. Roof spaces are used for summer roosts, when females form communal nurseries. The young are born in early summer (typically 1 per female) and they become independent after 6 weeks or so. Hibernation takes place from October to April and cellars and caves are preferred. OBSERVATION TIPS – Grey Long-eared Bats sometimes hawk for insects around outside lights to which moths are attracted.

BROWN LONG-EARED BAT

RABBIT *Oryctolagus cuniculus*

BODY LENGTH 35–50cm; TAIL LENGTH 5–8cm; ADULT WEIGHT 1.5–2.5kg

A distinctive, long-eared burrowing mammal. The Rabbit is an alien introduction to our region that is now widespread and common, sometimes even locally abundant. At an individual level, a Rabbit is an engaging and almost adorable creature. But in the context of the countryside at large, the species' grazing and nibbling habits cause considerable environmental and economic damage. Consequently, many people consider them to be an unwelcome addition to our native fauna. **ADULT** has mainly greyish-brown fur with a rufous patch on the nape, and pale greyish underparts. The ears are long with rounded tips and the tail is dark above and white below. The location of the eyes gives the Rabbit all-round vision. Compared to both hare species, the Rabbit's legs and ears are proportionately shorter; the ears are tipped brown, not conspicuously black as is the case with a Brown Hare. In the absence of ground predators on some offshore islands, black (melanic) rabbits are encountered occasionally. **JUVENILE** is similar to an adult but with a proportionately larger head and shorter ears. **VOICE** – When seriously threatened, a Rabbit will squeal loudly in alarm. HABITAT AND STATUS – Rabbits are found a wide range of habitats but do best where areas of short vegetation, such as grassland or arable fields, are sited close to scrub-covered banks where burrows can be excavated. Farmland and downland invariably support thriving populations of Rabbits but scrub-fringed roadside verges are becoming familiar haunts for the species as well. The Rabbit probably made its first appearance in Britain some 900 years ago, brought here by the Normans and encouraged for its meat and fur. Introductions were not restricted just to the mainland but also occurred on offshore islands. Consequently, Rabbits are now found throughout almost the whole of the region, although they are least common in, or absent from, upland districts. In an effort to control numbers – 100 million is not an unrealistic estimate of numbers that were present in the mid-20th century – the *Myxoma* virus was released in the region and in 1953 alone the disease is thought to have wiped out 99 per cent of the British population. Inevitably, however, a degree of resistance to the disease developed and numbers have crept up steadily ever since. Currently, several tens of millions of Rabbits are thought to be present in the region as a whole, despite the occasional crash in numbers, at the local level at least, due to myxomatosis and Rabbit haemorrhagic disease (RHD). HABITS AND NATURAL HISTORY – Rabbits live in social groups that range in size according to the availability of food and the presence of suitable ground for excavation. In prime locations, burrow complexes (known as *warrens*) can be extensive with numerous entrance holes. Animals are essentially crepuscular or nocturnal in their habits although they do become bolder and partially diurnal where they are not persecuted. They seldom graze more than a few hundred metres from their warren and are extremely alert to danger, their senses of hearing, sight and smell being acute. Rabbits are capable of breeding year-round although most litters (4–8 young per litter) are born between March and August. In theory, a healthy female could produce 6 or 7 litters each year so their reproductive potential is prodigious. Unsurprisingly, Rabbits have plenty of predators, not least of them being humans. Badgers, Stoats, Foxes and Buzzards all take their quota of Rabbits as well. OBSERVATION TIPS – These days, Rabbits are probably easiest to observe beside roads, and will often feed during daylight hours, seemingly oblivious to the roar of passing traffic. If you want to watch them in more natural settings, find a warren where you can observe the entrances from a downwind position. You will need to conceal yourself and sit quietly and still because the slightest hint of danger will result in the Rabbits remaining underground. Late afternoons offer the best opportunities for observation.

black/melanic form

baby rabbits in nest

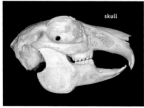
skull

RABBIT
⊙ ABOVE **adult**
⊙ BELOW LEFT **droppings**
⊙ BELOW **burrow entrance**

BROWN HARE *Lepus europaeus*

BODY LENGTH 45–65cm; TAIL LENGTH 7–12cm; WEIGHT 2.5–6.5kg

A superficially Rabbit-like animal but with proportionally longer legs and ears. The Brown Hare is a fast runner; unlike its cousin, it does not burrow. **ADULT** has a yellowish-brown coat that is grizzled with grey and black hairs, especially on the back. The coat is thicker in winter than in summer and often slightly darker and more reddish in appearance. The ears are long and black-tipped and the legs are long too. The tail has a dark upper surface with a pale fringe, and it is whitish underneath; it is held down when the animal is running. The eyes, which are rather large and 'wild' looking, are located high on the sides of the head and allow near all-round vision. **JUVENILE** (*leveret*) is similar to an adult but with a proportionally larger head. VOICE – Mainly silent but will some-times scream in terror. HABITAT AND STATUS – Brown Hares are usually thought of as animals of arable farmland. However, in part this may be because they are far easier to see in this habitat than in others, particularly when the crops are short. They are also found in meadows and in open woodland, especially in sites with adjacent areas of grass-land and arable crops. Numbers have declined markedly over the past 50 years or so, the most noticeable reduction in numbers taking place on arable farmland; changes in agricultural practices are assumed to be responsible. The Brown Hare is essentially a lowland animal. It is least common, or absent from, the West Country and upland areas in northern Britain; it is extremely local in Ireland, having been introduced there. A few hundred thousand animals are thought to be present in the region as a whole. HABITS AND NATURAL HISTORY – In areas where they are disturbed by people (or more usually their uncontrolled dogs) Brown Hares can be almost exclusively nocturnal and crepuscular, spending the hours of daylight hidden in a shallow depression (called a *form*) that they have excavated for themselves. However, when disturbance is not a factor, they are sometimes active in the mornings and afternoons too, especially in the summer months. Brown Hares are primarily grazing animals, eating grassland vegetation and arable crops, the latter in the early stages of growth. In woodland and scrub areas, they will nibble shoots and strip tree bark. Like Rabbits, they engage in refection, pellets from the first digestive cycle being consumed again to extract extra proteins. They tend to be solitary for much of the year, although individuals' home ranges do overlap and several animals will sometimes form what appears to be a loose association if the feeding is good. So-called 'mad March hare' behaviour ('boxing' bouts and frantic chases) usually involves unreceptive females chasing off suitors, rather than sparring males. Although Brown Hares will breed throughout much of the year the majority of young are born between March and September. A female will usually produce 3 lit-ters a year, each containing 3–4 young. For the first few weeks of life, leverets spend much of the time crouched motionless in sep-arate forms. The mother suckles them once every 24-hour period, usu-ally after dark. Understandably, infant mortality is high. OBSERVATION TIPS – Brown Hares are engaging animals to watch. In the spring, 'boxing matches' are a frequent sight and are extremely entertaining. In locations where they are not disturbed or persecuted (a relatively rare thing these days) Brown Hares can become remarkably tolerant of people on foot, often preferring to crouch, with their ears flat, in the hope of not being seen, rather than flee. If you stand and stare at a crouching Brown Hare for any length of time you are likely to unnerve it but if you don't change your direction or speed of walking it may well sit tight. Brown Hares are usually tolerant of vehicles and so, when driving around farmland, your car becomes the perfect mobile hide.

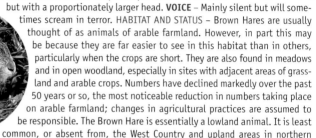

leveret

boxing match

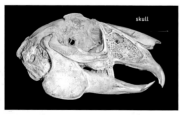

skull

BROWN HARE
ABOVE **adult**
RIGHT **droppings**
MAIN PIC **regularly used trail**

MOUNTAIN HARE *Lepus timidus*

BODY LENGTH 45–55cm; TAIL LENGTH 4–8cm; WEIGHT 2.5–5.5kg

Superficially similar to the Brown Hare but with proportionately shorter ears and a more compact body. Mountain Hares also have uniformly whitish tails and, in some regions, entirely different coat colours in summer and winter. The distributions of the two species seldom overlap, Mountain Hares usually being found on more rugged, upland terrain than their lowland cousins. **ADULT** Scottish race (*L. t. scoticus*) has a mainly greyish-brown coat in summer, which is palest on the underparts and most rufous on the head. Note the blackish tips to the ears. The underfur is blue-grey and this can lead to the animal

Irish Hare, summer

assuming a rather bluish hue in some lights, which explains one of its alternative names, Blue Hare. In winter, Mountain Hares (in Britain) acquire a thick coat of mainly white hair; the nose usually remains buffish, as do the ears, which are dark-tipped. Adult Irish race (*L. t. hibernicus*, often referred to simply as the Irish Hare) has a rather reddish-brown coat in summer (closer to a Brown Hare than a Mountain Hare from Scotland). In winter, the coat does not become completely white: the back and the head are usually variably and extensively tinged with buffish brown. **JUVENILE** (*leveret*) is born fully furred with a grey-brown coat. **VOICE** – Mainly silent but screams when in great distress. HABITAT AND STATUS – As the English name suggests, Mountain Hares are associated with upland areas, typically grassy mountain slopes and windswept heather moorland. Occasionally they will be encountered in grassy fields on the fringes of moorland habitat and in Ireland they are more likely to be seen in open, grassy and stony places. Mountain Hares are fairly common and widespread in suitable habitats in Scotland and Ireland. Scottish animals have been introduced at various times to England, and persist in the Peak District. To confuse matters, Mountain Hares from Ireland have been introduced to various sites in Scotland! Several hundred thousand individuals are probably present in the region as a whole.

winter adult (Scotland)

HABITS AND NATURAL HISTORY – Typically, Mountain Hares lead solitary lives although the range of an individual usually overlaps with those of

summer adult (Scotland)

its neighbours, and several may gather together if the feeding is particularly good. Most feeding activity takes place at dawn, dusk and after dark. The hours of daylight are often spent crouched in a depression known as a *form*, usually located in the lee of a clump of Ling (*Calluna vulgaris*) or a rock. Mountain Hares feed on the young shoots of Ling, as well as moorland vegetation generally. Like their cousins, they engage in refection, consuming for a second time those faecal pellets produced by the first digestive cycle. They are capable of running at great speeds and of astonishing leaps and changes in direction. The Mountain Hare breeding season extends from late winter to late summer. A female may produce up to 3 litters a year, each containing on average 2–4 leverets. For the first few weeks of life, the young spend the hours of daylight concealed in an underground den at the end of a short, excavated tunnel. Mortality among leverets is high. OBSERVATION TIPS – Often the first glimpse you will get of a Mountain Hare is of an animal that you have disturbed from cover sprinting for its life away from you. However, if you persevere you can usually eventually spot one crouching in the moorland vegetation. Once in a while an animal will stand up to survey its surroundings, allowing human observers to pinpoint its location. With care, crouching Mountain Hares can sometimes be approached closely on foot, but the best views are often obtained from a car, on minor roads across the moors. Look out for dust baths; particularly good sites may be used by a number of different individuals.

droppings

MOUNTAIN HARE
⌃ ABOVE **adult in spring (Scotland)**
⌄ MAIN PIC **tracks**

RED SQUIRREL *Sciurus vulgaris*

BODY LENGTH 20–25cm; TAIL LENGTH 15–20cm; WEIGHT 300–350g

Our only native squirrel. The Red Squirrel has an emblematic – almost iconic – appearance and its outline is also a frequently encountered heraldic device. **ADULT** has a compact body with a proportionately large head and ears. The tail is bushy – almost wispy towards the tip. In summer, the coat is rather uniformly reddish brown or orange-brown, although the underparts are contrastingly creamy white. Short ear tufts are present. Initially the tail is usually similar in colour to the body upperparts, but it bleaches to a noticeably paler hue with time. In winter, Red Squirrels possess a thicker coat; typically the back is greyish brown while the legs and head are reddish brown. Strikingly long ear tufts are noticeable features in winter. Observers should bear in mind that not only does the precise coloration of an individual vary according to the time of year but that its genetic origins may have a bearing on its appearance too – mainland European Red Squirrels, which have been introduced to Britain, are typically darker overall than native animals, particularly so on the tail. **JUVENILE** is similar to an adult but smaller. **VOICE** – Utters a variety of chattering calls. HABITAT AND STATUS – Prior to the introduction of the Grey Squirrel to Britain in 1876, the Red Squirrel was common and fairly widespread in both deciduous and mixed forests across the region. Today, however, it is numerous only in the north of the region, being restricted to conifer forests – Scots Pines are particularly favoured – in Scotland, Northumberland and Cumbria. Isolated populations are also found in central and north Wales, Norfolk (Thetford Forest), Lancashire, the Isle of Wight, and Brownsea and Furzey islands in Poole Harbour, Dorset. Elsewhere in England it is extinct. There are thought to be around 120,000 or so Red Squirrels in Britain, the vast majority in Scotland. Direct competition between Red and Grey Squirrels is cited as the main cause of the former's demise and its effective restriction to coniferous habitats. More recently, Greys have spread *Parapox* virus to a few populations of Reds, causing local extinctions. However, habitat destruction, fragmentation and degradation in England probably also played their parts, certainly when it came to disadvantaging the native species. Red Squirrels are locally common in Ireland and, so far, the introduced Grey Squirrel has had less of an impact on their numbers there than it has in England. HABITS AND NATURAL HISTORY – Red Squirrels are typically solitary animals although there is sometimes a degree of overlap between the territories of neighbouring individuals. Although they will forage on the ground, they are mainly arboreal animals, feeding on nuts extracted from pine cones, as well as acorns, fungi, berries, buds and shoots, in season. The front paws are used to manipulate food and feeding animals typically sit on their haunches with their tail pressed against their backs. Most feeding activity takes place in the early morning and late afternoon. At other times of the day, Red Squirrels usually rest in their drey – a nest constructed from twigs and lined with grasses and mosses. The drey is usually located close to the trunk of tree, 10–15m off the ground. Mating usually occurs in the first few months of the year and the young (usually 3–5 per litter) are born 7 weeks or so later. They remain with the mother for a few months before beginning to disperse. OBSERVATION TIPS – Red Squirrels are fairly easy to see if you visit a conifer forest in the Scottish Highlands or the Lake District. In a few locations, animals may visit forested car parks and campsites in search of food; early mornings provide the best opportunities for observation. Sometimes Red Squirrels will even come to woodland feeding stations. Elsewhere in the region, Brownsea Island offers opportunities for observation in southern England. The species' presence in an area is indicated by the discovery of characteristically gnawed pine cones.

adult,
late summer

gnawed pine cones

RED SQUIRREL
⊙ BELOW adult, winter

GREY SQUIRREL *Sciurus carolinensis*

BODY LENGTH 25–30cm; TAIL LENGTH 20–25cm; WEIGHT 450–600g

A widespread and abundant alien. This is the familiar squirrel species of urban parks and gardens. **ADULT** has a plump but relatively elongated body and a long, bushy tail. Note the rather rounded ears that lack ear tufts. The coat, including the tail, is mainly grizzled grey with a whitish chest and belly. Individuals are variably tinged with brown on the back, flanks and legs; some animals can appear almost reddish, so there is potential for confusion with a Red Squirrel if a poor or partial view is obtained. During the winter months the coat is thick and uniformly grizzled grey, lacking the brown tinge. **JUVENILE** is similar to a summer adult but the tail usually appears more scrawny than bushy. **VOICE** – Utters a teeth-smacking *tchack* when alarmed, and various chattering calls. HABITAT AND STATUS – The Grey Squirrel is native to North America. It was first introduced to our region in 1876 and for the subsequent 50 years or so a succession of people continued this harebrained strategy. Since then the species has expanded its range, and its numbers have increased dramatically. Today, several million individuals may be present in the region as a whole, although it has yet to make its mark in northern Scotland and Ireland. Although it is easy to appreciate why some people think of the Grey Squirrel as adorable and a welcome addition to our fauna, the reality is that its presence here is little short of an ecological disaster. The impact it has had on the native Red Squirrel is well known, but its effect upon other wildlife can be equally profound. In the case of coppiced Hazel, managed for Dormice, if Grey

drey

Squirrels are left to their own devices they will do an effective job consuming or destroying most of the nut harvest, leaving little or nothing for Dormice and other native species. Part of the reason for the Grey Squirrel's success in our region is its adaptability. Although they probably do best in deciduous woodlands, they are quite at home in rural and urban gardens, as well as city parks. In forestry circles they are considered a pest, because of their bark-stripping habits, and are treated as such. HABITS AND NATURAL HISTORY – Grey Squirrels are usually solitary animals although individuals' territories may overlap, and several animals may congregate in areas of good feeding. They are diurnal and active throughout the day. Much of the time is spent in the trees although they will descend to the ground, particularly in winter, to forage. A Grey Squirrel's diet is varied and includes nuts, berries, fruits, berries and tree bark; food is sometimes cached in times of

nut opened by inexperienced animal (see p.219)

plenty. They have learned to visit bird feeders, and are not averse to taking the eggs and young of birds, sometimes even raiding bird boxes. The hours of darkness are spent in a drey, constructed from twigs, lined with leaves and placed high in a tree. Grey Squirrels do not hibernate, although in winter, several hours of daylight may be spent in the drey and on cold, wet days they may not emerge at all. Mating usually occurs in late winter and early spring, the young being born after a gestation period of 6 weeks or so. The litter size is usually 2 or 3 and the young become independent after around 4 months. OBSERVATION TIPS – You should have little difficulty seeing Grey Squirrels, except if you live in the north of Scotland, on an island, or in the western half of Ireland. They are frequent visitors to gardens, sometimes making a nuisance of themselves. In urban parks, where the public often feeds them, Grey Squirrels can become remarkably bold and inquisitive.

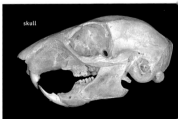

skull

GREY SQUIRREL
⌄ BELOW adult

HAZEL DORMOUSE *Muscardinus avellanarius*
BODY LENGTH 7–9cm; TAIL LENGTH 6–8cm; WEIGHT 15–30g

Arguably the region's most 'cute' mammal. The image of a Hazel Dormouse (often referred to simply as a Dormouse) is familiar to almost all naturalists, even though its retiring and mainly nocturnal habits ensure that few have actually seen one in the wild. **ADULT** has a thick and mainly golden-brown coat, the colour being almost unique among British rodents (only the diminutive Harvest Mouse comes close in terms of colour); the throat and belly are typically paler than the rest of the body. The body is rather plump-looking, although post-hibernation animals in spring do look comparatively slim. Note the rather large, beady eyes and rounded ears. The feet have relatively long, flexible toes that provide a good grip when the animal is climbing. The tail is covered in a thicker layer of rather long hairs that are the same colour as the body. **JUVENILE** is similar to an adult but with a proportionately larger head and a less rufous coat. **VOICE** – Mainly silent. HABITAT AND STATUS – The Hazel Dormouse is associated with ancient woodlands, or perhaps more accurately woodlands that have an ancient history. The difference lies in the fact that continuity in woodland management, rather than ancient trees *per se*, is probably the most important factor. Dormice like a varied woodland structure in order to provide them with food and shelter throughout the year. Mature trees (particularly Pedunculate Oak) are important at all times but particularly in the spring when flowers, pollen and associated insects feature in the diet. A closed canopy is vital, too, because Hazel Dormice are strictly arboreal and will not willingly visit the ground in order to move from tree to tree. As the season progresses, berries, fruits and nuts become important, particularly with regards to fattening up for hibernation, and the presence of Hazel

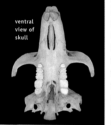

ventral view of skull

lower jaw

(for its nuts) is crucial, coppiced sites being the optimum Dormouse habitat. Honeysuckle is vital, too, the berries being consumed and the bark stripped to construct the nest. Hazel Dormice are widespread in Wales and southern and central England; the northernmost populations are in the Lake District. Although the species is local (due to habitat fragmentation) there are probably several hundred thousand individuals in the region. However, because Dormice will not cross open ground, isolated populations will remain that way and, in the event of a catastrophe, natural recolonisation will not occur. HABITS AND NATURAL HISTORY – The Hazel Dormouse is well known for the fact that it hibernates. Typically this takes place between October and April although, in reality, there is scant knowledge about what goes on in the wild and much of what is known is based on anecdotal evidence. Hibernation takes place in an underground nest and those that have been discovered are usually sited among a tangle of underground roots. Animals appear in spring, often having lost half their body weight during their winter sleep; the flowers of willows, and the associated insects, are important for regaining their reserves at this time of year. During spring and summer, Dormice spend the hours of daylight (in a state of torpor) in spherical nests (typically 12–15cm in diameter), constructed mainly of stripped Honeysuckle bark, and often located in a tangled mass of the climber. They will also use nest boxes at this time of year. Mating occurs in early summer and most females give birth in late July or August (usually 3–7 young per litter). The young remain with their mother for around 2 months. Very occasionally a second litter is produced in September but the survival rate for second-brood young is not good – in some seasons they do not have enough time to achieve a satisfactory pre-hibernation weight. OBSERVATION TIPS – Because they are secretive, wary and essentially nocturnal, you are most unlikely to stumble across Hazel Dormice in the wild by chance. Look for evidence of their presence in the form of stripped Hazel bark and old summer nests (which become visible during the winter months when the leaves have fallen). The most conclusive proof of the species' presence is the discovery of nibbled hazelnuts: unlike other rodents, Dormice make a perfectly round hole that has chisel-like tooth marks on the outer rim, but a perfectly smooth inner surface. Since Dormice usually tackle the nuts at the blunt end, the finished article often resembles a miniature clog. If you want to encourage Dormice, put up nest boxes (see p.204). Wildlife Trusts and the various mammal organisations regularly organise Dormouse courses where the animals can be seen under licence.

HAZEL DORMOUSE
- ⊙ ABOVE **adult**
- ⊙ LEFT **nibbled Hazelnut** (*see also* p.219)
- ⊙ RIGHT **hibernating adult**

EDIBLE DORMOUSE *Glis glis*

BODY LENGTH 15–18cm; TAIL LENGTH 13–15cm; WEIGHT 80–250g

A plump rodent that is relatively large, at least by Dormouse standards. The Edible Dormouse has a passing resemblance to a miniature Grey Squirrel. In the past, it has gone by the names of Fat Dormouse and Glis. **ADULT** has something of the body proportions of a Brown Rat, and indeed sometimes achieves a size comparable to a medium-sized rat. However, its appearance is rather variable: in autumn, just prior to hibernation, the body weight can be almost double that of the same animal post-hibernation; unsurprisingly, the body appears sleek in spring but plump and rather rounded in autumn. Perhaps the most distinctive feature of an Edible Dormouse is its greyish coat (sometimes

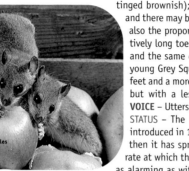

juveniles

tinged brownish); in most animals, the throat and belly are whitish and there may be hint of a dark vertebral stripe down the back. Note also the proportionately large eyes and rounded ears, and the relatively long toes. The presence of a long, bushy tail (brownish grey and the same colour as the body) could lead to confusion with a young Grey Squirrel but the latter has proportionately larger hind feet and a more rounded head. **JUVENILE** is similar to a small adult but with a less bushy tail and a browner coat in most cases. **VOICE** – Utters various chattering grunts and squeals. HABITAT AND STATUS – The Edible Dormouse is not native to Britain but was introduced in 1902 to Tring Park in Hertfordshire. Inevitably, since then it has spread into the surrounding countryside. However, the rate at which the population and range has expanded has not been as alarming as with some other introduced aliens and it is still more or less confined to the Chilterns. In parts of Europe where it is native, the Edible Dormouse is usually associated with mature deciduous woodlands, and indeed this sort of habitat is often occupied by the species in England. Being essentially arboreal in habits, it does require an almost continuous canopy of mature trees in order to thrive. However, it also finds large, mature gardens in the Chilterns area much to its liking, especially where fruit trees supplement its diet and loft spaces provide ready-made accommodation. There are probably several tens of thousands of individuals in the region. HABITS AND NATURAL HISTORY – Edible Dormice earned their name because, in Roman times, they were a prized dish and captive animals were fattened for human consumption. This ability to put on weight is a survival adaptation, allowing the animal to accumulate sufficient body reserves to see it through its winter hibernation, which lasts from October to April. Hibernation takes place in a hollow tree or underground burrow, or very occasionally in a building. From spring to autumn, when Edible Dormice are active, they are essentially nocturnal; the daytime is spent, often communally, in a nest. This may be constructed in the cover of dense tree foliage, or in a tree hole; the species will sometimes use a nest box or loft cavity for this purpose. The diet is varied and includes nuts, fruits and invertebrates. Comparatively little is known

plump adult,
in late summer

about the private life of the Edible Dormouse in the wild but the young are born during the summer months and there are usually 4–8 babies per litter. Animals are known to strip tree bark as a source of food, and chew through electrical cables (for who knows what reason). As a consequence of its occasionally destructive habits, house owners and foresters do not always view the species' presence with favour. OBSERVATION TIPS – Edible Dormice are hard to observe in the wild. However, if you live in the Chilterns area and have them lodging in your loft or garden shed you are sure to know about it: their nocturnal antics have a reputation for being noisy affairs. If you want to encourage the species in your garden, and you live in the right area, you could put up a nest box. However, the likelihood is that, in time, you will come to regret your actions.

EDIBLE DORMOUSE
△ ABOVE **juvenile**
◁ LEFT **hibernating adult**
▷ RIGHT **emerging from nest hole**

BANK VOLE *Clethrionomys glareolus*

BODY LENGTH 9.5–10.5cm; TAIL LENGTH 3.5–7cm; WEIGHT 15–35g

A plump and rather richly coloured vole. The Bank Vole is a familiar species to many naturalists and is sometimes encountered in broad daylight. **ADULT** has a compact body and fur that is mainly reddish brown, although it usually grades to greyish brown on the flanks and is paler still on the chest and belly. Note the proportionately large (by vole standards) ears and the relatively long tail. The various subspecies that occur on islands are, on average, larger and heavier than their mainland counterparts. **JUVENILE** is similar to an adult but the coat is greyer and it lacks the adult's intense reddish hue. **VOICE** – Utters a variety of squeaking calls if alarmed or distressed. HABITAT AND STATUS – Bank Voles are found in a variety of wooded and scrub habitats, including deciduous woodland, mature hedgerows and field margins. They are widespread and native in England, Wales and lowland areas of Scotland; the species has been introduced to southern Ireland. Bank Voles also occur (possibly as early introductions) on several islands and distinct subspecies are recognised from Skomer (*C. g. skomerensis*), Jersey (*C. g. caesarius*), Mull (*C. g. alstoni*) and Raasay (*C. g. erica*). Although Bank Vole populations fluctuate greatly with the seasons, and in response to climatic extremes, many millions of individuals occur in the region as a whole at any one time. HABITS AND NATURAL HISTORY – At the heart of a Bank Vole's home range is a nest, woven from plant fibres (typically grass) that have been gathered close to hand. The nest is usually underground in a burrow but occasionally it may be sited under a piece of corrugated iron or a log. Shallow burrows and surface tunnels radiate from the nest area and form the basis of the vole's feeding range. The diet includes plant shoots and leaves, as well as berries, nuts and fungi, in season. Bank Voles are usually active throughout the 24-hour period. Although they spend much of the time feeding on the ground, they are adept climbers, often clambering through bramble patches in search of blackberries. Once in a while they will take up residence in a bird nesting box sited several metres above the ground. The breeding season extends from early spring until late autumn and females have the potential to produce as many as 5 litters a year, each comprising 3–5 young. Needless to say, infant mortality is extremely high and Bank Voles seldom achieve their breeding potential. OBSERVATION TIPS – Sit quietly beside a blackberry-covered bramble patch, or on a woodland floor covered with fallen nuts, and eventually you should hear the telltale rustle of Bank Voles moving through the vegetation or leaf litter. On occasions they can be surprisingly bold; Skomer Voles, which seem particularly easy to observe, can be almost ridiculously oblivious to what is going on around them. Bank Voles are caught regularly in live traps set for small mammals and feature heavily in the diet of many predators; Tawny Owl pellets often contain their remains. Field signs include dark, stubby and cylindrical droppings. Hazelnuts that have been nibbled by Bank Voles show teeth marks only on the inner rim (the cut surface) of the hole; the outer surface of the nut is more or less unmarked.

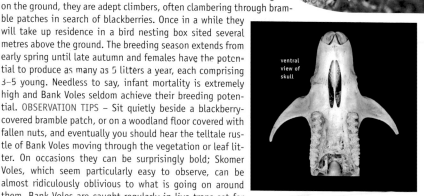

adult foraging

juvenile

ventral view of skull

lower jaw

BANK VOLE
⊙ ABOVE **adult**
◐ LEFT **Skomer vole**
◑ RIGHT **nibbled hazelnut (***see* **p.219)**

FIELD VOLE *Microtus agrestis*

BODY LENGTH 9–12cm; TAIL LENGTH 2.5–4.5cm; WEIGHT 30–40g

A widespread and occasionally locally abundant rodent that sometimes goes by the name of Short-tailed Vole. Although it is superficially similar to the Bank Vole, fur colour and the proportions of body to tail lengths allow accurate differentiation of the two species. **ADULT** has a plump body and a proportionately much shorter tail than a Bank Vole. Note also the rather small ears that are usually partially masked by hair. The coat colour is mainly grey-brown but it grades paler across the flanks to the chest and belly; it is thicker in winter than in summer. **JUVENILE** is similar to an adult but smaller. **VOICE** – Utters a range of shrill squeaking calls. HABITAT AND STATUS – As its common name suggests, the Field Vole is primarily a grassland species. It favours ground that has not been disturbed and will thrive in a range of different habitats from lowland meadows and pasture to upland grassy moors. Occasionally it is also found in hedgerows and woodland margins. The species is widespread in England, Wales and Scotland but is absent from Ireland and most islands except some in the Hebrides. It is impossible to assess the population size of the Field Vole in the region and, in any case, numbers fluctuate greatly throughout the year, and in response to climatic extremes. However, it would not be unreasonable to put the overall figure at several tens of millions of individuals. HABITS AND NATURAL HISTORY – Field Voles patrol their home ranges via a network of concealed surface runways and tunnels that run just below the surface of the soil, or more precisely, that run through the compacted roots of grasses that mat the surface of meadows and pastures. The diet is almost exclusively vegetarian and grass roots are the most important component. Field Voles are active throughout the 24-hour period. Males are distinctly territorial but females tend not to be. At the heart of a vole's home range is a nest of woven grasses, usually sited in the base of a grass clump. The breeding season extends from early spring to autumn and a female is capable of having 4 or 5 litters per year, each containing 4–6 young. However, the Field Vole's full breeding potential is seldom if ever achieved in the wild: mortality is high among both adults and young animals. Field Voles are on the menu for a wide range of predators, including Foxes, Weasels, Kestrels, Hen Harriers and Barn Owls. Indeed, the fluctuating cycles in vole numbers have a profound influence on the breeding success of many of these mammalian and avian carnivores. OBSERVATION TIPS – Field Voles do not venture out into the open as willingly as do Bank Voles, preferring the cover of their tunnels and runways. On occasion you may see evidence of their progress through a subterranean runway: look for a progression of telltale twitching grass stems as a passing vole brushes past the roots below. Animals are sometimes discovered by turning over sheets of corrugated iron that have been lying in a meadow for some time; Field Voles sometimes avail themselves of this form of shelter in order to build a nest. Skull fragments are often discovered in owl pellets, and field signs include piles of oval droppings (green when fresh, reflecting the diet) that are deposited beside runways.

skull

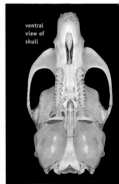

ventral view of skull

FIELD VOLE
⌃ ABOVE **adult**
⌄ BELOW **mother with babies**

ORKNEY and GUERNSEY VOLES *Microtus arvalis*

HEAD AND BODY LENGTH 9–12.5cm; TAIL LENGTH 3.5–4.5cm; WEIGHT 40–85g

Although the Orkney Vole (*M. a. orcadensis*) is not native to our region, it has been present here for thousands of years, its range restricted to the eponymous islands. It has a closely related cousin, the Guernsey Vole (*M. a. sarnius*), that is found only on Guernsey. **ADULT** Orkney Vole is relatively large by vole standards (often more than double the weight of a Bank Vole, for example). Most animals have a coat that is mainly reddish brown. However, extremely dark individuals are sometimes encountered and those found on the island of Sanday are invariably lighter than their counterparts on the other islands. The Guernsey Vole is paler and greyer than its Orcadian cousins, as well as being appreciably smaller (50g is a good adult weight for this subspecies). **JUVENILE** is similar to its adult counterpart but smaller. **VOICE** – Utters high-pitched squeaks. HABITAT AND STATUS – *Microtus arvalis* is a widespread species across mainland Europe, and in that context it is known as the **Common Vole**. In our region, it is restricted to a few islands and represented by two subspecies. Although it is difficult to be absolutely certain, it is generally accepted (in the case of the Orkney Vole at least) that it is not native to Britain. However, archaeological evidence indicates that voles have been present on Orkney for at least 5,000 years and it is assumed that they accompanied (presumably inadvertently) the first Neolithic human settlers to those islands. During the time they have spent in isolation, Orkney Voles have evolved into a distinct subspecies, on average plumper and darker than their mainland European counterparts. Given the amount of grazing pasture, hay meadows and non-specific grassland found on the Orkneys, it might be supposed that this would be the sort of terrain favoured by its voles. However, odd though it may seem, Orkney Voles shun these sorts of habitats, favouring instead more natural sites such as heather moorland; in particular, they like patches of rushes (*Juncus* sp.) and grasses that colonise old peat cuttings in amongst the dense carpet of Ling (*Calluna vulgaris*). Orkney Voles are found on the Orcadian islands of Mainland, Westray, Sanday, Rousay and South Ronaldsay. Their population is certainly numbered in the high hundreds of thousands. The status and origins of the Guernsey Vole are open to speculation, but given the proximity of the island to mainland France (where the species is common) it is not inconceivable that its occurrence there is natural, although its range and numbers are restricted and small. Guernsey Voles have similar habits and natural history to their Orkney cousins, although they are associated with undisturbed grassy, not moorland, habitats and are more exclusively nocturnal. HABITS AND NATURAL HISTORY – Given the frequently waterlogged nature of their favoured moorland habitat, it is not surprising that Orkney Voles are mainly active at the surface. Their home ranges are explored via a network of surface runways through Ling, rushes and grasses. Tunnels, as such, are usually shallow, penetrating the compacted roots of moorland vegetation and usually restricted to areas of ground elevated slightly above the water table; suitable terrain is often created as a consequence of small-scale peat working. Orkney Voles are active, off and on, throughout the 24-hour period; that they are at least partly diurnal is inevitable during the summer months because of the extended day length. They have a mainly vegetarian diet, and are particularly fond of the roots of rushes and grasses. The breeding season extends from early spring to late autumn and potentially a female could have 3 or 4 litters a year, each comprising 4–7 young. Needless to say, mortality is high. Orkney Voles feature prominently in the diet of avian predators and their presence presumably explains why Hen Harriers and Short-eared Owls breed so successfully on the islands. OBSERVATION TIPS – If you visit a moorland habitat suitable for Orkney Voles it is usually relatively easy to detect their presence: look for surface runways through the vegetation. You may even discover 'latrines' of greenish, cylindrical droppings. If you find a suitable area, and are prepared to sit quietly for an hour or so, you stand a reasonable chance of catching a glimpse of an animal as it explores its territory; the fact that the species is partially diurnal obviously helps in this respect.

Hen Harrier – Orkney breeders are dependent on vole numbers for their breeding success

adult Guernsey Vole

ORKNEY VOLE

⌃ ABOVE **adult**
⌄ BELOW **adult**

WATER VOLE *Arvicola terrestris*

BODY LENGTH 15–22cm; TAIL LENGTH 9–14cm; WEIGHT 150–300g

A charming and endearing waterside mammal, equally at home in water or on a river bank. Sadly, the Water Vole has declined catastrophically in recent decades and nowadays is perhaps best known, in the literary sense at least, as 'Ratty' from Kenneth Grahame's book *Wind in the Willows*. **ADULT** has a plump body that is covered with coarse, rich reddish-brown fur. The head is proportionately large and rounded, a feature that helps distinguish it from the Brown Rat. The front feet, which have 4 toes, are often used to grasp vegetation while eating. The hind feet, which have 5 toes, are relatively large and are used for swimming; the 1st and 5th toes on the hind foot are splayed and hence tracks in mud are distinctive. The tail has a coating of hairs and is proportionately shorter than that of a Brown Rat, which has a naked tail. **JUVENILE** is similar to an adult but smaller, with a proportionately larger head and shorter tail. **VOICE** – Generally silent, but occasionally utters a grating call in alarm. HABITAT AND STATUS – Water Voles are typically associated with clean, slow-flowing or still waters with an abundance of marginal vegetation and steep, muddy banks into which they can burrow. Perhaps as recently as 100 years ago, there could hardly have been a lake, pond, canal, slow-flowing river or ditch in England, Wales or Scotland in which the species did not occur; it has never occurred in Ireland. However, since that time, the story has been rather different. In the latter half of the 20th century, numbers began to decline, probably due to competition from increased numbers of grazing animals. If that were not enough, Water Voles then had to contend with habitat loss or degradation, the result of insensitive waterway management, land drainage and pollution from industry and agricultural run-off. By the 1990s the species' range and numbers were in catastrophic decline. The final nail in the coffin has come in recent years in the form of the American Mink, which has spread alarmingly and caused local extinctions in Water Vole populations that were already in serious decline. Today, it is difficult to estimate Water Vole numbers and the species is absent from many of its former haunts, including western England, the East Midlands, south Wales and lowland Scotland. A few valiant attempts are being made to combat the trend by encouraging appropriate management regimes for rivers and lakes, and by attempting to control, if not exterminate, American Mink. HABITS AND NATURAL HISTORY – Water Voles are primarily vegetarian and eat roots, shoots and grasses among other things. They are fond of Yellow Iris stems and tubers, and excavate burrow complexes in muddy waterside banks. Typically, Water Voles live as adult pairs although the social order is disrupted periodically by the presence of young animals; 2–4 litters a season (each containing 4–6 young) are usual and the breeding season extends from April to September. The young are usually weaned after 14 days and then evicted from the parental territory, the boundaries of which are often marked and defined by latrine-type deposits of the cylindrical droppings. Water Voles swim well and, if alarmed, will dive into the water with an audible 'plop'. OBSERVATION TIPS – If you live in an area where Water Voles still thrive, observing them is usually relatively straightforward. Sit quietly beside water, close to a spot where droppings have been deposited, or where burrow entrances can be seen, and it will not be long before one swims past you. They love apple.

young animal

droppings

adult feeding

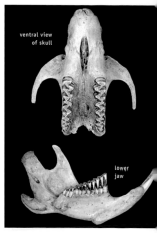

ventral view of skull

lower jaw

WATER VOLE
ABOVE **adult feeding**
BELOW **swimming**

HARVEST MOUSE *Micromys minutus*

HEAD AND BODY LENGTH 5–8cm; TAIL LENGTH 5–7cm; WEIGHT 6–11g

A charming and diminutive mouse. The Harvest Mouse is the smallest rodent in the region and indeed it is among the tiniest of all our mammals; its only rivals to this claim are the Pygmy Shrew and Common Pipistrelle. **ADULT** has a tiny, compact body with a mainly golden-brown coat; only the throat, chest and belly are white. The ears are rounded and relatively prominent, and the feet possess an excellent grip, essential for the species' climbing habits. To assist in this latter respect, the tail is prehensile and serves as a 5th limb. **JUVENILE** is similar to an adult although the coat lacks the adult's striking golden hue. **VOICE** – Mainly silent. HABITAT AND STATUS – As its common name hints, the Harvest Mouse was once widespread and common (in England at least) in fields of wheat. Sadly, changes in farming practices have meant that it has all but disappeared from arable land that is in production. Today, the Harvest Mouse is associated mainly with hay meadows that are managed with wildlife in mind, as well as bramble patches and dry reed-beds. In areas of farmland (i.e. much of the lowland countryside) it is now restricted to field margins and grassy hedgerows. There is little doubt that Harvest Mice have declined nationally over the last century, although their small size and secretive nature means they are easy to overlook. Nowadays, they are distinctly local, occurring mainly in southern and central England, and in south Wales. The increasingly fragmented nature of habitats suitable for the Harvest Mouse means that there is little hope of the species ever becoming as common and widespread as it was, say, 100 years ago. HABITS AND NATURAL HISTORY – Being so secretive and essentially nocturnal, the Harvest Mouse is a difficult animal to study in the wild although many observations have been made on captive populations. During the summer months at least, they seldom visit the ground, spending much of their lives moving acrobatically through the swaying stems and flower heads of meadow vegetation. They are usually solitary, each animal constructing a tennis ball-sized spherical nest, woven among the stems, at the heart of its home range. The breeding season extends from spring to autumn and a female is capable of producing 3–6 litters a year, each comprising 4–8 young. The vegetation of the Harvest Mouse's favoured habitats is often cut in late summer and, indeed, even in areas where this does not happen the vegetation tends to compact down naturally. Consequently, they spend more time at ground level from autumn to spring, with winter nests being constructed in bramble patches or even in an underground burrow. Although Harvest Mice are mainly vegetarian, eating, in season, seeds, berries and fruits, they will supplement their diet with insects and spiders. OBSERVATION TIPS – The usual way that the presence of Harvest Mice is detected is by the discovery, in the autumn or winter, of abandoned summer nests in grassy areas that have not been cut. However, if you do discover one, resist the temptation to take it home. There is just an outside chance that it might still be in use – you would never know because the owner would have left the vicinity long before you noticed the nest. Extremely fortunate observers may discover an occupied nest during the summer months. With patience, it can be possible to observe the occupants coming and going at dusk, but usually only if the nest is viewed from a distance and with the aid of binoculars.

climbing adult

emerging from nest

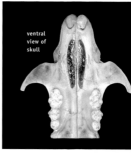

ventral view of skull

lower jaw

HARVEST MOUSE
ABOVE **adult and nest**
BELOW **climbing adult**

WOOD MOUSE *Apodemus sylvaticus*

HEAD AND BODY LENGTH 9–11cm; TAIL LENGTH 7–11cm; WEIGHT 15–30g

A widespread and common rodent. The Wood Mouse is the most familiar mouse in the region and, nowadays, the species you are most likely to encounter in the rural house and garden. **ADULT** has a classic mouse-shape with a rather pointed head, a compact body and a long tail. Compared to a House Mouse, note the relatively large eyes, ears, hind legs and tail. The coat colour is mainly yellowish brown on the upper parts, with a dark vertebral band along the dorsal surface of the head and body. The yellowish colour on the flanks grades into the whitish underparts with less of a clear demarcation than is seen in the Yellow-necked Mouse. In some animals, there is a small yellowish spot on the throat. **JUVENILE** is similar to an adult but smaller. The coat is greyish brown and lacks the adult's yellowish hue. **VOICE** – Mainly silent but utters frantic squeals in distress. HABITAT AND STATUS – The Wood Mouse is catholic in its choice of habitats. As its name suggests, it is generally most numerous in deciduous woodland. However, it can also be found in hedgerows, areas of scrub and mature gardens and, to a lesser extent, in almost every other terrestrial British habitat except perhaps mountain summits and the seashore. The Wood Mouse is also a frequent visitor to garden sheds, greenhouses and loft spaces, particularly during the cold, wet winter months. It is widespread throughout mainland Britain and Ireland, and also occurs on many of our larger islands. Many tens of millions of individuals must be present in the region as a whole. HABITS AND NATURAL HISTORY – Wood Mice lead mainly solitary lives although there is a degree of overlap between the home ranges of individuals (less so between females and other females, and during the summer months). At the heart of the home range is a small network of tunnels, one of which will lead to a nest chamber; several mice may share the same nest in the winter. Wood Mice are mainly nocturnal and seldom venture out of their burrows until dusk has fallen. Thereafter, they forage on the woodland floor and climb with ease. They are opportunistic feeders and their diet includes, in season, seeds, nuts, fruits and fungi, as well as insects and other invertebrates.

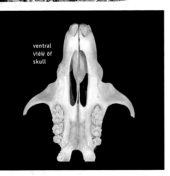
mother with babies

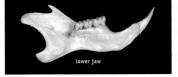
adult

ventral view of skull

lower jaw

The breeding season extends from early spring to the autumn and a female is capable of producing 4–6 litters a year, each containing 3–8 young. This prodigious breeding potential is seldom achieved in the wild because Wood Mice of all ages feature prominently in the diets of most avian and mammalian predators, notably Tawny Owls, Stoats, Weasels and Foxes. OBSERVATION TIPS – Wood Mice can sometimes be observed scurrying across the woodland floor at dusk. They are frequently captured in small-mammal live traps and will visit rural houses and sheds in the autumn and winter. Signs of their presence include nibbled nuts, which bear chisel-like tooth marks around the rim of the opening as well as on the cut surface.

droppings

WOOD MOUSE
⌃ ABOVE **adult**
⌄ BELOW **adult**

YELLOW-NECKED MOUSE *Apodemus flavicollis*

HEAD AND BODY LENGTH 9–13cm; TAIL LENGTH 9–13cm; WEIGHT 15–50g

A rather large and impressive mouse. The Yellow-necked Mouse is the largest of its kind in the region. **ADULT** is superficially similar to a Wood Mouse and a slightly flippant, and decidedly non-scientific, way of looking at the species is that it is like a Wood Mouse, *only more so*. The Yellow-necked is heavier for its size than a Wood Mouse, has proportionately larger ears, eyes and feet, and a longer tail; the coat colour is richer on the upper parts and there is a clearer demarcation between the coat colour above and the white underparts (which are cleaner looking than with the Wood Mouse). Although the above description may sound rather subjective, the overall impression is of an animal that is much more robust and substantial than its cousin. However, there is one reasonably objective distinction between the two species: as the common name suggests, the Yellow-necked Mouse has a rather broad, prominent and richly coloured yellow band that runs across the throat; it links to the brown fur on the upper parts. In Wood Mice, the yellow on the throat is, at most, restricted to a discrete spot. **JUVENILE** is similar to an adult but smaller, and often with a less well developed yellow throat and a duller coat colour generally. **VOICE** – Mainly silent in the wild but will squeal loudly in distress. HABITAT AND STATUS – The Yellow-necked Mouse has a rather restricted range in the region. It occurs patchily across the southern half of England and, locally, in Wales, particularly along the English border. Yellow-necked Mice are associated mainly with ancient deciduous woodlands or, perhaps more accurately, with woodlands that have an ancient history: the trees themselves don't have to be particularly old but continuity in woodland presence is a key factor. The species is reasonably common in those areas where it does occur (one autumn I live-trapped 14 individuals in my house, in the space of just 4 weeks); several hundred thousand individuals may be present in the region as a whole. HABITS AND NATURAL HISTORY – Yellow-necked Mice lead mainly solitary lives for most of the year, although individuals' home ranges may overlap and animals can lead seemingly communal lives in winter, especially if they visit human habitation. They are essentially nocturnal animals and, during the spring and summer months, the daytime is spent in a nest, sited in an underground burrow or perhaps in a tree hollow (Yellow-necked Mice are regularly found nesting – usually females with babies – in nest boxes designed for birds and Dormice). After dark they forage on the woodland floor and in the trees themselves (radio-tracking indicates that they are excellent climbers). The diet is varied and includes, in season, nuts, fruits, berries, fungi and invertebrates. The breeding season extends from early spring to autumn and a female is capable of producing 2 or 3 litters a year, each containing, on average, 4–7 babies. OBSERVATION TIPS – The Yellow-necked Mouse is particularly inclined to visit human habitation with the onset of winter and, indeed, the urge to seek sanctuary around harvest festival time means that this species merits the description 'church mouse'. Unsurprisingly then, if you live in a relatively rural area, within the range of the Yellow-necked Mouse, there is a good chance that one or more will take up residence in your house, garage or garden shed from September to March. For an animal that, presumably, is so alert to the dangers associated with sound (making a noise is likely to attract the attention of predators), Yellow-necked Mice can be amazingly noisy creatures when living in a loft space. From personal experience, a single mouse can make enough commotion in the dead of the night to convince you that you are being burgled! If you live-trap a Yellow-necked Mouse, either for research purposes or to remove it from your house, handle it at your peril: for all their small size, they are remarkably agile and ferocious in the hand, and will bite, squeal and wriggle with alarming vigour.

adult

adult

YELLOW-NECKED MOUSE
ⓐ ABOVE **adult**
ⓥ BELOW **droppings**

HOUSE MOUSE *Mus domesticus*

HEAD AND BODY LENGTH 7–10cm; TAIL LENGTH 7–9cm; WEIGHT 10–20g

A relatively small rodent, the House Mouse is the archetypal mouse and the ancestor of domesticated pet mice. **ADULT** has a compact head and body that is roughly the same length as the tail. The coat is rather uniform in colour although generally slightly darker above than below. Individuals vary from yellowish brown to grey-brown. Note the beady eyes and the relatively large ears. **JUVENILE** is similar to an adult but smaller. **VOICE** – Utters high-pitched squeaks, barely audible to the human ear. HABITAT AND STATUS – The House Mouse is thought not to be native to Britain and Ireland but to have been introduced, inadvertently, during the Iron Age; archaeological evidence indicates that they were present, in some numbers, by Roman times. Although it occurs in the countryside at large (along hedgerows and in woodlands) at low densities, typically it does best in locations where humans live and work. In particular, it thrives at sites where food is stored, processed or distributed, and in terms of its association with humans the species is truly commensal. In rural regions, it occurs in the vicinity of farms while in urban areas it is found in buildings where food is stored, processed or cooked; to a lesser degree it takes up residence in domestic housing. Over the last 50 years or so, House Mice numbers across the region have undoubtedly declined markedly. Legislation regarding the storage and processing of food materials has been tightened up and increasingly effective rodenticides are now deployed. In the 1970s I remember seeing House Mice at such densities in an arable farm grain store that not a square inch of the floor was visible. Today, that would be a rare sight. That is not to say that the species is not common: it is just not as numerous or widely distributed as it once was, although countless millions are probably present in the region as a whole at times of plenty. HABITS AND NATURAL HISTORY – Numbers of House Mice, and the densities at which they live, are extremely variable and governed by external forces beyond their control, namely the presence or absence of food supplies, its accessibility, and the availability of shelter. Unsurprisingly, therefore, House Mouse behaviour is extremely flexible and adaptable. At low densities, the home ranges of individuals usually overlap and there is little sign of territoriality. However, as densities increase, so signs of aggressive behaviour appear, particularly when it comes to the arrival of strange mice in currently occupied territories, the boundaries of which are scent-marked. In the absence of human disturbance, House Mice are usually active, off and on, throughout the 24-hour period. Their diet includes a wide range of food materials, but they show a preference for stored grains; occasionally, substances with seemingly no nutritional value (e.g. soap) are consumed. Using their front paws to manipulate grain, House Mice will remove the husk and eat just a portion of the item: nibbled grain is a classic sign of their presence. They also contaminate stored food with urine and droppings and since this can render the food in question unusable the House Mouse is clearly important in economic and public hygiene terms. Periods of rest are spent in a nest, constructed in an inaccessible (to predators) recess or cavity. The species has a prodigious reproductive rate and a female is capable of producing as many as 10 litters per year (young can be born at any time of year), each comprising on average 5–7 babies. Infant mortality is high though, and females will abandon their litters readily if unduly disturbed. OBSERVATION TIPS – Changes in building construction, and an increased awareness of domestic hygiene, mean that the House Mouse is a comparatively rare visitor to the modern home. However, owners of most large buildings where food is stored or served will have colonies.

adult

mother with babies

pet mice

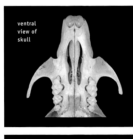

ventral view of skull

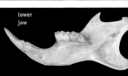

lower jaw

HOUSE MOUSE
⌃ ABOVE adult
⌄ BELOW droppings

BROWN RAT *Rattus norvegicus*

HEAD AND BODY LENGTH 20–27cm; TAIL LENGTH 16–23cm; WEIGHT 300–500g

A widespread and all too familiar rodent. The Brown Rat is reviled on account of its habits and the sight of one is guaranteed to bring a shudder to most people. However, if a detached and dispassionate viewpoint can be maintained, a fascinating and adaptable animal is revealed. **ADULT** recalls an outsized mouse, but note the proportionately larger, plumper body and shorter ears; a Brown Rat also has relatively shorter legs (but larger feet) and a thicker tail. The fur appears rather coarse and is mainly brown, although it grades to grey on the underparts. The tail has a scaly appearance and is sparsely armed with bristles. **JUVENILE** is similar to an adult but with a more slender body and a proportionately larger head. **VOICE** – Utters various screams and whistles in dire distress. HABITAT AND STATUS – The Brown Rat has its origins in the Far East and presumably spread westwards, into Europe, as the human population expanded in numbers and developed trade routes. It was first recorded in our region in 1720, having arrived as an uninvited stowaway on boats. Since then the species has never looked back, here or abroad, following in the wake of people as they visited, and colonised, even the remotest parts of the globe. Throughout their range, by and large Brown Rats maintain their association with humans and highest densities are found in sewers, rubbish dumps, urban locations where food is discarded, and farm buildings. There is little doubt that, if the Brown Rat is a 'problem' animal, then the problem is one of our own making. Thanks to the way we, as a society, live our lives today we provide them with shelter and an almost limitless supply of food. Many millions of animals are probably present in the region as a whole. HABITS AND NATURAL HISTORY – Where feeding is good and shelter is available, sizeable colonies of Brown Rats can develop, individuals of which are often closely related to one another. Boundaries are scent-marked and a sense of 'ownership' is demonstrated by unwillingness on the part of occupants to allow 'strange' rats to intrude into their domain. However, in farm and domestic locations, Brown Rat colonies are seldom allowed to persist for any length of time without human intervention. On the whole, they are mainly nocturnal animals and being able to climb and swim allows them to exploit a wide range of resources. The diet is omnivorous and includes all manner of stored foodstuffs, along with fruit, berries, insects and other invertebrates, birds' eggs and amphibians, not forgetting their predilection for discarded food and rubbish generally. As well as competing directly for the food we eat, Brown Rats are important agents of contamination and, via their urine and faeces, can transmit diseases such as *Salmonella* and *Leptospirosis* (Weil's disease). A female Brown Rat is capable of producing 5–10 litters per year (each containing 6–9 babies) and the breeding season is defined more by the availability of food than the seasons themselves. OBSERVATION TIPS – Few tips are needed in order to see Brown Rats. Visit almost any location where people congregate and leave food scraps and the species is sure to be close to hand. Field signs include oval droppings that are usually pointed at one end, and 'greasy' looking trails (especially around burrow entrances and access holes to buildings) where oil from the fur and urine have left their mark.

droppings

foraging in rubbish

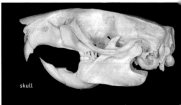

skull

BROWN RAT

ⓐ ABOVE **adult**
ⓑ BELOW **mother with babies**

BLACK RAT *Rattus rattus*

HEAD AND BODY LENGTH 15–22cm; TAIL LENGTH 12–25cm; WEIGHT 150–250g

A scarce and declining rodent. It recalls its Brown cousin, but the Black Rat has a sleeker body outline and a much darker coat. **ADULT** has mainly blackish fur although the chest and belly are usually paler than the upper parts. Close up, the coat has a shaggy appearance due to the bristle-like guard hairs. Note also the rather large, naked ears and the relatively long slender tail. **JUVENILE** is similar to an adult but smaller. **VOICE** – Squeals when in dire distress. HABITAT AND STATUS – The Romans did many positive things for Britain but leaving a legacy of Black Rats was not one of them. The species soon assumed pest proportions in the region, with numbers boosted by regular boat-borne stowaways. To make matters worse, in the Middle Ages plague epidemics were transmitted by Black Rat fleas. Until the 18th century, the Black Rat was the only one of its kind in the region. But following the arrival of the Brown Rat, its numbers dwindled and by the end of the 20th century it was restricted to dockland areas of London and Bristol, and on the Shiant Islands in the Outer Hebrides. The small population on Lundy was erad-icated in 2003/2004 in an attempt to safeguard the future of breeding seabirds (rats are predators of nesting birds, eggs and chicks). Black Rats are recorded occasionally in mainland Ireland but their status there is uncertain. Surviving mainland populations of Black Rats are associated with buildings. Unlike Brown Rats, they seldom venture below ground, have an aver-sion to water and favour warmer, drier situations overall. HABITS AND NATURAL HISTORY – Black Rats live in social groups of mixed sex and age with clear dominance hierarchy. They are nocturnal and have a var-ied omnivorous diet; stored human food is important. The breeding season extends from early spring to late autumn and a female can produce 3–5 litters per year, each containing up to 12 or more babies. OBSERVATION TIPS – Today you are unlikely to encounter a Black Rat. You might see one in the London docklands after dark, but most people are willing to forego this particular mammal-watching experience!

WALLABIES | Order *Diprotodontia* – Family *Macropodidae*

RED-NECKED WALLABY *Macropus rufogriseus*

HEAD AND BODY LENGTH 60–70cm; TAIL LENGTH 60–70cm; WEIGHT 7–16kg

A large and unmistakable marsupial mammal with a diagnostic hopping gait. **ADULT** has a greyish-brown coat overall but note the strong reddish hue on the nape and shoulders. The outline of the head is vaguely deer-like and the ears are prominent. Note the relatively tiny front legs, and huge, powerful hind legs and thickset tail. The female has a pouch in which the baby is carried. **JUVENILE** has a similar coat coloration to an adult from about 6 months onwards. **VOICE** – Mainly silent. HABITAT AND STATUS – Red-necked Wallabies first appeared on the British scene around 1940 when they escaped from Whip-snade Zoo. Around the same time, various people had the 'bright' idea of introduc-ing the species to the Peak District, Sussex and various other locations; these 'wild' pop-ulations have either died out or are on the verge of extinction. HABITS AND NATURAL HISTORY – Red-necked Wallabies favour a mosaic of open habitats (grassland and moorland) for feeding, and scrub and woodland for cover. They are mainly crepus-cular and nocturnal, and have a vegetarian diet. Compared to other mammals, mar-supials give birth to young at a premature stage. In the case of the Red-necked Wallaby, gestation lasts barely a month and the baby is then carried around in the pouch for a further 9 months. OBSERVATION TIPS – You are unlikely to see a Red-necked Wallaby at large in the British countryside nowadays. If you want to see free-roaming (but nevertheless captive) animals then visit Whipsnade Zoo.

mother with baby

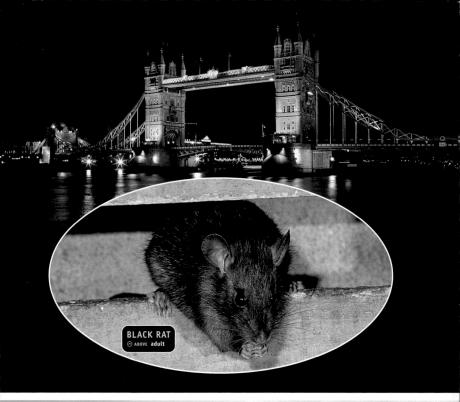

BLACK RAT
⊘ ABOVE **adult**

RED-NECKED WALLABY
⊘ ABOVE **adult**

COMMON SEAL *Phoca vitulina*

LENGTH 1.2–1.9m; WEIGHT 50–120kg

A rather small seal with a relatively small, 'friendly'-looking face. Elsewhere in the world it is referred to as Harbour Seal. The Common Seal frequently basks on the seashore making it comparatively easy to observe. A thick layer of blubber provides insulation against cold seas. **ADULT** is variable in appearance, but typically the coat is greyish brown but mottled with darker grey, brown or blackish spots. The underside is usually appreciably paler than the upper side. When completely dry, Common Seals can look pale and shiny, especially if the body is coated in windblown sand. In profile, the bridge of the nose has a concave outline (convex

in the Grey Seal) and the muzzle is blunt, creating a rather doglike appearance. Seen from the front, the nostrils are close together at the base and splayed in a V-shaped fashion (they are separated from, and more parallel to, one another in the Grey Seal). The front flippers are armed with claws and the powerful hind flippers effect propulsion when swimming. Males are larger and heavier than females. **PUPS** are born with a faintly marbled and mottled coat that is greyish above and paler buffish grey below. The coat becomes darker and more mottled with age. **VOICE** – Mainly silent. HABITAT AND STATUS – Common Seals are associated with sheltered seas and are widespread on the east coast of England, and on coasts generally around Scotland and Ireland. They are least common, or locally absent from, much of the Irish Sea and southern and south-west England. Estuaries and sea lochs are particularly favoured, the animals hauling out to bask on sandbanks and beaches. In northern waters, Common Seals also occur on sheltered rocky shores but they are usually absent from locations that are exposed to the full force of the sea. Several tens of thousands of individuals are probably present in the region as a whole. HABITS AND NATURAL HISTORY – One look at the dentition of a Common Seal's skull will leave you in little doubt that it is a carnivore. Fish are the preferred prey, but they will also tackle crabs and other marine crustaceans. Where animals can haul out onto a beach independent of the state of the tide, then they tend to feed, off and on, during the day. Elsewhere, Common Seals tend to feed when the tide is high and haul out onto exposed sandbars when it is low. At prime sites, several dozen individuals may haul out together. Mating occurs during the summer months but implantation is delayed until the winter, ensuring that pups are not born until the following summer. The young are weaned after a month or so, at which point their mother abandons them to their fate. OBSERVATION TIPS – Common Seals tend to be rather nervous and wary animals and in most circumstances they are much less inquisitive than their Grey cousins. However, superb views can be obtained at certain locations, notably Blakeney Point on the north Norfolk coast; here the animals are accustomed to daily boat trips that visit their hauling-out sites. Mousa, in the Shetland Isles, is another location where Common Seals seem particularly tolerant of human observers. Here they can sometimes be seen hauled out alongside Grey Seals for comparison.

skull

COMMON SEAL
- TOP **adult**
- ABOVE **adult**
- BELOW **young animal**

GREY SEAL *Halichoerus grypus*
LENGTH 2.2–3.2m; WEIGHT 125–300kg

A large and well-built marine mammal. The Grey Seal has a proportionately large head and is usually more inquisitive, when it is in the water, than its Common cousin. **ADULT** has a bulky body with a thick layer of blubber that insulates the animal against the cold sea. As its common name suggests, the overall colour is greyish, but the body is marked with dark blotchy spots; there are fewer, larger spots than on a Common Seal. Males tend to be darker than females and they are the larger and heavier of the sexes. Seen in profile, a Grey Seal is often described as having a 'Roman nose' appearance: the bridge of the nose is convex (concave in the Common Seal); this feature is

more pronounced in males than females, the latter having relatively slender muzzles. From the front, the nostrils are more widely separated than those of a Common Seal and they are more parallel to one another, not distinctly V-shaped. There are numerous long, bristly whiskers on the upper lip and above the eye. The fore flippers are armed with sharp claws and the hind flippers are used to propel the animal through the water. **PUP** is born with a white coat of fur. After a few weeks this is moulted and replaced by a coloration reminiscent of an adult, but less well marked. **VOICE** – Adults utter low, moaning calls. Pups utter squealing cries. HABITAT AND STATUS – The Grey Seal is more usually associated with rocky shores than its Common cousin and it is not deterred by exposure to rough seas and heavy waves. Consequently it is widespread on western coasts in the region (including much of Ireland), as well as on shores that face the North Sea. The species also occurs on more sheltered stretches of coasts, hence its occurrence south to the Wash and East Anglia. There are probably 100,000 or more individuals in the region as a whole, the largest proportion of which occur in the north. HABITS AND NATURAL HISTORY – Grey Seals are carnivores and specialise in catching fish. Obviously, the precise species taken depends upon availability and location, but in some areas both salmon and cod can be important in their diet; unsurprisingly, where this happens Grey Seals are brought into conflict with fishermen. Seabirds, squid and crabs are among the other animals eaten when the opportunity arises. Grey Seals are consummate and graceful swimmers, capable of diving for several minutes at a time. In many parts of their range, they favour hauling out onto rocky outcrops and usually do so at low tide during daylight hours, and at sunset. Typically, at larger hauling-out sites there is a lot of coming and going and jostling for position. In the sea, Grey Seals frequently engage in so-called 'bottling' behaviour, where the animal in question remains stationary and vertical, the head and neck rising above the water in order to survey the surroundings. Mating occurs in autumn and early winter, but delayed implantation ensures that the pups are not born until the following autumn. Pregnant females congregate at regularly used sites for pupping where conditions afford them a degree of protection from disturbance, land predators and inclement weather. The pups are weaned after as little as 3 weeks, after which time they soon take to the sea. OBSERVATION TIPS – Grey Seals can be seen on suitable rocky shores and from cliffs around the Scottish and Irish coasts, their moaning calls alerting observers to their presence. They are often inquisitive animals and if you sit quietly and still on a rock next to the sea, they may come and investigate you. Excellent views can be obtained of hauled-out animals on boat trips to the Farne Islands in Northumberland, and Grey Seals regularly haul out on beaches along the Lincolnshire coast. Although usually rather sedentary, occasionally they are seen from ferries, beyond the sight of land.

pup

skull

GREY SEAL
◎ TOP **adult male** ⌃ ABOVE **adult male** ⌄ BELOW **adult female**

MINKE WHALE *Balaenoptera acutorostrata*
LENGTH 8–10m; WEIGHT 8–10 tonnes

The smallest of the baleen whales but still a large and impressive animal. The Minke (pronounced *Minky*) Whale is the only 'great' whale species that is regularly encountered in inshore waters and occasionally it can even be seen from land. **ADULT** has a streamlined body with a rather narrow, pointed snout. The upper parts are dark grey, although in poor or high-contrast light conditions the colour can appear almost black. The under-parts are whitish and broad bands of paler coloration extend up the flanks and are sometimes visible on animals at the surface. Note the curved dorsal fin that is set relatively far back on the body. Seen from above there is a single ridge running from the nostrils to the tip of the rostrum. Arguably the most distinctive feature (and one that is diagnostic) is the broad white spot or band on the upper surface of the flipper; this is striking enough to be noticeable in submerged, swimming animals seen from a boat. **JUVENILE** is similar to an adult but smaller. **VOICE** – Mainly silent. HABITAT AND STATUS – Minke Whales favour the relatively shallow waters of the continental shelf, or at least this is where they are most frequently encountered in our region. Unsurprisingly, they concentrate where the feeding is good and so western and northern waters are particularly productive for the species. HABITS AND NATURAL HISTORY – The Minke Whale is a fast swimmer that spends comparatively little time at the surface. The blow is rather indistinct, partly because it is relatively small but also because it starts while the whale's head is still partly submerged. However, if the blow is observed it is often at the same time as the dorsal fin appears.

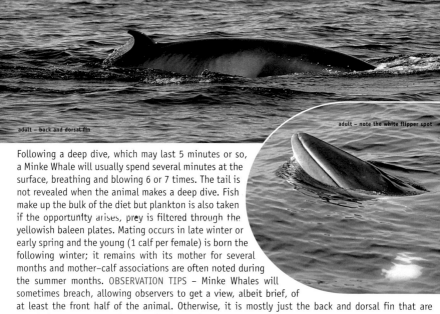

adult – back and dorsal fin

adult – note the white flipper spot

Following a deep dive, which may last 5 minutes or so, a Minke Whale will usually spend several minutes at the surface, breathing and blowing 6 or 7 times. The tail is not revealed when the animal makes a deep dive. Fish make up the bulk of the diet but plankton is also taken if the opportunity arises, prey is filtered through the yellowish baleen plates. Mating occurs in late winter or early spring and the young (1 calf per female) is born the following winter; it remains with its mother for several months and mother–calf associations are often noted during the summer months. OBSERVATION TIPS – Minke Whales will sometimes breach, allowing observers to get a view, albeit brief, of at least the front half of the animal. Otherwise, it is mostly just the back and dorsal fin that are revealed. Very occasionally, an individual will show an interest in a boat and swim alongside it for a short period; at such times the pointed head and white flipper spot can usually be seen. The most reliable locations for the species in the region are The Minches (and indeed the Hebrides generally), the seas between the Orkney and Shetland islands, and the west coast of Ireland. Whale-watching trips operate from Mull and a few other locations. Prolonged observation from headlands on the south and west coasts of Ireland, northwest Scotland and southwest Cornwall will occasionally reward the observer with a brief glimpse. Given the relatively small size of a Minke Whale, and the fact the views are bound to be distant, you only have a realistic chance of seeing one from land if the sea is flat calm.

MINKE WHALE
⌃ ABOVE **mother and calf – note the latter's faint 'blow'** (*see p.196*)
⌄ BELOW **adult, showing dorsal fin**

BLUE WHALE *Balaenoptera musculus*
LENGTH 25–30m; WEIGHT 100–150 tonnes

The longest and heaviest of all cetaceans, the Blue Whale is also the largest animal alive on the planet. Extraordinary anatomical statistics abound for the species. **ADULT** has a huge, streamlined body that is bluish grey overall but mottled and marbled with greyish white. Seen just below the surface of the water, a Blue Whale does indeed look blue. The underside, particularly the throat, is paler than the rest of the body, as are the flippers, which are small relative to the body size. There is a single ridge that extends from the nostrils to the tip of the broad rostrum and the throat has 70–90 pleats that allow a huge expansion when feeding. The tail stock is thick and the dorsal

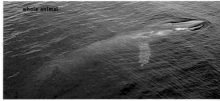

blow

fin is relatively small and set rather far back on the body. **JUVENILE** resembles a small adult in relative terms – a newborn calf weighs around 7 tonnes. **VOICE** – Utters a variety of high-pitched and deep calls but these are inaudible to observers on the surface. HABITAT AND STATUS – Blue Whales were decimated by 20th-century whaling and it is unclear whether numbers are recovering, despite the cessation of hunting; females probably calve every 3 or 4 years so inevitably any increase in numbers, if it happens, will take time. Estimates of Blue Whale populations can never be truly accurate but there are probably several hundred individuals in the northeast Atlantic. They are found mostly in deep waters, typically in places where upwelling occurs, such as at the edge of the continental shelf. They are seen regularly in the Bay of Biscay and, more occasionally, in the Western Approaches. HABITS AND NATURAL HISTORY – Blue Whales feed on tiny planktonic crustaceans (generically referred to as *krill*) that occasionally swarm in vast numbers, and at huge densities, in surface waters. As with other baleen whales, this species is a filter feeder – it engulfs a huge volume of water containing food, the throat pleats expanding to a grotesque extent. Water is expelled under pressure from the tongue, the krill being retained in the mouth by the baleen plates. In many parts of the

whole animal

world Blue Whales are migratory, spending the summer months feeding in polar seas and travelling to tropical waters for the winter. In better studied populations than our own, mating and birth occur in tropical seas (gestation lasts around 1 year). In the northeast Atlantic, Blue Whales occur in June and early July in the Denmark Strait (between Iceland and Greenland) and later in the summer there are occasional sightings in the Bay of Biscay. It is a matter of conjecture as to the status of individuals seen to the south and west of Great Britain and Ireland: perhaps they are merely migrants or maybe regular feeding grounds exist. Blue Whales are fast swimmers, capable of speeds of up to 25kph, although the usual cruising speed is much slower. OBSERVATION TIPS – Because of the species' scarcity, and its predilection for oceanic

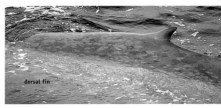

dorsal fin

waters, frankly it is impossible to plan with any certainty to see a Blue Whale in the seas around Great Britain and Ireland. However, using ferries that operate between southern England and northern Spain, you stand a chance (not a particularly good one, it has to be said) of seeing one. If a Blue Whale is seen in good light (with the sun behind you) then its coloration and markings, not to mention its size, make identification relatively easy. The species is often first detected by its blow, which can reach a height of 10m and is accompanied by an exhalation that is audible over a considerable distance. As the blow disperses, a long extent of back appears at the surface before finally the relatively tiny dorsal fin can be seen. The proportionately small tail fin is sometimes observed just as the whale glides beneath the surface; it is raised highest just before the whale dives deeply. Typically, a Blue Whale spends 10 minutes or so near the surface, making 15–20 shallow dives, before diving deeper and for up to 30 minutes.

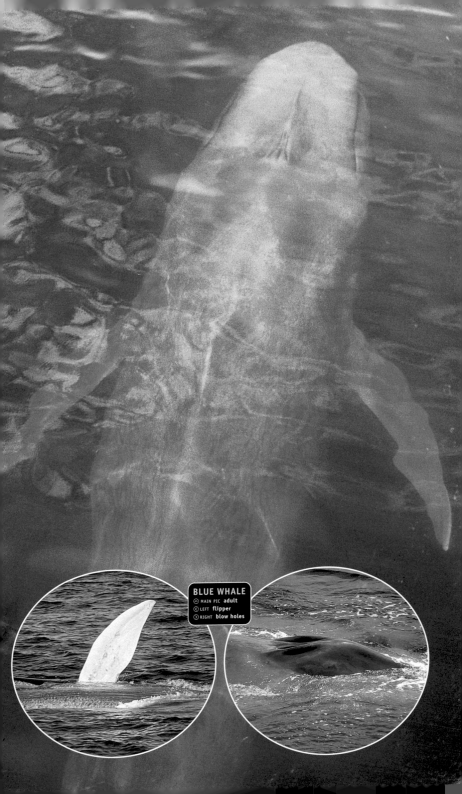

BLUE WHALE

MAIN PIC **adult**
LEFT **flipper**
RIGHT **blow holes**

FIN WHALE *Balaenoptera physalus*
LENGTH 18–22m; WEIGHT 40–50 tonnes

A large and streamlined whale, second only in terms of size to the Blue Whale. The Fin Whale is unique among our mammals for the asymmetrical markings on its head: symmetry is the norm in the animal kingdom. **ADULT** has a long and relatively slender body with a rather narrow, pointed head. Overall the body colour is a rather uniform dark grey, although the underparts, including the throat, are distinctly paler, which presumably affords the animal a degree of counter-shading when seen from below. Uniquely, the right side of the lower jaw is whitish (as indeed is the front half of the right side of the baleen plates and tongue) whereas the left side is the same colour as the rest of the body. A single median ridge extends from the nostril to the tip of the rostrum and the flippers are relatively long. The dorsal fin is recurved and rather large, set a long way back on the body. The tailstock is thick and the tail fin is large. **JUVENILE** is similar to an adult but smaller. **VOICE** – Utters various high-pitched and low calls that are inaudible to observers on the surface. HABITAT AND STATUS – Fin Whales are by no means restricted to deep, oceanic waters and, if the feeding is good, they can be found in the relatively shallow waters of the continental shelf. There are probably several thousand individuals in the northeast Atlantic and the species is regularly encountered in small numbers off the Irish coast and in the Western Approaches. HABITS AND NATURAL HISTORY – The Fin Whale is a fast swimmer, essential when you consider its feeding habits: although krill feature in the diet, shoaling fish are particularly important and speed is essential to ensure capture of prey that itself is fast and evasive. Typically a feeding Fin Whale rolls onto its right side, opening its mouth to engulf the shoal;

back and dorsal fin

the asymmetrical jaw and baleen markings are presumed to aid feeding efficiency. The species usually lives in social groups (*pods*) comprising half a dozen or so individuals. Populations in the northeast Atlantic are presumed to spend the summers in Arctic seas, wintering and breeding in more southerly, warmer seas near the tropics. British and Irish observations occur mainly in summer and autumn. These sightings could relate to migrants, but the fact that pods often linger in the same general area for several days hints at a brief residency when feeding is good. OBSERVATION TIPS – Fin Whales are seen occasionally during the summer months off the northern Scottish coasts and off southwest Ireland in summer and autumn. These days, Ireland would appear to be the most reliable location for the species. Weather permitting, regular trips operate from a few locations and it is just conceivable that you could see a Fin Whale from a prominent headland, with the aid of a telescope. Anecdotal evidence from fishermen indicates that the species occurs in some numbers in the Western Approaches and it is regularly seen from ferries crossing the Bay of Biscay. A Fin Whale's blow can reach 6m. A long extent of gently curving back is seen before the curved dorsal fin appears. The tail is seldom raised above the surface of the water, even preceding a deep dive.

FIN WHALE
⊙ ABOVE **head and blowholes – note the white lower jaw**

SEI WHALE *Balaenoptera borealis* LENGTH 12–15m; WEIGHT 15–20 tonnes

Superficially similar to a Fin Whale but smaller and with a characteristic blow and dive sequence. **ADULT** has a streamlined body but is not as elongated as a Fin Whale. Overall the body of a Sei (pronounced *Say*) Whale is blue-grey in colour, palest on the underside. The head is broader and less pointed than that of a Fin Whale and the colour is symmetrical. There is a single median ridge on the rostrum, the flippers are uniformly coloured and the dorsal fin is relatively tall and strongly recurved. **JUVENILE** is similar to an adult but smaller. **VOICE** – Silent in the context of surface observations. HABITAT AND STATUS – The Sei Whale is a rather enigmatic species and comparatively little is known about its status in our waters. However, it does occur in seas off northwest Scotland, and around the Shetland and Orkney islands during the summer months. Later in the season there are irregular sightings from the Western Approaches and the Bay of Biscay. HABITS AND NATURAL HISTORY – The Sei Whale feeds on krill, which are usually harvested close to the surface. They are fast swimmers, capable of bursts of speed up to 50kph, and hence able to avoid close encounters with boats if they wish. OBSERVATION TIPS – Sightings of this species are invariably chance encounters and brief ones at that. To be sure of identification, you need to rule out the possibility of Minke and Fin Whales. Rather than the gliding, arching way in which these species blow and dive, typically a Sei Whale will rise almost horizontally to the surface. In calm weather you should see the blow, head, back and dorsal fin simultaneously.

SEI WHALE
⊙ BELOW **adult – note the dorsal fin, back and blow can be seen at the same time**

HUMPBACK WHALE *Megaptera novaeangliae*
LENGTH 12–15m; WEIGHT 20–30 tonnes

A large and impressive cetacean. The Humpback Whale is often active at the surface and as a consequence of this, and because it possesses several distinctive features, it is one of the easiest large whale species to identify with certainty. **ADULT** has a streamlined but bulky body, the broad head being covered in lumpy tubercles. The pectoral fins are extremely long and mainly white, while the dorsal fin is comparatively short and stubby. The tail is typically dark on the upper surface and white with black markings on the underside, the precise pattern being unique to an individual and the whale equivalent of a fingerprint. When diving, the back arches strongly and the tailstock comes clear of the water before a deep dive. **JUVENILE** is similar to an adult but appreciably smaller (calves are invariably seen in the company of their mothers) and it has proportionately shorter pectoral fins. **VOICE** – An extremely vocal whale during the winter breeding season (spent in tropical waters) but typically silent in our region. HABITAT AND STATUS – If the feeding is good, the Humpback Whale will tolerate comparatively shallow seas and consequently it is occasionally seen from land. However, having said that, they seldom linger for any length of time. Once in a while a stray individual will spend a few days – occasionally weeks – in comparatively sheltered, inshore waters; these sightings are presumed to relate to sickly animals. The north-east Atlantic population of Humpback Whales was decimated by 19th- and 20th-century whaling and now probably numbers just a few hundred animals, although accurate figures are not available. As if past direct exploitation were not enough, they now have to contend with the industrial scale of the modern fishing industry destroying their food stocks. HABITS AND NATURAL HISTORY – Humpback Whales feed primarily on schooling fish and planktonic crustaceans that concentrate in surface seas from time to time. Having swallowed a huge volume of water – food included – in the capacious mouth, the whale then uses its tongue to expel the water, sieving out the fish and plankton using the baleen plates in the mouth. A Humpback's blow can reach 3m and typically it is broad and billowy at the top. At the risk of sounding anthropomorphic, Humpback Whales appear to be extremely 'playful' animals, although in reality the various behavioural patterns probably have more to do with communication, or concentrating food, than fun. They are well known for 'breaching', and it is not uncommon for individuals to leap out of the water 20–30 times repeatedly. Other traits include 'flipper-slapping' and 'tail-slapping' where the relevant part of the body is lashed repeatedly against the surface of the sea. Humpbacks are present in the north-east Atlantic mainly during the summer months, the bulk found off Iceland and north Norway. Individuals seen in British waters are presumed to be migrants travelling to and from their winter quarters in more tropical seas to the south. These warmer waters are favoured for mating, which occurs in late winter. Gestation lasts 10–12 months and so pregnant females give birth the following winter. OBSERVATION TIPS – Because the Humpback Whale is so scarce in British waters it is difficult to plan to see one. Southwest Ireland is probably the most reliable location for the species and the relative regularity of observations hints at the existence of an established migration route; over the last couple of years, the Irish Whale and Dolphin Group has recorded a dozen or so sightings annually off the south coast, from late summer to early winter. Humpback Whales are sometimes encountered in the seas around the Shetland Isles, and on ferry trips across the Irish Sea and the Bay of Biscay in late summer.

HUMPBACK WHALE
⌣ MAIN PIC **breaching adult** ⌣ ABOVE **tail fluke**

SPERM WHALE *Physeter macrocephalus*
LENGTH 16–20m; WEIGHT 20–40 tonnes

A huge and distinctive whale with a disproportionately large and bulbous head. The Sperm Whale is famed for its ability to dive to great depths. **ADULT**

head

is blackish grey overall, but mature animals often bear numerous whitish scars as testimony to fights with one another and violent encounters with their prey. The head is blunt-ended and huge, accounting for roughly one-third of the length and mass of the body. By comparison, the lower jaw is small relative to the size of the body and it is armed with a series of sharp teeth. There is no dorsal fin as such but instead note a dorsal 'hump' beyond which is a series of undulating, knobbly lumps. The flippers are rather small while the tail is proportionately large. Unlike baleen whales, which have 2 blowholes, the Sperm Whale has just one. It is sited at the front of the head and angled slightly forward and to the left, thus creating an asymmetrical appearance. **JUVENILE** is similar to an adult but smaller. **VOICE** – Utters various clicking sounds, but these are inaudible to observers at the surface without the aid of a hydrophone. Living beached whales produce a deafening roar. HABITAT AND STATUS – The Sperm Whale is a truly oceanic species and it is usually associated with waters overlying the edge of continental shelf and the abyss beyond. Healthy individuals are seldom found in shallow, inshore waters. HABITS AND NATURAL HISTORY – Sperm Whales have been recorded diving to depths of 2,000m and beyond, where they hunt prey such as giant squid and deep-sea shark species. Deep dives typically last 30–40 minutes and on its return to the surface the whale exhales explosively. A further 10 minutes is spent at the surface, the whale loafing and breathing every 15 seconds or so. Females and young animals typically live in social groups comprising around 20–30 individuals; these groups tend to live in warm, tropical and subtropical seas. Mature males live in 'bachelor groups' that migrate to polar seas during the summer months, returning to the tropics in winter to breed. As they age, males are increasingly likely to lead solitary lives. Group-living animals tend to dive and surface together. It is likely that several tens of thousands of individuals live in the North Atlantic as a whole. OBSERVATION TIPS – Groups of Sperm Whales are sometimes encountered by ferries that cross the Bay of Biscay from southern England, and by others that ply the seas between mainland Scotland and the Shetland Isles. Just occasionally Sperm Whales are seen in the Western Approaches and off the west coast of Ireland. Sightings in British and Irish waters are presumed to relate to migrating males. The species is relatively easy to identify, even at a distance, if sea conditions are fair. Uniquely among the great whales, the blow is angled forward and off to the left of the animal, and the huge, bulbous head is often visible at the same time as the blow is seen. Prior to a deep dive, the tail is raised clear of the water as the whale embarks on its vertical dive into the abyss. Sperm Whales are sometimes washed up on our shores, their appearance on a beach usually occurring post-mortem. The fact that strandings occur not infrequently on North Sea coasts hints at the possibility of a migration route through those waters.

tail fluke

scrimshaw carved on tooth

spermaceti soap

SPERM WHALE
⊙ ABOVE **head and blow** ⊙ BELOW **dorsal 'fin'**

CUVIER'S BEAKED WHALE *Ziphius cavirostris*
LENGTH 6–7m; WEIGHT 5–6 tonnes

A medium-sized whale with an unusual appearance to the head and mouth. **ADULT** is an overall bluish-grey colour, the back marked with pale scars and the belly and flanks with pale blotches. In profile, the head, which is paler than the rest of the body, has a steeply angled forehead and a rather short beak. Seen in isolation, the beak bears a fanciful resemblance to the beak of a goose; at close range, note the 2 teeth that jut upwards, externally, from the tip of the lower jaw. The eye is relatively large, the dorsal fin small and set quite far back on the body, and the flippers are small and oval. **JUVENILE** is similar to an adult but smaller. **VOICE** – Silent to observers above the water. HABITAT AND STATUS – Cuvier's Beaked Whale occurs throughout the northeast Atlantic but it is a deep-water species that seldom, if ever, comes close to land. It is impossible to assess its population with any accuracy. HABITS AND NATURAL HISTORY – Cuvier's Beaked Whale is capable of long dives to catch deep-sea fish and squid. Little is known about its breeding biology. Since it is usually encountered in small groups it can be inferred that it is, to a degree, a social animal. OBSERVATION TIPS – Your only realistic chance of seeing a living animal in our region is to take a ferry across the Bay of Biscay. Even then you will need calm weather and more than a little luck. Typically, the rounded top of the head is seen first as the whale blows, followed by the appearance of the gently arching back and small dorsal fin.

NORTHERN BOTTLENOSE WHALE
Hyperoodon ampullatus LENGTH 7–9m; WEIGHT 5–7 tonnes

A medium-sized whale with a streamlined body and a distinct head. **ADULT** is variable in colour, although the throat and belly are typically always paler than the rest of the body. Young animals can be bluish grey or brownish, marked with paler blotches on the flanks. Older animals are often pinkish buff overall with a distinctly pale head. Note the strikingly bulbous, rounded forehead, single blowhole and pronounced beak. The flippers are relatively small and the dorsal fin is curved, rather small and set roughly two-thirds back along the body. The tail fluke is broad. **JUVENILE** is similar to a small adult but uniformly brown in colour. **VOICE** – Silent to observers above the water. HABITAT AND STATUS – The Northern Bottlenose Whale is a deep-water cetacean that is seldom seen close to land. It is difficult to assess the population size of such an elusive species but there are probably several thousand individuals in the northeast Atlantic as a whole. HABITS AND NATURAL HISTORY – The Northern Bottlenose Whale is capable of deep dives in order to catch squid. It probably migrates past the west coasts of Britain and Ireland, following the edge of the continental shelf. It is usually seen in small groups of 2–5 individuals. The species is relatively easy to identify: animals rise steeply, often exposing their diagnostic heads. OBSERVATION TIPS – Observations are usually restricted to chance encounters from ferries crossing the Irish Sea, the Bay of Biscay or the seas north of the Scottish mainland. Sometimes the species lingers in inshore waters. Most recently, in the summer of 1998, a pair spent a month off Skye.

NORTHERN RIGHT WHALE *Eubalaena glacialis*
LENGTH 14–18m; WEIGHT 45–55 tonnes

A rare and impressively bulky whale. Named by whalers because it was the 'right' whale to kill – it is slow and indifferent to boats (hence easy to catch) and it floats when dead. **ADULT** has a mainly dark body that is stout, with a proportionately huge head and curved mouth. The flippers are relatively small and triangular and the tail fin is broad. A dorsal fin is absent. At close range, note the so-called callosities on the head, comprising barnacles and whale lice. **JUVENILE** is similar to an adult but smaller, and lacking callosities. **VOICE** – Silent to observers above the water. HABITAT AND STATUS – In the past, Northern Right Whales would have migrated past our coast between summering grounds in the Arctic and wintering quarters from the Bay of Biscay southwards. However, this no longer happens because the species has been driven to the point of extinction by whaling. The few hundred individuals found in the west Atlantic probably represent the species' entire world population and any individual seen in the east Atlantic is likely to be a wanderer from this population. HABITS AND NATURAL HISTORY – Northern Right Whales are rather slow swimmers that spend long periods of time cruising at the surface of the sea. OBSERVATION TIPS – Consider yourself extremely privileged if you get to see a Northern Right Whale in European waters.

CUVIER'S BEAKED WHALE
⌃ ABOVE **adult**

NORTHERN BOTTLENOSE WHALE
⌃ ABOVE **adults**

NORTHERN RIGHT WHALE
⌃ ABOVE **adult breaching**

KILLER WHALE *Orcinus orca*
LENGTH 4–9m; WEIGHT 3–5 tonnes

A distinctive and well-marked cetacean. The Killer Whale is the largest member of the dolphin family. Males are appreciably larger and heavier than females but both share the same streamlined body and blunt, conical snout. **ADULT MALE** has mainly blackish upper parts and often this is the only colour that can be discerned in swimming animals seen in poor light. At close range, a grey saddle-like patch can be seen behind the dorsal fin. The underparts are white and a band of white extends onto the flanks. Note also the white patch behind the eye. There is a clear demarcation between the black and white elements. The dorsal fin is up to 1.8m tall, triangular and upright, sometimes even forward-leaning. The flippers are broad and paddle-shaped. **ADULT FEMALE** is similar to the male but smaller and with a proportionately much shorter dorsal fin that is curved and rather shark-like. **CALF** is similar to an adult female but much smaller and with a proportionately shorter dorsal fin. **VOICE** – Utters a complex range of clicks and whistles, some associated with echolocation, others with communication. A hydrophone is needed to appreciate these calls. HABITAT AND STATUS – The Killer Whale is a widespread species in the northeast Atlantic and occurs from time to time in British and Irish waters. Although it could turn up almost anywhere, it is least likely to be found in the English Channel or southern North Sea. Killer Whales are not averse to feeding in comparatively shallow water and are occasionally seen at close range from coastal headlands. There are probably several thousand Killer Whales in the northeast Atlantic as a whole and a few dozen are recorded in our range each year. HABITS AND NATURAL HISTORY – Killer Whales are social animals that live in stable groups, known as 'pods', typically comprising 5–20 animals of mixed sex and age. Pods seen in coastal British and Irish seas tend to be small and lone individuals are also encountered. As their English name suggests, Killer Whales are carnivores, taking a variety of prey including fish, seals, squid and even other cetaceans. Females give birth, on average, every 3–4 years. Calves (1 per female) are usually born in autumn or early winter, mating having taken place the previous autumn. The young animal is weaned after a year or so but typically it will remain in its mother's pod for several years, perhaps even for life. OBSERVATION TIPS – With its uniquely tall dorsal fin, a mature male Killer Whale is instantly recognisable. With a female, there is an outside risk of confusion with, for example, a Long-finned Pilot Whale, but since they are usually found in the company of at least one male, identification is usually relatively straightforward. Killer Whales also breach regularly and at such times their distinctive and diagnostic black-and-white markings are easily seen. As with most cetacean species, it is difficult to plan to see Killer Whales in British and Irish waters, despite the fact that they do occur on a regular basis. Pods or individuals tend to be transient and so are seen briefly by lone observers. However, just occasionally, they linger in the same general area for a few days if the feeding is good. When this happens, it is usually in the summer months, in places where Mackerel are running and seals are common. The south and west coasts of Ireland, and the seas around the Shetland Isles seem to be particular hotspots. Killer Whales are also encountered by ferry crossings of the Irish Sea, between the Scottish mainland and the northern isles, and from routes that cross the Bay of Biscay from southern England. If you are lucky enough to encounter Killer Whales from a small boat you are likely to be treated to spectacular views, because they often swim close, seemingly as curious about the encounter as their human observers.

male and juvenile

KILLER WHALE
⌃ ABOVE **mother and calf** ⌄ BELOW **male**

RISSO'S DOLPHIN *Grampus griseus*
LENGTH 3–3.5m; WEIGHT 300–400kg

A rather large and blunt-nosed dolphin. Risso's Dolphin is a distinctive colour and, in good light, identification should be a relatively straight-forward matter. **ADULT** is typically greyish brown overall, darkest on the dorsal fin, flippers and tail, and palest on the face, throat and belly. Older animals are often quite pale (almost chalky grey) and the upper surface in particular becomes heavily criss-crossed with white scars (presumed to be the result of aggressive encounters with others of their kind) and circular to oval marks, possibly caused by squid suckers. The head is blunt-ended and the forehead is split down the middle – from the upper lip to the blowhole – by a deep crease. The dorsal fin is tall, pointed and slightly recurved. The flippers are relatively long and narrow, and the tail fin is broad. **JUVENILE** is similar to an adult but smaller and with fewer scars on the back. **VOICE** – Mostly silent. HABITAT AND STATUS – Despite the fact that Risso's Dolphins are often associated with deep water, and are capable of diving to considerable depths, they are encountered in relatively shallow, coastal water on a regular basis. In fact, at locations where the seabed shelves steeply from shore, they can sometimes be seen just a few hundred metres from land. It is almost impossible to gauge the population size of such a transient and nomadic species but it is likely that several thousand individuals are present in the north-east Atlantic as a whole. HABITS AND NATURAL HISTORY – Risso's Dolphins live in groups (known as *pods*) comprising 3–15 animals on average, typically of mixed sex and age. Calves are born (1 per female) from late winter to early summer, mating having occurred the previous spring. Mother and juvenile pairs are frequently seen so it is likely that parental associations persist for months, if not years, after weaning. Like many cetacean species, Risso's Dolphins live rather nomadic lives, but it is likely that the northeast Atlantic population remains within the same general area year-round. In the open sea, the main prey would appear to be squid and octopus, but in inshore waters the likelihood is that fish feature heavily in the diet too. OBSERVATION TIPS – Risso's Dolphins are regularly observed at classic seabird migration hotspots in the south and west of the region. So, if you were to visit coastal headlands in Cornwall, west Wales or south and west Ireland in late summer or early autumn you would stand a good chance of seeing the species. You would need to be vigilant, however, and would probably have to spend several days staring out to sea in order to be lucky. Risso's Dolphins are also seen from ferries crossing the Irish Sea, and those plying routes from mainland Scotland to the northern isles, and from southern England across the Bay of Biscay. Identification should be relatively straightforward: look for the tall dorsal fin that typically looks darker than the diagnostically scarred greyish back. Risso's Dolphins are often quite active at the surface of the sea. Lucky observers may see one breach clear of the water, or spy-hop, the animal raising its head (and occasionally flippers too) clear of the water in order to see what is going on above the surface of the sea.

tail fin and tailstock

dorsal fin

RISSO'S DOLPHIN
⌃ ABOVE **breaching adult**

LONG-FINNED PILOT WHALE *Globiocephala melaena*
LENGTH 4–6m; WEIGHT 1–3 tonnes

A medium-sized cetacean. Despite its impressive size, the Long-finned Pilot Whale is more closely related to dolphins than to true whales. The distinctive shapes of the head and dorsal fin make for relatively straightforward identification. **ADULT** has a mainly blackish body. There is a greyish saddle-shaped mark behind the dorsal fin but this feature is not always easy to discern in the field, especially if light conditions are harsh. A white, thighbone-shaped mark adorns the underparts, running from the throat to the vent; note, however, that this feature can be seen only if an animal breaches. The head is blunt-ended, the forehead is domed and the flippers are relatively long and

sickle-shaped. The dorsal fin is broad-based and curved, and is set relatively far forward on the body. Males are longer and heavier than females and usually have a more pronounced bulbous forehead. **JUVENILE** is similar to an adult but smaller, with a less strikingly domed forehead. **VOICE** – Utters a wide range of whistles, squeaks and clicking sounds. HABITAT AND STATUS – The Long-finned Pilot Whale is widespread in the northeast Atlantic and occurs on a regular basis in British and Irish waters, typically being seen in sizeable groups. It often occurs in deep water and is capable of diving to considerable depths, but occasionally it can be seen in comparatively shallow seas, such as those surrounding offshore islands and prominent headlands. It is impossible to assess the population in the northeast Atlantic with any degree

large pod with partly breaching animal

of accuracy but it is likely that several tens of thousands are present in the region as a whole.

HABITS AND NATURAL HISTORY – The Long-finned Pilot Whale is a gregarious cetacean and typically it is encountered in social groups (known as *pods*) of 10–50 animals; much larger congregations have been recorded elsewhere in the world. Each pod comprises a mixture of sexes and ages. Long-finned Pilot Whales feed mainly on squid, but fish are important in the diet as well. Mating takes place in spring and early summer and the young are born in autumn. Each female produces a single calf every few years and it is likely that the juvenile's association with its mother persists beyond the point of weaning, which occurs at just under 2 years of age. When cruising at the surface, typically the head, back and dorsal fin are visible at the same time; members of a pod seem to surface and blow with a degree of synchrony. Prior to a deep dive, the tail and tailstock are sometimes lifted clear of the water. Long-finned Pilot Whales are occasionally washed up dead on beaches but are also renowned for seemingly deliberately beaching themselves while still alive. In such cases, several animals may be involved, a testament perhaps to the strength of the bonds that exist between pod members. OBSERVATION TIPS – Long-finned Pilot Whales lead rather nomadic lives and no predictable patterns can be discerned with regards to their appearance in British and Irish seas. So seeing this species is really a matter of chance. The seas around the Shetland Isles and off southwest England and Ireland appear to be particular hotspots for land-based observations. Pods are occasionally seen from ferry crossings between the Scottish mainland and the northern isles, and from those sailing across the Bay of Biscay from southern England.

LONG-FINNED PILOT WHALE
⌃ ABOVE pod with animals showing dorsal
fins, backs and blowholes

COMMON DOLPHIN *Delphinus delphis*
LENGTH 1.8–2.3m; WEIGHT 80–110kg

As its English name suggests, the Common Dolphin is probably the most widespread and numerous cetacean worldwide, and that includes the northeast Atlantic. It is also the yardstick by which other dolphin species should be judged: get to know the Common Dolphin well and you will greatly improve your chances of correctly identifying its less numerous and unfamiliar cousins. **ADULT** is a streamlined cetacean that is adorned with a distinctive pattern of overlapping stripes and bands of pigmentation. Note, however, that only breaching animals reveal the complete pattern – for most of the time you will see only part of the animal and a range of different views will be needed to complete the overall picture. Broadly speaking, the body is dark grey above and whitish below. However, a broad, tapering yellow band runs along the flanks from the eye and mouth to just behind the dorsal fin; a band of grey continues along the flanks towards the tail. The overall effect of the yellow and grey patches, with their tapering intersection, recalls an hourglass. A striking dark patch surrounds the eye. There is a long beak; the upper jaw is black while the lower jaw is grey. The flippers are narrow and black, with a black line running forward from the base to the throat. The dorsal fin is broadly triangular and curved backwards slightly. Overall, males are larger than females. **JUVENILE** is similar to an adult but smaller. **VOICE** – Mainly silent to observers above the water. HABITAT AND STATUS – The Common Dolphin is essentially an open-sea cetacean and typically it is encountered from boats, out of sight of land. It is likely that populations in the northeast Atlantic remain in the same general area year-round but, having said that they are, by necessity, nomadic, their movements dictated by their search for prey. It is difficult to assess the numbers of such a mobile species with any degree of accuracy but it is likely that many tens of thousands of individuals are found in the northeast Atlantic as a whole.

dorsal fin and head

tailstock and dorsal fin

Like other small dolphin species, the Common Dolphin suffers at the hands of the fishing industry, being caught and killed in nets. Fixed nets have always been a problem, but increasingly the practice of pair-trawl fishing for Sea Bass is having a tragic impact on the species. A unilateral ban is likely to be imposed in British waters but it is hard to imagine French or Spanish fleets willingly complying with any restrictions on their activities in their own waters. It is impossible to assess the true extent of the killing, but extrapolation from recorded by-catch figures would suggest that thousands of Common Dolphins are killed each year in the northeast Atlantic alone. HABITS AND NATURAL HISTORY – This is one of the most social of all cetaceans and you are most unlikely to encounter a solitary Common Dolphin, or at least not a healthy individual. Typically, the species forms schools of 10–40 individuals, but aggregations of several hundred are not unprecedented and elsewhere in the world several thousand have been recorded. The schools comprise a mixture of ages and sexes. Common Dolphins feed on shoaling pelagic fish and squid. Each female is likely to give birth to a single calf every few years. Most are born in early summer with mating having occurred 10–12 months earlier. OBSERVATION TIPS – During the winter months in particular, Common Dolphins are

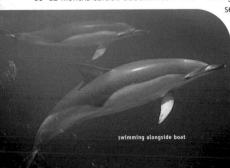

swimming alongside boat

seen occasionally from headlands in southwest England and Ireland. At such times, views are typically rather distant and observation from a boat in spring or summer is needed for closer encounters. Ferries crossing the Irish Sea, the Bay of Biscay, and from mainland Scotland to the northern isles, can all yield sightings. Pelagic birdwatching trips from Cornwall and the Scilly Isles also encounter the species and it is often seen from lone yachts too. Common Dolphins show little fear of boats and will often approach closely, sometimes bow-riding for several minutes.

COMMON DOLPHIN

⌃ ABOVE **dorsal fin**
⌄ MAIN PIC **school**

BOTTLENOSE DOLPHIN *Tursiops truncatus*
LENGTH 2.5–4m; WEIGHT 100–300kg

A medium-sized dolphin with a near-cosmopolitan distribution, absent only from polar seas. The body is bulky and muscular, yet still streamlined. **ADULT** is essentially greyish brown overall, darkest on the upper surface and palest on the throat and belly; a mid-grey band can sometimes be discerned on the flanks. The beak is relatively short and blunt (fancifully bottle-like) with the lower jaw extending beyond the upper one. The flippers are rather long and pointed, and the dorsal fin is relatively tall, curved backwards and almost shark-like in outline. The tailstock is thick and the tail fin is broad. **JUVENILE** is similar to an adult but smaller.

VOICE – Utters a variety of clicks for echolocation and whistles for communication. HABITAT AND STATUS – Although some Bottlenose Dolphins are essentially pelagic, seldom venturing close to land, other groups spend much of their lives in coastal waters; some even venture into estuaries and river mouths. Several hundred individuals probably live in inshore waters around the British and Irish coasts. Numbers in the open seas of the northeast Atlantic as a whole are not known but the species is certainly nowhere near as numerous as the Common Dolphin. HABITS AND NATURAL HISTORY –

dorsal fins

Bottlenose Dolphins are social animals that are usually found in schools comprising 3–15 individuals. They have a catholic diet that includes fish, squid, cuttlefish, crabs and shrimps, and this eclectic range of prey may help explain why some individuals can spend their lives in the open sea while others restrict their range to inshore waters. The species is known to engage in cooperative feeding on occasions. When swimming at a leisurely pace, Bottlenose Dolphins usually only reveal the arched back and the tall dorsal fin. Typically, their swimming action appears relaxed and controlled, and there is little of the frantic, splashing activity seen with Common Dolphins. On occasions, however, Bottlenose Dolphins will breach clear of the water in a manner familiar to anyone who has seen the species in captivity. Females give birth to a single calf every few years. Gestation lasts around a year and mating and birth seem to occur at any time of year. The ties between mother and calf appear to persist beyond the point of weaning, which usually occurs after a year and a half. OBSERVATION TIPS – Although Bottlenose Dolphins could not be described as common in British and Irish waters, certain groups are broadly faithful to the same general area. Consequently, observation of the species, although by no means guaranteed, is more predictable and reliable than for other dolphins. The Moray Firth in Scotland and the Shannon estuary in Ireland are hotspots, but Bottlenose Dolphins also occur in the western English Channel (the range extending east to Durlston in Dorset), off west Cornwall and Cardigan Bay. The species typically shows no fear of boats, or of swimmers for that matter, and some individuals appear persistently interested in the company of humans.

dorsal fin

BOTTLENOSE DOLPHIN
⌃ ABOVE **breaching** ⌄ BELOW **dorsal fin**

WHITE-BEAKED DOLPHIN *Lagenorhynchus albirostris*
LENGTH 2.4–2.8m; WEIGHT 180–220kg

A relatively large and well-marked dolphin. **ADULT** has a black back and dorsal fin. There is usually a broad, pale band behind the eye and an oblique greyish-white stripe on the flanks running backwards from a point above the flippers and grading into a greyish-white area behind the dorsal fin. The snub-nosed beak is strikingly pale, as are the throat and belly. Seen above the water, the beak usually looks pale pinkish grey but when submerged it appears gleaming white. The flippers are broadly triangular and the dorsal fin is tall and sickle-shaped. **JUVENILE** is similar to an adult but smaller. **VOICE** – Silent to observers above the surface of the sea. HABITAT AND STATUS – The White-beaked Dolphin favours cool seas. Several thousand individuals probably live in the region as a whole. HABITS AND NATURAL HISTORY – White-beaked Dolphins usually live in schools comprising 3–15 individuals. They sometimes consort with other dolphin species. OBSERVATION TIPS – White-beaked Dolphins are fast swimmers. They occasionally come close to vessels but tend to come and go rapidly. The northern North Sea is the best area for the species in our region. You are unlikely to see it from land.

ATLANTIC WHITE-SIDED DOLPHIN
Lagenorhynchus acutus LENGTH 2–2.5m; WEIGHT 170–210kg

A relatively large dolphin with distinctive markings. **ADULT** has a dark back and dorsal fin. On the flanks, a grey band runs the length of the body. Above this lies a white stripe (below the dorsal fin) and a yellowish stripe (from the dorsal fin to the tailstock). Below the grey flanks, the belly is white and this colour extends forward as a band to the eye. The beak is short and stubby; the upper jaw is dark while the lower jaw is pale. The flippers are relatively small and the dorsal fin is tall and curved backwards. **JUVENILE** is similar to an adult but smaller. **VOICE** – Silent to observers above the surface of the water. HABITAT AND STATUS – Typically associated with deep waters. However, it does occasionally venture into inshore waters (presumably following fish shoals). Several thousand are probably resident in the northeast Atlantic. HABITS AND NATURAL HISTORY – Atlantic White-sided Dolphins live in schools the size of which, as a general rule, is inversely proportional to the proximity of land: groups of 5–20 might be encountered within sight of land whereas pelagic schools may comprise hundreds of individuals. They are probably present year-round and are more likely to occur close to land during the summer months. OBSERVATION TIPS – Atlantic White-sided Dolphins are sometimes seen from sea-watching sites in southwest England and Ireland, northern Scotland and the northern isles; from ferries in those regions; and on pelagic trips from Cornwall and the Scilly Isles. Summer and early autumn are the best seasons.

STRIPED DOLPHIN *Stenella coeruleoalba*
LENGTH 2–2.5m; WEIGHT 90–130kg

A streamlined and relatively long-beaked dolphin. **ADULT** has longitudinal stripes and bands of black, grey and white. The back and dorsal fin are blackish. A broad, grey band runs the length of the flanks but it is partly interrupted by a striking black streak that extends forward from the dark back beneath the dorsal fin. The lower margin of the grey flank-stripe is defined by a black margin; 2 narrow black stripes run back from the eye; the anterior one connects with the dark flipper. The dorsal fin is tall and sickle-shaped. **JUVENILE** is similar to an adult but smaller. **VOICE** – Silent to observers above the water's surface. HABITAT AND STATUS – The Striped Dolphin prefers warm, oceanic waters and the Western Approaches probably represent the typical northernmost extent of its range in the northeast Atlantic. HABITS AND NATURAL HISTORY – Striped Dolphins live in schools, typically numbering 5–50 animals. They are extremely active at the surface. OBSERVATION TIPS – Ferries crossing the Bay of Biscay offer the best chances of seeing this species.

WHITE-BEAKED DOLPHIN
⊘ BELOW breaching adult

ATLANTIC WHITE-SIDED DOLPHIN
⊘ BELOW dorsal fin and flank stripes

STRIPED DOLPHIN
⊘ BELOW breaching adult

HARBOUR PORPOISE *Phocoena phocoena*

LENGTH 1.4–1.9m; WEIGHT 40–90kg

A small and plump-bodied cetacean that is the smallest of its kind in the region. In the past it was called Common Porpoise. **ADULT** has a stout but streamlined body, a blunt head and no beak. The flippers are rather small and oval and the dorsal fin is distinctly triangular, but with a concave trailing edge. The tailstock is thick and the tail fin is broad. The upper parts are mainly dark grey while the underparts are whitish. Note, in addition, the bluish-grey patch on the flanks, roughly between the eye and the start of the dorsal fin. **JUVENILE** is similar to an adult but smaller. **VOICE** – Silent to observers above the water. HABITAT AND STATUS – As its current English name implies, the Harbour Porpoise favours inshore waters. While it is seldom seen in harbours as such, it does occur in estuaries, river mouths and sheltered coastal bays, frequently within sight of land. However, it is also widespread across much of the North Sea and in seas that overlie the continental shelf around Britain and Ireland as a whole; water depths of less than 100m are preferred. It is

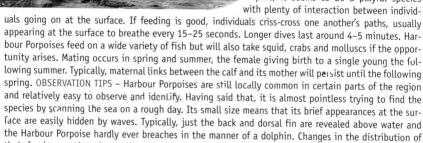

adults

likely that more than 100,000 Harbour Porpoises live in British and Irish waters. Despite this seemingly high figure the species is still vulnerable: it has been estimated that at least 7,000 are killed annually – as so-called 'by-catch' – by the North Sea fishing industry alone. Clearly, if this degree of mortality is maintained year after year a decline in numbers overall is inevitable. HABITS AND NATURAL HISTORY – The Harbour Porpoise is usually encountered in groups comprising 3–15 individuals. At the risk of sounding anthropomorphic, it seems to be a playful species with plenty of interaction between individuals going on at the surface. If feeding is good, individuals criss-cross one another's paths, usually appearing at the surface to breathe every 15–25 seconds. Longer dives last around 4–5 minutes. Harbour Porpoises feed on a wide variety of fish but will also take squid, crabs and molluscs if the opportunity arises. Mating occurs in spring and summer, the female giving birth to a single young the following summer. Typically, maternal links between the calf and its mother will persist until the following spring. OBSERVATION TIPS – Harbour Porpoises are still locally common in certain parts of the region and relatively easy to observe and identify. Having said that, it is almost pointless trying to find the species by scanning the sea on a rough day. Its small size means that its brief appearances at the surface are easily hidden by waves. Typically, just the back and dorsal fin are revealed above water and the Harbour Porpoise hardly ever breaches in the manner of a dolphin. Changes in the distribution of

their food mean that the species is more likely to be encountered in inshore waters in summer and early autumn. Harbour Porpoises could turn up almost anywhere around the British and Irish coasts but you are perhaps least likely to see one in the English Channel or the southern North Sea. Particular hotspots appear to be the Moray Firth, the seas surrounding the Inner Hebrides, and the north Devon coast, particularly the stretch between Hartland Point and Lundy.

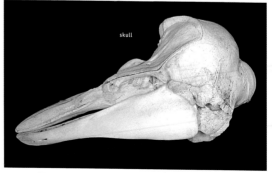

skull

HARBOUR PORPOISE
⌃ ABOVE **adult** ⌄ BELOW **mother and calf**

WILDCAT *Felis silvestris grampia*

BODY LENGTH 50–65cm; TAIL LENGTH 25–35cm; WEIGHT 3–7kg

Resembles a large, well-marked version of the familiar domestic cat (*Felis silvestris catus*). Both share common ancestry and, in classification terms, there is just a subspecies difference between the two. The true Wildcat is a wild and untamed animal that is endangered and restricted to rather remote areas of Scotland. Some domestic individuals are virtually indistinguishable from their wild cousins and to confuse matters further the two subspecies are known to interbreed. **ADULT** bears a passing resemblance to a large, tabby domestic cat, but subtle differences allow separation of the two in most instances. A Wildcat is a stocky animal with greyish-brown fur marked with rather uniform, vertical stripes along the side of the body; there is a dark vertebral line running down the back. The tail is thick, bushy and blunt-tipped, and marked with 3–5 dark and discrete bands. The eyes are orange-yellow and the nose is pink. Typically, the tail of 'wild'-type domestic cats is less bushy, tapers and has less distinct bands; the flanks are seldom striped and are usually marked with irregular dark blotches. **JUVENILE** resembles a small, well-marked adult with a proportionately larger head; the eyes are blue for the first few weeks of life. **VOICE** – Utters a variety of calls – mewing, purring, spitting and growling – similar to those of a domestic cat. HABITAT AND STATUS – In historical terms the Wildcat was once widespread, but today it is restricted to Scotland; it occurs on rather rugged moors, forest margins and the fringes of mountain slopes, the species' stronghold being central and northern areas. In all probability it has been marginalised to these seemingly less than optimal habitats by human persecution and the colonisation of more benign territories by feral domestic cats. Because of the difficulty of surveying such a secretive animal, and the potential for confusion (when assessing numbers on the basis of tracks, trails and signs) with domestic cats, it is not possible to place a reliable figure on the species' population. HABITS AND NATURAL HISTORY – Although Wildcats will patrol their territories and hunt at any time of the day or night, they seem to be most active at dusk and dawn. Prey animals include Rabbits, hares and small mammals but, like their domestic cousins, they are opportunistic and will seldom pass up the chance to tackle any mammal or bird of a suitable size that presents itself. Typically, adults are solitary and territorial; non-aggressive encounters are restricted to the mating season (late winter and early spring). Females give birth to 1 litter per year, usually in spring or early summer. The litter comprises 3–5 kittens and they are usually confined to an underground den for the first few weeks of their life. The young are usually weaned and fully independent after a period of 3–4 months. Adult territories are marked by the owner using scent: pungent urine is sprayed on vegetation, faeces is deposited in prominent places and special scent glands (such as those on the chin and at the base of the tail) are used to mark strategic spots. OBSERVATION TIPS – The Wildcat is a difficult animal to observe in the wild. Search carefully in suitable habitats and you might come across scratch marks on trees, or droppings; if you have a good sense of smell then you may pick up the scent of fresh urine. Most encounters are made by chance and not infrequently the species is caught in car headlights as it crosses a remote Scottish road after dark. If you spend enough time in the Abernethy and Rothiemurchus forests in the Scottish Highlands, you stand a chance of getting a fleeting glimpse. Unfortunately, the only completely reliable way to see a Wildcat is to visit one of the Scottish 'wildlife parks' where rather dejected-looking specimens are kept.

adult with rabbit prey

kitten

domestic tabby

skull

WILDCAT
◁ LEFT **typical partial view**   ⌒ ABOVE **adult**   ▷ RIGHT **dropping**

FOX *Vulpes vulpes*

BODY LENGTH 60–90cm; TAIL LENGTH 35–45cm; WEIGHT 5–10kg

A widespread and adaptable doglike mammal whose appearance and colour are familiar to most people, even if the animal itself is seen relatively infrequently. **ADULT** has a thick coat of orange-brown or reddish-brown fur on most of the body and tail. However, the jaws and underparts are white and there is a white tip to the tail. The feet and the backs of the ears are blackish. The male (known as a *dog*) is similar to, but marginally larger than, the female (referred to as a *vixen*). **JUVENILE** (known as a *cub*) has rather dark fur and a proportionately larger head than an adult. **VOICE** – The most characteristic call is a high-pitched yelping scream, uttered mainly by vixens for just a few weeks at most, in the dead of winter, to mark the breeding season. This scream is beloved of TV 'murder mystery' programmes, dubbed onto the soundtrack of scenes that take place after dark; in most instances it is used at completely inappropriate times of year. Adults utter barking sounds in the vicinity of the den, to warn the cubs of danger. HABITAT AND STATUS – The Fox is widespread and occurs in most mainland areas in our region. Originally it might have been thought of as an animal of woodland, farmland and moors. However, it has proved to be extremely adaptable and now occurs at surprisingly high densities in towns and cities, benefiting indirectly from small mammals that flourish in the wake of our wasteful society, and more directly from the food we discard. There are probably several hundred thousand Foxes in the region as a whole. Several tens of thousands of these are killed each year by people (shooting, trapping, road kills etc.) and natural mortality is also high in young animals. HABITS AND NATURAL HISTORY – Although the Fox is, in classification terms at least, a carnivore, to describe its dietary habits as solely predatory is to oversimplify things. It certainly kills and eats animals, but it is also an opportunistic feeder, taking carrion, fruits and berries when available. In urban areas, some individuals are adept at raiding dustbins, or at least they were until the introduction of wheelie bins. If a Fox is presented with readily available food, such as hens or reared pheasant poults confined to a pen, it will often kill far more than it can eat in one go. This behaviour is not unique to Foxes by any means and many predators will exhibit a similar response if presented with a freely available and seemingly limitless source of food. I include humans in this too – just think of fishermen on a 'Mackerel spree'. In Foxes at least the behaviour can be explained as an adaptation to unpredictable food supplies: in times of plenty prey is cached underground, to be retrieved at a later date in times of hardship. In most rural parts of the region, Foxes are essentially nocturnal animals. Where they are not unduly disturbed, particularly in urban areas, they are sometimes active from the late afternoon onwards. Much of the day is spent in shelter and in most instances this is achieved by excavating a burrow and den, collectively known as an *earth*. They are territorial animals, marking occupation of an area using conspicuously placed faeces, urine spraying and scent deposited from special glands. Territorial size depends upon the availability of food and shelter, as well as the amount of persecution and disturbance to which they are subjected. In areas where the population is relatively stable (these days, this tends to mean urban areas), a territory might be occupied by a male and female, and varying numbers of young females, presumably offspring from the previous year. Males are sexually active for a couple of months in midwinter and females are fertile for just 3 days. The young are born in early spring; there is 1 litter per year comprising 4 or 5 cubs. They are usually weaned after a couple of months. Both parents provide prey for the cubs at this stage. The young remain with the mother until the autumn. Thereafter dispersal is likely to occur if their natal territory is fully occupied. OBSERVATION TIPS – Observation is probably easiest in urban areas. If you want to watch them in a more rural setting, you will need to watch an earth from a safe distance. Remember to sit downwind and to remain silent – a Fox's senses of hearing and smell are acute.

cub

adult raiding bin

dropping

skull

FOX
⊕ ABOVE **young animal**
⊘ MAIN PIC **entrance to 'earth'**

STOAT *Mustela erminea*

BODY LENGTH 18–30cm; TAIL LENGTH 10–14cm; WEIGHT 100–400g

An extremely active animal with a long, sinuous body, the Stoat is a voracious predator of rodents and Rabbits. Its unobtrusive habits mean that, typically, views of the species are fleeting and occasional. Males are larger, and heavier, than females. **SUMMER ADULT** has rich orange-brown fur on the upper parts (and the outer sides of the legs), with a clear demarcation from the white under-parts. The tail is mostly rich orange-brown but the tip is black. **WINTER ADULT** has a thicker coat. In the southern half of the region, the colour remains the same as that seen in summer. However, further north a variably com-plete white coat is acquired (referred to as *ermine*) although the tip of the tail always remains black. **JUVENILE** is similar to an adult but smaller. **VOICE** – High-pitched calls are uttered in alarm, especially by adults with young. HABITAT AND STATUS – The Stoat is widespread in mainland Britain. It also occurs throughout Ireland where, confusingly, it is sometimes referred to as a *weasel*. A wide range of habitats are favoured by the species, including farmland, woodlands, marshes and moors, the key common factor being the pres-ence of prey. Several hundred thousand are probably present in the region as a whole. Significant numbers are killed each year by gamekeepers and road kills are not infrequent. HABITS AND NATURAL HISTORY– Stoats have an exclusively carnivorous diet. Males – the larger of the sexes – often specialise in catching Rabbits and hares, while females favour small mammals and birds. The sin-uous body form allows them to hunt underground and to move through comparatively dense vegetation with ease. Prey is typically killed by a bite to the back of the neck, which either severs the spinal cord or catastrophically impairs brain function. Stoats are active by day and by night and often concentrate their hunting activities along hedgerows and walls, as well as in the vicinity of the burrows of prey. When resting or breeding, burrows or chambers within stone walls are often favoured; Stoats will happily use the burrows of their prey, notably those of Rabbits. For much of the year they are solitary and territorial ani-mals. However, during the breeding season males tend to wander widely, abandoning their former territories in search of receptive females. Mating occurs in early summer, but delayed implantation ensures that females do not give birth until the following spring. There is 1 litter per year and this usually comprises 6–12 babies. The young become fully independent after 3 months or so, by which time they are capable of killing prey for themselves. OBSERVATION TIPS – Stoats are always difficult animals to observe and most sightings relate to chance encounters. The agonising squeals of a Rabbit often indicate that the terrified animal is the process of being killed by a Stoat. With caution, a stealthy observer can sometimes creep up on the act. If a female Stoat with young to feed discovers a litter of baby Rabbits, she will often 'clean out' the nest, removing the prey one by one and carrying them back to her own den. So if you see a Stoat drag-ging a young Rabbit along the ground, sit qui-etly and you may be rewarded by a repeat performance a few minutes later.

dropping

northern adult, winter

adult killing rabbit

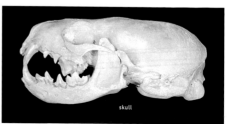

skull

STOAT
⌃ ABOVE **adult, summer**
› RIGHT **adult, summer**

WEASEL *Mustela nivalis*

BODY LENGTH 18–30cm; TAIL LENGTH 5–10cm; WEIGHT 35–55g

Recalls a diminutive version of a Stoat, with its long, sinuous body. Note, however-er, the proportionately shorter tail, which is uniform in colour, not black-tipped. **ADULT** has sleek orange-brown fur on the upper parts and sides of the body, the sides of the legs and the entire tail. The underparts, including the throat, are white and there is a clear demarcation between the two zones of colour. The coat colour remains the same in summer and winter. Males are appre-ciably larger than females. **JUVENILE** is similar to an adult. **VOICE** – Utters high-pitched hissing sounds in alarm. HABITAT AND STATUS – The Weasel is widespread throughout mainland Britain but it is entirely absent from most islands, as well as from Ireland. A wide variety of habitats are favoured, including woodlands, hedgerows, meadows, farmland and moors; the common factor is the presence of ground cover and an abundance of prey animals. Sev-eral hundred thousand individuals are probably pres-ent in the region as a whole. HABITS AND NATURAL HISTORY – Weasels are voracious predators with an exclusively carnivorous diet. Their senses of smell, hearing and vision are acute. Small mammals, notably voles and mice, make up the bulk of their prey, although rats, baby rabbits and birds will also be taken if the opportunity arises. The sinuous body form allows them to hunt underground in rodent burrows and to follow the runs of small mammals through dense vegetation. Above ground, a hunting Weasel often stands upright on its hind legs in order to view its surroundings. This agile little animal can also climb when the need arises and it is known to raid nest boxes for young birds. Prey is typically killed by a bite to the back of the neck, which either severs the spinal cord or catastrophically impairs brain function. Weasels are active by day and by night. When resting or breeding, the burrows of prey animals are often favoured. They tend to be solitary and territorial animals, although males seek out receptive females in early spring, when mating occurs. Delayed implantation does not occur and so females give birth 5 weeks or so later; 4–6 babies per litter is usual. In most years just 1 litter is produced but in seasons when small mammal numbers are high a second may be born in late summer. Parental care is undertaken by the female alone. The young become fully independent after 3 months or so, by which time they are capable of killing prey for themselves. OBSERVATION TIPS – Weasels lead unobtrusive lives and hence most encounters occur purely by chance, for example when an animal is seen running at speed across a road. In hunting mode, they are usually thorough and their persistence can sometimes aid observation. If, for example, you catch a glimpse of a Weasel hunting around a log pile, or some other fairly well-defined and restricted location for small mammals, sit qui-etly and watch: periodically the animal may emerge from cover as it systematically search-es every nook and cranny for prey.

hunting adult

dropping

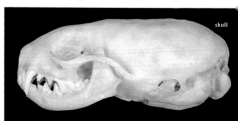

skull

WEASEL
⌃ ABOVE adult ⌄ BELOW adult

POLECAT *Mustela putorius*

BODY LENGTH 30–45cm; TAIL LENGTH 13–15cm; WEIGHT 600–1,500g

Resembles a large, bulky and dark ferret, and indeed the Polecat is now considered to be the likely ancestor of its domesticated cousin. **SUMMER ADULT** has rather coarse fur that is dark brown overall. However, the flanks and belly are typically paler, sometimes appearing buffish yellow. On the face, note the white marks on either side of the nose, following the line of the jaw upwards to a point between the eyes and the ears. These white markings contrast with, and help define, the rather dark 'mask' through the eyes. The tips of the ears are pale. **WINTER ADULT** is similar but overall the coat is paler, often rather buffish yellow. **JUVENILE** is similar to a winter adult. **NOTE** – Feral ferret populations

mother with young

exist in some parts of the country. While most individuals are typically slim, pale animals (albinos are not uncommon) a few have markings that are virtually indistinguishable from those of a genuine Polecat. **VOICE** – Utters various screams and hisses when alarmed. HABITAT AND STATUS – The story of the Polecat in our region has certainly had its ups and downs. As recently perhaps as a century ago the species was widespread throughout mainland Britain, but towards the latter half of the 20th century it had become extinct in most parts, its decline put down to a combination of human persecution and the virtual disappearance of Rabbits – an important prey species – from the scene owing to myx-

omatosis. Polecats became confined to central Wales and the future did not look promising. However, since the 1990s, there has been something of an upturn in their fate. Through a combination of legal protection, a recovery in Rabbit numbers (which not everyone welcomes, of course) and active species recovery and introduction programmes, it now occurs throughout Wales and central southern England, with isolated pockets in the Lake District and southern Scotland. Indeed, if observations and records (mainly of road kills) are anything to go by, Polecats are spreading back into formerly occupied parts of Britain. Today, several tens of thousands of individuals probably occur in the region as a whole. Favoured habitats include farmland, woodland margins, river margins and marshes. HABITS AND NATURAL HISTORY – Polecats are essentially nocturnal animals and spend the daylight hours in a burrow, often one previously occupied by Rabbits. They are primarily predators and prey includes Rabbits, small mammals, birds and amphibians. However, they are also opportunistic feeders and will take prey down to the size of insects and earthworms, as well as carrion and birds' eggs. Polecats are typically solitary and territorial, and occupied ground is marked using scent glands and droppings. Mating occurs in early spring and the young are born in early summer; typically, there are 4–6 babies per litter and there is 1 litter per year. By late summer the young Polecats are fully independent and disperse from their mother's territory. OBSERVATION TIPS – Unfortunately, you are far more likely to see a Polecat dead on a road than you are a live one. However, working on the basis that road kills do not account for the entire population, such sightings do at least indicate the presence of this rather secretive animal in a given area. Another telltale sign is the presence of rather pungent droppings that contain fur and bones; if you know what a ferret smells like then this will give you a clue. Once you know for sure that you have Polecats living in your area, observations at dawn and dusk should lead to a chance encounter sooner or later.

pet ferrets

adult Polecat

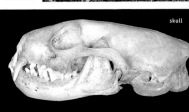
skull

POLECAT
⌃ ABOVE **adult** ⌄ BELOW **Polecat/ferret hybrid**

AMERICAN MINK *Mustela vison*

BODY LENGTH 30–45cm; TAIL LENGTH 15–22cm; WEIGHT 500–1,500g

An alien and unwelcome introduction to the region and one that has caused untold destruction to native wildlife. The American Mink is a lithe, active predator that is typically associated with aquatic habitats. **ADULT** has a long, slender body and a relatively long and rather bushy tail. The fur is soft and silky, and most individuals are uniformly dark brown except for variable white markings on the chin and throat. Males are larger, and heavier, than females. **JUVENILE** is similar to an adult. **VOICE** – Utters high-pitched calls when alarmed. HABITAT AND STATUS – As its name suggests, the American Mink comes from North America and it was brought here to be bred on fur farms for its pelt. The presence of an established population in the wild is the result of individuals having escaped from captivity or having been 'liberated' by people with animal welfare concerns. To anyone with the least grasp of ecology the devastation that has been unleashed by their release can never be justified, however unsavoury the reality of the fur trade. At the local level, American Mink are nothing short of an ecological disaster, causing widespread devastation to nesting birds and having executed numerous local extinctions of Water Vole populations. Shame on anyone naïve and ill-informed enough to think releasing American Mink into the British countryside could ever be a good idea. Ponds, lakes and slow-flowing rivers are ideal for the species and there are probably several tens of thousands of individuals in the region as a whole. It occurs throughout mainland Great Britain and Ireland, as well as on a few islands. Man remains the most significant predator of American Mink. Ironically, nowadays, most trapping and killing is undertaken by conservationists in desperate attempts to save dwindling Water Vole populations and other native wildlife. Total eradication from our region would seem to be an unrealistic proposition. Probably the most realistic prospect of keeping American Mink numbers in check comes from the recovery and return of Otters to many freshwater habitats: the two species do not coexist happily and the larger Otter dominates the scene. HABITS AND NATURAL HISTORY – American Mink typically hunt in the late afternoon and throughout the night. However, when disturbance is minimal they are often bold enough to venture out during daylight hours. They are competent swimmers, their partly webbed feed assisting with propulsion. Birds, Rabbits, rodents and fish are the main prey, but no opportunity is likely to be passed up and so frogs, insects and crustaceans will also be consumed. American Mink are solitary and territorial, resting and sleeping in an underground den. Mating usually occurs in late winter and the young are usually born in early spring. There is 1 litter per year comprising 4–6 babies. These are independent after 3 months or so, by which time they are capable of killing their own prey. OBSERVATION TIPS – Sightings of American Mink along waterways in the region are all too common these days. There is scope for confusing this species with an Otter. However, when swimming, only the head and shoulders of an Otter are revealed above water, whereas with the more buoyant Mink, most of the body, including the tail, can be seen. Look for pungent droppings deposited in a conspicuous waterside spot – they are long and pointed at one end – and footprints in mud.

adult

dropping

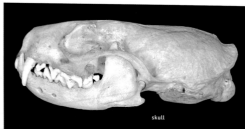

skull

AMERICAN MINK
⌄ ABOVE **adult**

PINE MARTEN *Martes martes*

BODY LENGTH 35–55cm; TAIL LENGTH 20–25cm; WEIGHT 500–2,000g

A secretive and generally rather scarce mammal. The Pine Marten is an active creature that is the subject of considerable conservation interest in Britain and Ireland. **ADULT** has a comparatively long, slender body and a long, bushy tail. The head is rather pointed and the ears are relatively large. The fur is thick and sleek, and rather uniformly dark orange-brown in colour. Note, however, the creamy yellow throat patch. **JUVENILE** is similar to an adult but appreciably paler. **VOICE** – Mainly silent. HABITAT AND STATUS – In historical terms, the Pine Marten was once widespread in Great Britain and Ireland. However, centuries of persecution (in recent times, both trapping and illegal poisoning) and loss of its favoured woodland habitat resulted in its extinction across much of the region. Even today, when the population appears to be recovering, it is still only locally common in more remote parts of Scotland and Ireland. The Pine Marten's status in England and Wales is unclear: evidence for the species' presence, in the form of tracks and signs, are occasionally discovered but numbers of these relict populations must be, at best, tiny. By contrast, in its Scottish and Irish strongholds, several thousand individuals are probably present. Pine Martens are usually associated with forested terrain – deciduous and mixed woodland on broken, rocky ground in Scotland. In Ireland, however, where less than 8 per cent of the land area is wooded, they are obliged to occupy areas of scrub and open rocky ground. HABITS AND NATURAL HISTORY – Pine Martens are mainly active after dark, spending the hours of daylight in a den, which may be underground or in a hollow tree. Their diet is mainly carnivorous, and small mammals, Rabbits, birds and frogs are important prey. They are fast and agile hunters, adept at climbing and even capable of catching Red Squirrels in active pursuit through the tree canopy. In addition, Pine Martens are opportunistic feeders and will take birds' eggs, berries, fungi and carrion when available. The latter source of food has been the species' downfall because of the ease with which they can be poisoned illegally. The species is solitary and territorial, although there is some overlap in the ranges occupied by the different sexes. Mating occurs in the summer months but delayed implantation means that the young are not born until the following

adult eating egg

dropping

adult

spring. There is 1 litter a year, comprising, on average, 2–4 babies. The young become independent after 3 months or so, by which time they are already adept hunters. OBSERVATION TIPS – Secretive habits and a nocturnal lifestyle mean that the Pine Marten is a difficult animal to observe. Once in a while, animals are seen crossing roads at night in their main Scottish and Irish ranges. A few individuals have learned to raid rubbish bins in Highland picnic areas and just occasionally Pine Martens have been known to visit garden bird tables for scraps of food.

PINE MARTEN
⌃ ABOVE adult, emerging from den ⌄ BELOW adult

BADGER *Meles meles* LENGTH 65–80cm; WEIGHT 8–12kg

A distinctive, mainly nocturnal mammal. The facial markings are unmistakable to the point of being iconic and hence most people can recognise a Badger, whether or not they have actually seen one. **ADULT** has coarse body fur that is greyish on the back and flanks, and blackish on the underside and legs. In close-up, the grey body hairs are in fact white at the base and tip, and black in the middle. The head is elongated into a snout and marked with longitudinal black bands that run through the ears and eyes to the nose; these contrast with otherwise whitish fur on the head. Note the white fringes to the ears. The legs are short, stout and powerful, and the rather short, blunt tail has a white tip. **JUVENILE** is similar to an adult but smaller, the grey fur often appearing less grizzled and worn. **VOICE** – Badgers are generally rather silent animals although adults will utter a variety of growls and snuffling sounds during social encounters. Cubs utter 'yickering' squeals on occasions. HABITAT AND STATUS – Badgers appear to do best where a mosaic of open habitats, such as farmland and meadows, are found alongside woodland, scrub and mature hedgerows. The species also occurs on the fringes of habitation, occasionally even visiting sub-urban gardens, and is by no means restricted just to lowland districts. It is widely distributed across mainland Britain and Ireland but least numerous in East Anglia and the far north. Several hundred thousand Badgers are probably present in the region as a whole. HABITS AND NATURAL HISTORY – Badgers have an omnivorous diet and are opportunistic feeders, typically snuffling along the ground, eating anything edible that comes their way. Earthworms and other soil invertebrates are a staple part of the diet and carrion and birds' eggs will also be consumed. Badgers have powerful front feet, armed with claws, and these are sometimes used to dig out the nests of wasps and bees, and to unearth bulbs and succulent roots. Small mammals are also killed and, in season, fruits and berries are eagerly consumed. The species lives in social groups, typically of 5–10 animals. They spend the daylight hours underground in an excavated network of tunnels and sleeping chambers, collectively known as a 'sett'. Active setts are easily identified by the presence of fresh spoil and tunnel entrances that are typically at least 25cm across. Other signs include the presence of old bedding that has been removed and discarded, and nearby dung-pits, which are often referred to as Badger 'latrines'. Badgers are almost exclusively nocturnal, although during the summer months animals will emerge from their setts while there is still a glimmer of light left. Mating occurs mainly in late winter and spring, but because of delayed implantation the cubs (usually 2–4 per female) are not born until the following January or February; they usually make their first appearance above ground in April or May. Sadly, most people have seen more Badgers dead beside roads than they have live animals, and road deaths are probably the most significant factor affecting mortality in adults. Despite being protected, to a degree, by the law, Badgers are still illegally dug out for 'Badger baiting'. In addition, under licence, the species has been the subject of local eradication programmes in parts of the country where it is perceived to play a part in the persistence of bovine tuberculosis in cattle. *See* p.26 for further discussion. OBSERVATION TIPS – Despite their essentially nocturnal habits, Badgers can be observed with care. *See* p.199 for further discussion. They are fond of peanuts and can sometimes be lured into rural gardens by the provision of these tempting treats.

emerging from sett

dung pit

skull

BADGER
⊙ ABOVE **adult** ⊙ RIGHT **paw print** ⊙ BELOW **sett entrance**

OTTER *Lutra lutra*

BODY LENGTH 60–90cm; TAIL LENGTH 35–45cm; WEIGHT 7–15kg

A relatively large and amphibious animal. The Otter is a lithe and sinuous swimmer and has a bounding gait on land. Its reappearance on many or our rivers has come to symbolise our increasing awareness of, and ability to reduce, the pollution we inflict on the countryside. Its position at the top of the freshwater food chain means that it is a barometer on the health of our waterways. **ADULT** has a long, rather cylindrical body, with short legs and a relatively long, thickset tail. The head is blunt and tapering and the external ears are relatively small. The muzzle is armed with sensitive bristles. The toes on both the front and back feet are webbed, which aids swimming. The coat is mainly dark brown although the chin, throat and belly are whitish. The fur is luxuriously thick, an outer layer of long guard hairs affording the coat its water-repelling properties and giving it a sleek appearance when wet. On drying in air, the guard hairs create a characteristic 'spiky' look to the coat. **JUVENILE** is similar to an adult but smaller. **VOICE** – Occasionally utters thin whistling calls but otherwise mainly silent. HABITAT AND STATUS – A history of persecution meant that at the start of the 20th century the Otter was a scarce animal in lowland Britain. Worse was still to come: in the 1950s and 1960s poisoning from the accumulation of agricultural pesticides appeared to be the final nail in its coffin, at least where lowland Britain was concerned. Consequently, by the mid-1980s the only reliable location for the species in Britain was northern Scotland and the Scottish isles, where coastal populations still flourished. However, in recent years cleaner rivers and the use of safer (in Otter terms at least) pesticides have caused a revival in its fortunes. It has recolonised many of its former inland, freshwater haunts across England and Wales. In Ireland, the species has always fared rather better, partly because, in the 1960s at least, agriculture was less intensive; today, it is locally common and widespread. Throughout their range, Otters are always associated with water, but they can be found on both freshwater sites such as rivers and lakes, as well as on the coast. HABITS AND NATURAL HISTORY – Otters are generally nocturnal animals. However, the feeding habits of coastal populations, particularly those in Scotland, are often tied to the state of the tide or dependent upon the feeding patterns of their prey. Hence, on Scottish coasts, animals are not infrequently seen during the day. Fish are the most important component in their diet but Otters will also take small mammals, birds and invertebrates when the opportunity arises; those that live on Scottish coasts are partial to Common Sea-urchins, undeterred by their spiny exteriors. Periods of rest are spent in an underground den, referred to as a 'holt'. Adult Otters tend to be solitary and territorial, although cubs typically remain with their mother for up to a year. Mating and the birth of the cubs can occur at almost any time of year, although the further north you travel, the more likely it is that these events will occur in spring and summer. Each female can produce 1 litter per year comprising 2–4 cubs. They are cared for by the mother alone and are weaned after 4 months, by which time they are competent swimmers and can hunt for themselves. OBSERVATION TIPS – Although Otters are still scarce in southeast England, there is a good chance that large and unpolluted freshwater bodies elsewhere in the region will host the occasional animal, or even a resident population. Unfortunately, however, this does not mean that you are going to see one because, particularly at inland locations, they are wary and essentially nocturnal animals. With luck you may find droppings (called 'spraints') deposited conspicuously on waterside stones or logs. Otters are playful animals and another telltale sign is a mudslide on the bank of a river. If you want to get more than a fleeting view of an Otter then you must visit the Scottish coast – the Shetland and Orkney islands are particularly good. Look for piles of fish bones and the shattered remains of sea urchins deposited on grassy slopes above the tideline and you will almost certainly have found an Otter territory. Scan the shore and sooner or later, and with a bit of luck, one will make its appearance.

adult on seashore

tracks

spraint

OTTER
ABOVE **adult** · BELOW **swimming**

RED DEER *Cervus elaphus* SHOULDER HEIGHT 105–130cm (MALE), 100–115cm (FEMALE); WEIGHT 200–250kg (MALE), 120–150kg (FEMALE)

A large and impressive, long-legged deer. Adult male Red Deer are the heaviest of their kind in the region. The size and bulk of individuals of a given age varies across the region, influenced by factors such as the quality of feeding and the climate. On average, Scottish animals are smaller than their southern England counterparts. **ADULT** has a coat of rather short hair that is reddish brown in summer but dark brown in winter. Note the whitish rump patch and the uniformly buffish-brown tail. Male Red Deer (*stags*) have rather thick necks. They grow antlers in spring and summer; initially they are covered in a fleshy layer of skin known as *velvet*. This is shed in autumn, revealing the bare antlers, which themselves are shed in the spring. Antlers increase in size and the number of points they bear each year until the animal reaches an age of 7–8 years; 10 or 11 is usually the maximum number of points. Note, however, that antler size and point number give only a rough idea of a stag's age because environmental quality and an animal's health are influential factors. Female Red Deer (*hinds*) are similar to stags but smaller and more elegantly proportioned; they do not develop antlers. **JUVENILE** (*calf*) is reddish brown, the upper parts adorned with whitish spots. The spots are lost, with the first moult, in the summer months. **VOICE** – Hinds bleat and utter a sharp barking sound when alarmed, while stags are renowned for the bellowing roars uttered during the autumn mating season (the *rut*). HABITAT AND STATUS – Red Deer do best in areas where a mosaic of woodland, heather moorland and grassland offer varied feeding and plenty of cover. The species has a disjunct distribution in the region. Populations in the Scottish Highlands and northern England, and possibly those in Ireland, are thought to be descendants of genuinely wild animals. Isolated populations elsewhere are probably descended from animals that were either released into the wild, or which escaped from captivity. Scotland is the species' stronghold in the region and a few hundred thousand individuals occur here; the population elsewhere may number several thousand animals overall. Away from Scotland, Red Deer are found in the Lake District, Exmoor, the New Forest and Norfolk. HABITS AND NATURAL HISTORY – For much of the year, adult males and females lead separate lives, forming separate-sex herds. Male calves remain with their mothers for a couple of years, but with the onset of maturity they leave to join a male herd. Red Deer graze grasses, rushes and Ling, browse tree foliage and strip bark. Feeding can take place at any time, but in areas where human disturbance is a factor, they tend to be more crepuscular or nocturnal. The main event of the year (for human observers at least) is the annual rut (the mating season), which occupies much of September and October. At this time, dominant stags defend a harem of hinds against rivals and interlopers. Relative strength, and hence dominance, is determined by ritualised fights involving contending stags linking antlers and pushing for all they are worth. All this is accompanied by a great deal of showmanship and rutting roars. Calves are born in late spring (usually 1 per female). OBSERVATION TIPS – You should have little difficulty seeing Red Deer in the Scottish Highlands. In summer, many herds move to more inaccessible upland terrain. The best time of year to see them is autumn when the rut is in full swing. The same applies to populations elsewhere in the region, including those in Richmond Park and other leafy London venues. Signs include clusters or strings of droppings that are roughly the size and shape of an acorn. Hoofprints are up to 7cm across; the anterior outer margins of the slots curve symmetrically inwards.

hoofprints

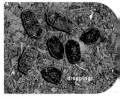

droppings

RED DEER
△ ABOVE **stag** ▽ BELOW **hind**

SIKA DEER *Cervus nippon* SHOULDER HEIGHT 80–90cm (MALE), 70–80cm (FEMALE); WEIGHT 45–65kg (MALE), 35–40kg (FEMALE)

A well-marked, introduced species with body proportions and markings that recall a Fallow Deer but, in the case of males, antlers that are pointed in the manner of a Red Deer (not palmate). Confusingly, Sika Deer will happily hybridise with Red Deer. **ADULT** has a reddish-brown coat adorned with whitish spots on the flanks and back during the summer months. In winter, males are dark grey-brown and females are marginally paler; pale spots are at best indistinct. At all times, in both sexes, the rump is whitish, bordered by a black rim, and the tail is mainly white with a dark median line on the upper surface. Male Sika Deer (*stags*) have rather thick necks. Compared to both Red and Fallow Deer, a Sika Deer stag has a proportionately shorter neck and legs, and a smaller, less elongated head. Antlers are grown in spring and summer; initially they are covered in a fleshy layer of skin known as *velvet*. This is shed in late summer, revealing the bare antlers, which themselves are shed in the spring. Antlers increase in size and the number of points they bear (to a maximum of 8) each year until the animal reaches an age of 6–7 years. Note, however, that antler size and point number only give a rough idea of a stag's age because environmental quality and an animal's health are influential factors. Female Sika Deer (*hinds*) are similar to stags but smaller and more elegantly proportioned; they do not develop antlers. **JUVENILE** (*calf*) is reddish brown and adorned with whitish spots. **VOICE** – Males utter piercing screams during the rut. HABITAT AND STATUS – The Sika Deer is essentially a woodland species, venturing from cover into clearings and adjacent farmland to feed. It is native to the Far East and animals (initially from Japan) were first introduced to the region from the mid-19th century onwards to adorn deer parks. Some escaped from captivity and established themselves in the wild; in a few locations, active attempts were made to create feral populations. Several thousand individuals are probably present in the wild in the region as a whole, although their precise distribution is patchy and in many cases reflects the location of the deer parks from which their ancestors escaped. HABITS AND NATURAL HISTORY – For much of the year, adult males and females lead separate lives, forming small separate-sex herds. Male calves remain with their mothers for a couple of years, but with the onset of maturity they leave to join a male herd. Sika Deer graze grasses and browse brambles, shrubs and tree foliage; they also strip bark. They are active throughout the 24-hour period but, in areas where human disturbance is a factor, they tend to be more crepuscular or nocturnal. The rut occurs in August and September. At this time, dominant stags defend a territory into which they attract females. Relative strength among stags, and hence dominance, is determined by ritualised fights. However, the dominant male is usually more tolerant of the presence of subordinates within his territory than is the case with other large deer species. Calves are born in late spring (usually 1 per female). OBSERVATION TIPS – The blood-curdling scream of a Sika Deer stag will soon alert you to the presence of the species in a given area. In most locations the species is easiest to observe at dusk. However, in locations where they are not disturbed, they are sometimes seen during daylight hours. The small herd on Lundy must be one of the easiest groups of 'wild' animals to observe, along with the more significant population at the RSPB reserve at Arne in Dorset.

J F M A M J J A S O N D

stag, winter

calf

droppings

hoofprint

SIKA DEER
⊘ ABOVE **stag, winter** ⊘ BELOW **hind, summer**

J F M A M J J A S O N D

FALLOW DEER *Dama dama* SHOULDER HEIGHT 90–100cm (MALE), 80–85cm (FEMALE); WEIGHT 70–90kg (MALE), 40–50kg (FEMALE)

A medium-sized deer, males of which have distinctive antlers. Fallow Deer are the most likely species to be encountered grazing the grasslands of stately homes and deer parks. **ADULT** usually has a reddish-brown coat in summer, marked with whitish spots. In winter, the coat is usually dark grey-brown; pale spots, if visible, are likely to be indistinct. However, there is considerable variation, with some animals appearing almost black, especially in winter, while others are creamy white in summer. On average, 'wild' animals tend to be darker than ones in captive populations: pale, well-marked individuals are often encouraged in captivity by selective culling. In all animals,

fawn

the rump is whitish and usually defined by a dark rim, and the tail is blackish with a white margin. A male Fallow Deer (*buck*) develops broad, palmate antlers in spring and early summer; these are initially coated in *velvet,* which is shed by early autumn. The antlers themselves are shed in each spring. Antler size and complexity increases with age over the first 5 years of life. In deer-shooting circles, various phrases have evolved to describe males of different ages: in its 1st year it is a *fawn*; it is a *pricket* in its 2nd year; in its 3rd year it is a *sorel*; in its 4th year it is a *sore* or *bare buck*; only in its 5th year is it called a *buck*. However, for the purposes of this book, males of all ages are referred to as *bucks*. A female Fallow Deer (*doe*) is smaller and more elegantly proportioned than a male; she does not develop antlers. **JUVENILE** (*fawn*) is reddish brown with whitish spots on the back and flanks. **VOICE** – Female utters a barking alarm call and, during the rut, the male's belching groan is a familiar sound. HABITAT AND STATUS – The Fallow Deer is not native to the region, having been introduced here first by the Romans. At one time restricted to royal forests and parks, encouraged there for hunting purposes, the species inevitably escaped and colonised new territories. Today, it is widespread in England, Wales, Ireland and southern Scotland, although its precise distribution is distinctly patchy. Many tens of thousands of Fallow Deer are found in the region as a whole. They seem to do best where a mosaic of woodland, farmland and scrub coexist side by side. HABITS AND NATURAL HISTORY – If they are disturbed, Fallow Deer are often crepuscular or nocturnal in their habits, lying up in deep cover during the daytime. However, undisturbed and left to their own devices they will often feed diurnally: they graze grasses and arable crops and browse tree foliage, brambles and shrubs. For much of the year, adult Fallow Deer live in separate-sex herds. Young (of both sexes) from the previous year usually consort with their mothers in female herds; after a year and a half, young males leave to join male herds. The autumn rut extends throughout October and November, during which time the male defends an area known as a '*stand*', to which he attracts females with his belching calls. The stand is defined by branch stripping, trampling and scent marking. Fawns are born the following June and are cared for by the mother alone. OBSERVATION TIPS – Fallow Deer are easy to observe in deer parks, and in many comparatively urban venues such as London's Richmond Park. However, seeing them in the wild, or at least seeing them well, can be a bit more problematic. They tend to be wary and alert animals and, despite their size, they can be surprisingly difficult to spot in wooded habitat. In the summer, their spotted coats blend in well with the dappled light that filters through the foliage; even in winter, when the leaves have fallen from the trees, their dark coats are almost invisible when seen through a tangle of grey-brown stems and branches. Signs include clusters (sometimes compacted) of seed-like, broadly cylindrical droppings, 15–16mm long; these are pointed at one end and indented on one side. Hoofprints are up to 5cm across and rather parallel-sided.

buck, dark individual

droppings

hoofprint

FALLOW DEER
⌃ ABOVE **buck, pale individual** ⌄ BELOW **doe**

ROE DEER *Capreolus capreolus*

SHOULDER HEIGHT 65–70cm; WEIGHT 23–25kg (MALE), 15–20kg (FEMALE)

An elegant and attractive native species. The Roe Deer is familiar to many people who walk in the countryside. **ADULT** has a coat that is reddish brown in summer; this is moulted in the autumn to produce a thick and dense greyish-brown winter coat. Throughout the year note the striking black-and-white markings on the muzzle (the black nose and 'moustache' contrast with the white 'chin'). A male Roe Deer (*buck*) develops relatively short, branchlike antlers in late winter and early spring. The initial coating of *velvet* is shed in April or May and the antlers themselves are lost in early winter. Antlers increase in size and complexity with age, to a maximum of around 25cm in length and 3 points. There is a whitish mark on the rump that is oval to kidney-shaped and an external tail is absent. A female Roe Deer (*doe*) is similar to a male but less stocky. Antlers do not develop and the whitish marking on the rump is shaped like an inverted heart. In winter, a Roe doe develops a white tuft of anal hairs (known as a *tush*) that resembles a tail. **JUVENILE** (*fawn*) is reddish brown with white spots on the back and flanks.

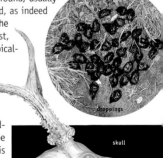

VOICE – Utters a barking call in alarm. During the rutting season, females attract the attention of males with their rhythmic, high-pitched cries. A male will utter a rasping call while pursuing a female in the latter stages of courtship. HABITAT AND STATUS – The Roe Deer is widespread in Scotland and locally common in England, being scarce in, or absent from, the southeast and Midlands. They are rare in Wales and entirely absent from Ireland. Several hundred thousand individuals probably live in the region as a whole. In lowland areas, Roe Deer seem to do best where a mosaic of woodland copses, arable farmland and grassland coexist. In Scotland, they are also found on heather moorland. HABITS AND NATURAL HISTORY – Roe Deer are primarily browsers, their diet including the leaves of deciduous trees and shrubs (and their twigs and shoots throughout the year) and bramble sprays; grassland vegetation and arable crops are also grazed. When undisturbed, they can be active throughout the 24-hour period, but in many areas they tend to be crepuscular and nocturnal. Typically, for a large part of the year, adult Roe Deer are rather territorial, at least with regards to members of the same sex. However, the home ranges of females do overlap those of males. Territory size varies according to habitat quality but typically in a lowland area it might be 7–10ha in size. Roe Deer tend to be solitary animals, although this is not a hard and fast rule because young animals often accompany their mothers for several months; young males are usually driven out of their mother's territory before young females. During the winter months, Roe Deer are sometimes encountered in small groups, which may comprise a few adult females, an adult male and several yearlings. The rutting season lasts from June to August. At the heart of a male's territory will be a so-called rutting ring, a worn area of ground, usually around the base of a tree. The whole area is heavily scent-marked, as indeed are the male's territorial boundaries, which are defined by fraying the bark of trees and bushes. Although mating occurs in July and August, implantation is delayed until midwinter and hence the young (typically twins) are not born until May or June. OBSERVATION TIPS – Roe Deer are usually fairly easy to observe. In areas where they are not unduly disturbed by people (or their out-of-control dogs) they can be amazingly indifferent to human observers. The winter months are best for observation, in part because of the absence of leaf cover in deciduous woodlands; however, do not underestimate the ability of Roe Deer to blend in with their surroundings. Often the whitish rump is the easiest thing to spot. Signs include tufts of hair (from the tush) and frayed bark. Hoofprints are usually around 3–4cm across and are narrowly pointed at the front. Droppings are scattered liberally on the ground and individually are shiny, black, cylindrical and pointed at one end; they are usually around 1.6–1.8cm long.

ROE DEER
- ABOVE **buck, summer**
- MAIN PIC **frequently used track**
- BELOW **doe, winter**

MUNTJAC *Muntiacus reevesi* SHOULDER HEIGHT 43–45cm (MALE), 38–40cm (FEMALE); WEIGHT 18–20kg (MALE), 13–15kg (FEMALE)

Strictly speaking this introduced species goes by the name Reeves' Muntjac, although nowadays most people customarily drop the prefix. When seen for the first time, most people are amazed just how tiny a Muntjac is – barely a match for a medium-sized dog. **ADULT** has a mainly reddish-brown coat although the chest and belly are whitish. The head is proportionately large and the legs are rather short. The tail is relatively long and reddish brown above but whitish below; it is strikingly conspicuous when raised, rather like a flag, in alarm. Note the converging dark stripes on the forehead. An adult male Muntjac (*buck*) develops tusk-like upper canine teeth (up to 2cm long) and these project outside the closed mouth. Antlers are grown in late summer and autumn and are shed in early summer the following year. They comprise a single spike (up to 8cm long) and they are borne on permanent, skin-covered pedicles. An adult female (*doe*) is similar to an adult male but smaller; she does not grow antlers. **JUVENILE** (*fawn*) is tiny and reddish brown with white spots on the back and flanks. **VOICE** – Utters a loud and piercing coughing bark, which, to the uninitiated, sounds just like an animal in distress. This is heard most frequently during the rut. HABITAT AND STATUS – The Muntjac is native to China and the Far East and was first introduced to this country (to Woburn Park) at the start of the 20th century. Inevitably, it escaped from this location, and from other sites where subsequently the species was kept in captivity; these animals gave rise to the Muntjac population that we see today. Currently there are probably several tens of thousands of individuals in the region as a whole; the majority are found in southern and central England. Muntjac favour areas of dense scrub, often lurking unseen in woodland undergrowth and even in mature gardens. HABITS AND NATURAL HISTORY – Although Muntjac are something of a pleasing curiosity for most naturalists, in the eyes of some sectors of society they have achieved a pariah status in the brief time they have been with us. It is certainly true that they do cause damage to forestry and farming interests, and to owners of show gardens. However, there is suspicion that in some instances they get the blame for damage caused by other mammals, notably other deer species and Rabbits. Muntjac have a rather varied vegetarian diet: they browse low-growing vegetation including brambles and shrubs, strip tree bark and shoots, but will eat grasses and forage for fungi and fallen fruit as well; they have an alarming predilection for Bluebells. Muntjacs are territorial and usually solitary, although young animals – particularly young females – will often stay with their mother beyond the point of weaning. There is no fixed breeding season as such and mating, and birth, can occur at almost any time of year. Muntjac reproductive potential is high because sexual maturity is reached towards the end of the 1st year and females have the capacity to give birth every 7–8 months. OBSERVATION TIPS – Because of their small size and relatively retiring habits, Muntjac lead unobtrusive lives. They are perhaps easiest to see at dawn and dusk, and in areas where they are common it is not unusual to see them after dark beside country roads, caught in the headlights of a car. Muntjac leave small, narrow tracks, perhaps 1.5cm across; typically, the outer toe is longer than the inner one. Look for scattered deposits of droppings that, individually, are cylindrical and pointed at one end (sometimes rather like a hazelnut in shape) with one side indented; they are usually around 1cm long. Other signs include stripped tree bark and browsed shoots (even those of garden herbaceous perennials).

buck feeding on willow

antler

hoofprint

droppings

MUNTJAC
ⓐ ABOVE **buck** ⓑ BELOW **doe**

CHINESE WATER DEER *Hydropotes inermis*
SHOULDER HEIGHT 55–60cm; WEIGHT 10–15kg

A small and rather dainty-looking alien species that has established itself in a few places in England. **ADULT** has a reddish-buff coat in summer and a much thicker greyish-brown coat in winter. The black nose is distinctive and highlighted by the otherwise white muzzle. Similarly, the beady black eyes are set off by a white surround. The ears are proportionally large and antlers are absent in both sexes. With age, the upper canines develop into tusks, which project externally beyond the closed mouth; these are longer (up to 7cm) in males (*bucks*) than in females (*does*). The tail is short and there is no pale rump patch. **JUVENILE** (*fawn*) is reddish brown with white spots on the back and flanks. **VOICE** – Will bark at intruders and utters a piercing scream in alarm. Males have a whistling call during the rut. HABITAT AND STATUS – Chinese Water Deer were introduced to Whipsnade Zoo early in the 20th century. Inevitably, a few escaped and as a result a feral population numbering 1,000 or more individuals has been established. Currently, their range extends from Buckinghamshire to East Anglia. There is a horrible irony to the fact that while the British population may be tiny it is probably equivalent to 10 per cent of the entire population surviving in its native China. Chinese Water Deer are often associated with marshy habitats, although they can also be found in drier, scrubby areas. HABITS AND NATURAL HISTORY – Much of what is known about the species' habits is derived from observations in captivity, albeit in semi-wild situations. Chinese Water Deer appear to be mainly crepuscular and nocturnal. They feed on grasses, shoots and roots, and will browse bramble sprays too. The rut is in midwinter and the young (usually 2–3 per female) are born in late spring. OBSERVATION TIPS – Chinese Water Deer are secretive and their small size and predilection for dense cover means they are difficult to spot. Occasionally one will be seen venturing out of cover at dusk, but a more typical view will be of a head and neck emerging from the grass momentarily to peer at you.

fawn

droppings

REINDEER *Rangifer tarandus* SHOULDER HEIGHT 1.1–1.2m (MALE), 0.9–1m (FEMALE); WEIGHT 90–150kg (MALE), 50–100kg (FEMALE)

A distinctive and long-legged species. Unusually for deer, both sexes have antlers. **ADULT** has a grey-brown coat that is thickest and palest in winter. Adult male (*bull*) has a thickset appearance and sports irregularly branched and asymmetrical antlers from early spring to the following midwinter. The antlers are broadly palmate towards the tip. An adult female (*cow*) is more elegantly proportioned than the male. Although branched, her antlers are relatively short and lack the male's palmations; they are shed in May. **JUVENILE** (*calf*) is greyish brown and unspotted. **VOICE** – Utters various grunting sounds. HABITAT AND STATUS – Travel back in time a millennium and wild Reindeer would have roamed the north of Scotland. However, hunting and habitat destruction drove them to extinction by the 12th century. The Reindeer that now roam the slopes of the Cairngorms, and very locally elsewhere in the Scottish Highlands, are domesticated animals introduced from Scandinavia in the mid-20th century. HABITS AND NATURAL HISTORY – Although Scottish Reindeer are far from 'wild' in the strict sense, aspects of their behaviour are akin to that which might be observed in natural populations – apart from their tolerance of people, of course. Female reindeer are gregarious animals, and in the wild herds would be accompanied by young animals of both sexes. Adult males are solitary except during the rut and during migration. The rut takes place in September and October, with a dominant male defending 'his' herd against rivals and interlopers. Reindeer feed primarily on low-growing plants, notably the lichen *Cladonia rangifer*, known confusingly as 'Reindeer Moss'. The antlers are used to clear snow, allowing access to their food in winter; hence, the presence of antlers in both sexes. OBSERVATION TIPS – Reindeer can sometimes be encountered by chance if you wander the slopes of the Cairngorm Mountains. However, for guaranteed sightings, pay your money and watch them being fed!

cow and calf

CHINESE WATER DEER
BELOW buck, winter

REINDEER
ABOVE bull

GOAT *Capra hircus* SHOULDER HEIGHT 80–90cm (MALE), 60–70cm (FEMALE); WEIGHT 45–55kg (MALE), 25–35kg (FEMALE)

A familiar domesticated animal, feral populations of which live in various parts of the region. **ADULT** Feral Goat differs from its domesticated cousins in being shorter and stockier. Typically, the coat is long and shaggy; the colour is rather variable and often a piebald mixture of grey, black and whitish. An adult male goat (*billy*) is larger and bulkier than a female, with an impressive set of recurved, ringed horns; these increase in size with age to a maximum of around 80cm. Unlike antlers, which are shed annually, horns are permanent fixtures; they are bony outgrowths that are covered in a layer of horn. Many animals possess a 'beard' and tassels on the chin. An adult female (*nanny*) is similar to a male but smaller; the horns are far shorter and the beard and tassels are shorter too. **JUVENILE** (*kid*) has a clean-looking coat and no horns. **VOICE** – Utters a warning whistle. Females will summon their kids by bleating in a familiar manner. HABITAT AND STATUS – Goats have been kept in domestication for more than 10,000 years, prized for their hair, milk, hide and meat. Their wild ancestors probably originated in

Anglo-nubian Goat

British Saanen Goat

the Middle East and it is likely that they were brought to our region with the first wave of Neolithic human settlers. Although, in Britain and Ireland at least, the importance of goats may be somewhat marginal today (largely limited to milk production), in the past their role in the rural economy would have been considerable. As anyone who has ever kept goats will testify, they are adept at escaping from confinement and escapes over the ages would have created some of the feral populations we see today. In more recent times, the Scottish land clearances in the late 18th and early 19th centuries liberated significant numbers when croft farmsteads were forcibly abandoned. Elsewhere, goats have also been deliberately released or translocated. Feral Goats are found mainly in mountainous districts as well as on rugged coastal cliffs and a few islands. They are widespread in Scotland and Ireland, and occur locally in Wales (mainly Snowdonia), northern England and a few islands (notably Lundy). Several thousand feral animals may exist in the region as a whole. HABITS AND NATURAL HISTORY – Feral Goats have a sure-footed confidence that allows them to negotiate even the most terrifying of cliffs and precipices with apparent nonchalance. Even youngsters show no fear of heights and will play

British Toggenburg Goat

with abandon on the narrowest of ledges or steepest of slopes. Feral Goats have a notoriously varied vegetarian diet that includes not only grasses and low-growing plants but tree bark and foliage too. Typically, they are found in groups of 4–10 females, to which a dominant male will attach himself during the rut (October and November). Sparring contests between rival males – they head-butt each other – are spectacular. The young (1–2 per female) are born in early spring and are usually weaned after 5–6 months. OBSERVATION TIPS – Visit Snowdonia, the Valley of the Rocks at Lynton in Devon, or Lundy if you want to get particularly good views of Feral Goats in stunning surroundings. Except in locations where they are accustomed to being fed, Feral Goats are usually wary and will not allow a close approach. DOMESTICATED FORMS – Among the goats kept captivity in Britain and Ireland there are several distinct breeds (as well as those that fail to qualify for breed status). The following are among the most regularly encountered: the British Saanen Goat (white and rather elegantly proportioned); the British Toggenburg (similar proportions to the Saanen but a brown and white coat); the Anglo-Nubian (Roman-nosed, short-haired and lop-eared); the British Alpine (black and white, with the proportions of a Saanen).

droppings

droppings

GOAT
⊙ ABOVE **feral billy, Scotland** ⊙ BELOW **feral Goat on Lundy**

SOAY SHEEP *Ovis aries* SHOULDER HEIGHT 60–70cm (MALE), 50–60cm (FEMALE); WEIGHT 20–25kg (MALE), 15–20kg (FEMALE)

The most ancient breed of sheep and undoubtedly the one that most closely resembles the earliest domesticated forms of this animal, or indeed their wild ancestors. Feral populations of Soay Sheep can still be found in a few remote parts of the region. **ADULT** has a dark reddish-brown summer coat; in winter, the coat is much thicker and darker still. The coat itself comprises both hair, which is thick and rigid, and wool, which is thin and curly. While moulting, animals look thoroughly moth-eaten. An adult male Soay Sheep (*ram*) has an impressive set of curved, ribbed horns with a slight spiral twist; they increase in length and curvature with age. An adult female Soay Sheep (*ewe*) is smaller than the male and has a much smaller set of horns. **JUVENILE** (*lamb*) resembles a small female, but with a shorter, cleaner coat that is a lighter shade of reddish brown. **VOICE** – During the lambing season, mothers and lambs utter the familiar 'baaing' and bleating calls respectively. Otherwise, Soay Sheep are mainly silent. HABITAT AND STATUS – As with goats, sheep have been domesticated for millennia, kept for their milk, wool, meat and hide. It is likely that the original ones arrived in our region along with the first waves of Neolithic human settlers, around 10,000 years ago. The general consensus is that Soay Sheep were brought to the island of Soay in

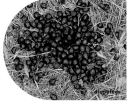

the St Kilda group by Viking settlers 1,000 years or so ago. Although their arrival on the scene is recent, relative to the overall scheme of things, they probably resemble the most primitive and ancient of domesticated sheep; a lack of genetic input from more recent breeds has ensured continuity in their appearance. Since people abandoned St Kilda in 1930, Soay Sheep have lived feral lives on the island of Soay, and on the neighbouring St Kildan island of Hirta where they were introduced. Feral populations can be found on a few other islands around the British coast and small flocks are kept on the mainland by enthusiasts, occasionally being employed for conservation grazing projects on nature reserves. HABITS AND NATURAL HISTORY – Feral populations of Soay Sheep live in flocks comprising both ewes and rams. They are hardy animals, much suited to the rigours of outdoor life on windswept offshore islands. Much of the day is spent grazing grasses and moorland vegetation. The mating season is in late autumn and most lambs are born in early April (1–2 per ewe). OBSERVATION TIPS – To see Soay Sheep on St Kilda requires a major expedition, not to mention a good pair of sea legs (the boat journey there is notoriously rough). A far easier alternative, if you want to see a genuinely feral population, is to visit the island of Lundy, off the north Devon coast. There, animals are not particularly bothered by the presence of human observers and good views can be obtained. DOMESTICATED FORMS – A huge range of sheep breeds has been developed worldwide and even in Britain and Ireland there are localised breeds (40 or more) to suit the varied climate and habitats of many of our regions. Typically, each breed is favoured either for its wool or its meat; milk yield is a minor concern in the region today. Invariably, all modern sheep breeds are significantly larger and heavier than Soay Sheep. Familiar breeds include the following: Dorset Horn; South Down; Welsh Mountain; Blackface; Suffolk; Cheviot; Hampshire Down.

Suffolk

Hampshire Down

Blackface

Dorset Horn

Welsh Mountain

South Down

SOAY SHEEP
Ⓐ TOP **moulting ram** ⬀ ABOVE **lamb** ⬁ RIGHT **hoofprint**

CATTLE *Bos taurus* SHOULDER HEIGHT 1–1.5m (MALE), 1–1.2m (FEMALE); WEIGHT 500–600kg (MALE), 400–450kg (FEMALE)

Familiar as a large, domesticated animal throughout the region and present in the form of a number of distinct breeds. Chillingham or White Cattle are the only animals that live as a truly feral population although, in more remote parts of our region, other breeds are sometimes allowed to roam freely in a semi-natural state. Cattle breeds are so variable in appearance that it is difficult to single out any particular one as being typical of the whole. Chillingham Cattle represent the closest thing to ancestral cattle in this region. **ADULT** Chillingham Cattle have shaggy white coats with a reddish line above the dark nose; the skin of the ears is also reddish. The male (*bull*) is larger and stockier than a female (*cow*). Both sexes have yellowish horns, although those of males are larger than in females. **JUVENILE** (*calf*) resembles a small, hornless adult but with a shorter, cleaner coat. **VOICE** – As with other cattle, Chillingham bulls bellow. HABITAT AND STATUS – No truly wild cattle survive in the region today. The ancestors of modern breeds were hunted to extinction in prehistoric times although, of course, domestication was taking place concurrently. Most European cattle are believed to have two ancestral origins: the Auroch *Bos primigenius*, which roamed the forests of Britain for a brief period

after the last Ice Age before being wiped out; and the so-called Celtic Ox *Bos longifrons*, which early Neolithic human settlers to our region brought with them, already domesticated, some 9,000–10,000 years ago. Chillingham Cattle have lived feral lives for the 700 years or so since Chillingham Park was created by enclosure of forested land and the animals it harboured. That these are direct descendants of ancient cattle is not in doubt. However, whether or not their ancestors were truly wild at the time the park was enclosed, or were themselves feral animals, is uncertain. HABITS AND NATURAL HISTORY – Chillingham Cattle roam the open pastures and woodland of Chillingham

Park in Northumberland. Typically, they graze grass but will also browse foliage on occasions. Unlike their domesticated cousins they are generally wary of humans and, if cornered or threatened, they can be aggressive and dangerous. The total population numbers just a few dozen animals so, apart from the fact that they live in a herd and have a dislike of people, any attempt to relate their behaviour to their truly wild ancestors must be treated with a degree of caution. OBSERVATION TIPS – If you are escorted by the warden, you can view Chillingham Cattle from a safe distance in Chillingham Park. You will have no difficulty seeing all manner of breeds of cattle in the region as a whole. DOMESTICATED FORMS – A wide range of breeds are found in Britain and Ireland, with characters to match their role in farming. Breeds of dairy cattle include Friesian, Guernsey, Jersey and Dairy Shorthorn. Breeds of beef cattle include Aberdeen Angus, Highland, Devon, Sussex, Hereford and Beef Shorthorn. Dual-purpose breeds include Belted Galloway and Red Devon.

skull

Jersey

part-Hereford

Highland

Friesian

Aberdeen Angus

CATTLE

⊕ ABOVE Chillingham bull
⊖ BELOW Chillingham calf

WILD BOAR *Sus scrofa* BODY LENGTH 100–150cm; TAIL LENGTH 20–30cm; WEIGHT 60–120kg

The Wild Boar is the ancestor of the domesticated pig. **ADULT** has a stocky body that is flattened laterally. The coat is grizzled grey-brown; in summer it comprises bristle-like guard hairs only, while in winter it is much more dense, with a thick layer of underfur. Hair and colour are often obscured by mud. The legs are relatively short and the head, which tapers to a blunt snout, is proportionately large. Note the rather small beady eyes and the relatively long ears. An adult male (*boar*) is larger and more powerfully built than a female (*sow*) and has protruding, upwards-pointing tusk-like lower canine teeth. **JUVENILE** (*piglet*) is undeniably adorable, being reddish brown with longitudinal pale stripes on the body. **VOICE** – Foraging animals utter various piglike grunts while feeding, and a barking call when alarmed.

wallowing pig

HABITAT AND STATUS – Wild Boar were native in the region until the Middle Ages, roaming forests until driven to extinction in the 17th century. Elements of the species' genetic makeup lived on in Britain and Ireland, in the form of domesticated pigs. In recent decades, attempts at reintroduction have been made; some animals have also escaped from captivity. Currently, perhaps 100 or so individuals live wild in the region, mainly in Sussex and Kent, with a few in Dorset. From time to time, further formal reintroduction programmes are considered. However, today habitats suitable for Wild Boar in our region are fragmented and small; and the activities of the animals will conflict with farming interests and those of nature conservation. Furthermore, the wisdom of reintroducing a potentially dangerous animal to our overcrowded islands has to be questioned from the point of view of Wild Boar welfare, as well as in human health and safety terms. HABITS AND NATURAL HISTORY – The Wild Boar does best in areas of deciduous woodland but will visit neighbouring farmland to forage. It is largely crepuscular and nocturnal, spending the daylight hours in dense cover, often in a favoured den of brushwood and dead leaves. Wild Boar forage on the ground and disturb the soil for fallen seeds (notably acorns and beechmast) as well as roots, shoots, invertebrates and carrion. Typically, females and young animals live in herds. Adult males are solitary, although during the extended mating season (autumn to early spring) dominant individuals pay close attention to potential mates. Litters of 4–8 piglets are born in spring and stay with their mother for their first few months. OBSERVATION TIPS – Its retiring nature and largely nocturnal habits make the Wild Boar difficult to observe well: often a glimpse of a fleeing animal is all you will get. Many people have to be content with looking for tracks and signs: rooting Wild Boar turn over the ground in an almost industrial manner; the droppings are sausage-like and 5–7cm long; the prints show splayed toes at the front and dew claws at the rear; mud-wallows are popular. When looking for Wild Boar, bear in mind they can be dangerous, especially if startled. DOMESTICATED FORMS – Pigs have been kept in domestication for centuries, being valued for their meat. Distinct breeds have evolved, among which the following are popular: Large White, with pinkish-white skin and an upturned snout; Berkshire, which is stocky and blackish; Middle White, with pinkish-white skin and snub-nosed; Tamworth, which is a sandy tan colour; Gloucester Old Spot, pinkish white with black blotches on the hindquarters; Saddleback, which is mainly blackish with a pale pinkish-white band around the shoulders and front legs.

Berkshire

Middle White

Tamworth

Saddleback

Gloucester Old Spot

Large White

WILD BOAR

⌃ ABOVE **boar** ⌄ BELOW **piglet**

PONIES *Equus caballus* SHOULDER HEIGHT 100–150cm; WEIGHT 150–500kg (DEPENDING ON BREED)
The name 'pony' is an imprecise one and in layman's terms it is often used simply to describe a small horse. However, a handful of recognised regional breeds qualifies more formally for this description. They are hardy animals that, in many instances, are allowed to roam their namesake regions in a state of semi-feral freedom. STATUS – As recently (in geological terms) as 9,000 years ago, Wild Horses (in the strict species sense) were probably still roaming our region. However, the arrival of the first Neolithic human settlers spelled disaster for them: genuinely wild animals soon became extinct, their place being taken by their domesticated cousins. Over the millennia, various horse breeds have come into being, all developed with specific functions in mind. The various pony breeds are the smallest and least developed of these. All are named after the region where they roam free, and all are hardy creatures that, for much of the year, are left to their own devices. By and large, human management (i.e. culling), rather than natural selection, controls their appearance. Some are losing their ancient genetic integrity owing to the introductions of other breeds. Among the more distinctive and regularly encountered pony breeds are the following:

DARTMOOR PONY has a shoulder height up to 1.25m and it may be black, brown or bay. It roams the moors of its namesake region in Devon.

EXMOOR PONY is usually dark reddish brown and up to 1.25m at the shoulder. The dark nose is offset by the rather pale muzzle and the eye is highlighted by a pale surround.

NEW FOREST PONY stands between 1.2m and 1.4m at the shoulder. The colour is rather variable, but reddish brown is typical.

SHETLAND PONY is the smallest of the bunch, usually standing around 1m at the shoulder. Herds wander the open moors on many of the larger Shetland islands.

WELSH MOUNTAIN PONY is a hardy upland breed that stands 1.1–1.2m at the shoulder. It is usually brown or grey in colour.

FELL PONY stands up to 1.3m at the shoulder and is found in the fells of Westmorland and Cumberland. It is usually brown or grey in colour.

DALES PONY is found east of the Pennines, mainly in County Durham and Northumberland. It is a stocky breed, usually dark brown or blackish in colour, and it stands around 1.4m at the shoulder.

HIGHLAND PONY is found in the Highlands of Scotland. It is usually black or brown in colour and stands 1.25–1.45m at the shoulder.

CONNEMARA PONY tolerates the wet and wild weather of its native Ireland, where it lives on moors and mountains. It is usually bay or grey in colour and is around 1.3–1.4m at the shoulder.

PRZEWALSKI'S HORSE, *Equus ferus przewalksii*, is the last remaining race of the otherwise extinct Wild Horse, the ancestor of modern domesticated breeds. It no longer occurs in the wild, in its native Mongolia, but small herds are kept in captivity in our region. Przewalski's Horse is a stocky, short-legged and pony-sized animal. It is grey brown or dun overall, often with a dark vertebral stripe and a mealy nose.

VOICE – Horses and ponies are usually silent but will 'neigh' when alarmed or excited. HABITS AND NATURAL HISTORY – By nature, horses and ponies are herd animals and the various breeds that are free-roaming usually tend towards a gregarious social life. Ponies are by and large grazing animals, but when food is in short supply they will browse tree foliage (often seen with New Forest Ponies) or even on the seashore, in the case of the Shetland Pony. A single foal is usual and most are born in the spring.

Dartmoor Pony

Shetland Pony

Connemara Pony

Exmoor Pony (mare with foal)

Przewalski's Horse (mare with foal)

New Forest Pony

PONY
⊙ MAIN PIC **New Forest Pony (mare)**
◁ LEFT **droppings** ▷ RIGHT **hoofprint**

COMMON LIZARD *Lacerta vivipara*

TOTAL LENGTH 10–15cm (60–65 PER CENT OF WHICH MAY BE TAIL)

The more widespread of our two native limbed lizard species. It sometimes goes by the alternative name of Viviparous Lizard. **ADULT** has a rather slender body with an angular, pointed snout. The ground colour is variable but brown is usual. Viewed from above, note the vertebral row of dark spots or patches, and parallel rows of dark markings on the flanks, the latter bordered above by a row of pale spots. Some individuals have a green or reddish flush to the head and anterior part of the body (sometimes even more extensive). A mature male has bright yellow or orange underparts studded with dark spots whereas the underparts of a female are usually rather dull yellow and unspotted.

JUVENILE resembles a miniature adult but with a proportionately much shorter tail. It is uniformly black for the first few weeks of life, becoming dark golden brown thereafter until it enters hibernation in its first autumn. **VOICE** – Silent. HABITAT AND STATUS – Despite its name, this species hardly deserves the epithet *common* these days. It may be widespread in terms of its overall occurrence in the region – it is still found in almost all mainland counties in Britain and Ireland – but locations where the Common Lizard is at all numerous tend to be fragmented and patchily distributed. Open habitats, notably heathlands, moors and sparse natural grassland (including chalk downland) are ideal, providing the animals with free-draining soils, a sunny aspect and an abundance of invertebrate food. Mature woodland and dense scrub areas are unlikely to harbour Common Lizards, and it goes without saying that the species is almost entirely absent from arable farmland and indeed agricultural land generally. Railway embankments are perhaps the one man-made habitat, if you can call it that, where Common Lizards thrive. HABITS AND NATURAL HISTORY – Common Lizards are sun-loving animals and frequently bask in sunshine, especially in the early spring or autumn. Occasionally, animals will bask on bare ground but a more usual site would be a log pile, or a compacted patch of dead twigs or bracken, into which they can disappear if alarmed. They are extremely active and alert animals, quick to respond to danger and agile enough to catch a wide range of invertebrates, some of which are themselves fast-moving. Like our other reptiles, Common Lizards hibernate, in their case typically from late October to early April. Hibernation sites include underground burrows and recesses under rocks and logs. Courtship, which is a fairly rough and tumble affair, starts soon after emergence from hibernation. Intriguingly, the fertilised eggs develop inside the body of the female. After a gestation period of around 3 months, she gives birth to wriggling young (4–10 is a usual number) which for the first few hours of life

shedding skin

are constrained by a thin egg membrane; a sharp egg-tooth soon allows them to break free. Common Lizard reproduction is, therefore, described as *ovoviviparous*. As a defence against predators, a Common Lizard can shed its tail (by a process know as *autonomy*), the theory being that the thrashing, disembodied tail will satisfy the attacker while the owner escapes. A replacement (much smaller) tail is grown in time. OBSERVATION TIPS – Common Lizards are easiest to observe closely in the spring, just after they have emerged from hibernation, and again in autumn just before they retire for the winter. Look for animals basking in the early morning sunshine but don't worry unduly if they scuttle away into cover: if you sit still they should soon reappear because most have favoured spots for sunbathing to which they will return time and time again.

COMMON LIZARD
⌃ ABOVE **basking adult** ⌄ BELOW **adult**

SAND LIZARD *Lacerta agilis*
TOTAL LENGTH 16–19cm (55–60 PER CENT OF WHICH MAY BE TAIL)

A robust and comparatively bulky lizard. The Sand Lizard is one of our most threatened reptiles, mainly on account of its restricted choice of habitats and the vulnerability of these to destruction and degradation. **ADULT MALE** is well marked and has a proportionately large head. The ground colour of the back is typically buffish brown, but note the 3 rows of white-centred dark spots that run the length of the body: a median row is flanked by 2 lateral ones. There is considerable variability in the extent and intensity of these darker markings; in some specimens, they may fuse to form longitudinal dark lines. In spring and summer (the only seasons when you stand a realistic chance of seeing the species), the head and flanks are flushed bright green. **ADULT FEMALE** has a proportionately smaller head and more bulky body than the male. The ground colour is pale to rich brown with 3 longitudinal rows of dark, ocellated spots, similar to that seen in the male but usually less intense. **JUVENILE** recalls a small, slender adult female. Note the presence of ocellated dark spots on the back and flanks. **VOICE** – usually silent. HABITAT AND STATUS – There are three disjunct populations of Sand Lizards in the region. In southern England, they are restricted to heathlands in Dorset and Surrey, the former county serving as the species' stronghold in our region. Not just any old patch of heathland will do, however, and in order for Sand Lizards to survive they need mature, undisturbed habitat with dense but low-growing vegetation, plus areas of bare, sandy ground for basking and laying eggs. The only other location for the species in our region is Merseyside, and here they favour undisturbed coastal sand dunes. HABITS AND NATURAL HISTORY – Sand Lizards hibernate and usually disappear below ground from September to March. Understandably, following their emergence in spring, sunbathing is a favoured pastime. Following a skin moult, after which males acquire their gaudy green colours, courtship and mating take place. Females lay up to a dozen eggs in a burrow in late spring; these hatch in late summer. During the summer months, adults are active mainly in the mornings and late afternoons; midday is usually spent in shade, or underground in a burrow. OBSERVATION TIPS – It should always be borne in mind that Sand Lizards are rare and are protected by law. So attempts to observe these fascinating reptiles should avoid any risk of disturbing them, or damaging their surroundings. Having said this, by keeping to well-trodden paths and trails as you walk across Dorset heathlands, you stand a reasonable chance of catching a glimpse of a Sand Lizard if you visit a suitable area in early spring. Your first sighting is likely to be of an alert individual scuttling to the safety of cover at your approach. Sit still and if you are patient you may be rewarded by the animal returning to its favoured basking spot, where it will continue to soak up the sun's rays.

female

courting pair

SAND LIZARD
◎ ABOVE **adult male**
◎ BELOW **adult male**

SLOW-WORM *Anguis fragilis* LENGTH 30–40cm

An intriguing and charming legless lizard that is superficially rather snakelike. The Slow-worm can close its eyelids, an ability that it shares with other lizards, but which snakes lack. **ADULT** has an elongated, shiny body roughly 50–60 per cent of which is tail (assuming it is intact). The body tapers smoothly along its length and there is no discernible 'neck'. An adult male is a rather uniform colour on the upper parts, the precise hue varying according to the individual; most are coppery brown or greyish brown. Occasionally, there are darker markings on the head. An adult female has a similar ground colour to the male, but generally there is a thin, dark vertebral stripe along the length of the back and a somewhat fragmented black line along the flanks. The anterior end of the vertebral dark stripe often ends in a faint 'V' on the head. In both sexes, the belly is bluish with a marbling of pale markings. Occasionally, individuals occur where the upper surface is adorned with blue spots, mainly towards the anterior end of the body. **JUVENILE** has a golden or silvery back with a thin, dark vertebral stripe along its length. The flanks are dark. **VOICE** – Silent. HABITAT AND STATUS – The Slow-worm can be found in a wide range of habitats, the common factors being a sunny, open aspect and an abundance of invertebrate prey. Consequently, the species does not occur in mature woodland or dense scrub, but woodland margins, along with undisturbed grassland, heathland and moors are ideal. Like Common Lizards, Slow-worms find railway and motorway embankments to their liking. They will also coexist quite happily with people in mature gardens but only thrive in the absence of domestic cats, which quickly exterminate Slow-worm populations, along with many other forms of native wildlife. Slow-worms are native to England, Wales and Scotland, and are most numerous and widespread in warmer southern districts. The species has been introduced to the Burren in western Ireland.

juvenile

stumpy, regenerating tail

HABITS AND NATURAL HISTORY – Slow-worms live rather secretive lives and were it not for the fact that they are relatively easy to discover resting under discarded objects lying on the ground, they would be seen only rarely. Little is known about their habits in the wild. However, since soil-dwelling slugs and earthworms feature heavily in their diet, it is safe to assume that they spend much of their lives underground and probably hunt above ground only after dark, when their prey is more likely to be active there. Slow-worms hibernate from October to March and, in spring, newly emerged individuals are sometimes observed sunbathing. Courtship and mating occur in late spring and the young are born (alive and wriggling, not in eggs) in early autumn; 5–10 young per female is usual. As a response to being attacked by a predator, a Slow-worm can shed its tail at will; the disembodied tail continues to wriggle for several minutes while the animal slips away into cover, or at least that's the theory. A stumpy replacement grows back in time. OBSERVATION TIPS – If you want to discover whether Slow-worms are present in your garden, or in an area of undisturbed grassland, turn over planks or pieces of corrugated iron that have been lying around for some time. Slow-worms love to rest under these shelters in the middle of the day and will take to newly provided retreats after only a short time. Newly exposed Slow-worms usually sit still for a while, allowing close inspection. Resist the urge to pick one up though: if handled incorrectly, a distressed animal will shed its tail, a traumatic experience in survival terms.

SLOW-WORM
ABOVE **adult female** BELOW **adult male**

GRASS SNAKE *Natrix natrix*
LENGTH 60–70cm (MALE), 70–90cm (FEMALE)

A large and impressive non-venomous snake. When full grown, a Grass Snake is the region's largest and longest terrestrial reptile. **ADULT** has a slender body that is thickest towards the middle of its length and tapers evenly towards the tail. The ground colour on the upper parts is usually olive-green; at intervals along the body there are vertical stripes on the flanks and a double row of somewhat indistinct dark spots down the vertebral line. The neck is clearly defined by striking black-and-yellow crescent-shaped markings on the sides; these are sometimes complete enough to give the impression of a collar. The scales on the undersurface of the body are whitish with a chequered pattern of darker markings.

Fangs are absent but the jaws are armed with backward-curved teeth that help retain struggling prey as it is swallowed. The eye has a round pupil. **JUVENILE** resembles a miniature adult but with a proportionately larger head and brighter colours. **VOICE** – Hisses alarmingly if distressed or annoyed. HABITAT AND STATUS – The Grass Snake can swim and has an amphibious lifestyle, with wetlands, in the general sense, being the habitats of choice. In the spring, truly aquatic sites such as ponds, lakes, marshes and fens are important to Grass Snakes because this is where their food (mainly amphibians) will be found. However, prime terrestrial terrain in the vicinity of freshwater habitats is also vital. During the summer months, they need dry ground for sunbathing, laying their eggs and for nocturnal refuges; besides which their prey typically abandon the water in summer and so the snakes must follow if they want to feed. In winter, they need somewhere dry to hibernate. Grass Snakes are widespread and locally common in lowland southern England. Their distribution becomes patchier, and their abundance diminishes, across Wales and the further north in England you travel. Grass Snakes do not occur in Scotland or Ireland. HABITS AND NATURAL HISTORY – Grass Snakes can move with surprising speed, both on land and in the water. Since their activity is related to air temperature and sunshine, it is hardly surprising that they are mainly diurnal animals, and that they hibernate during the colder months of the year (mainly October to April). Their prey comprises mainly amphibians (toads and frogs favoured) although small fish are sometimes taken. Prey is consumed whole and typically the snake manoeuvres it to swallow it head first. Like other reptiles, Grass Snakes slough their skin several times a year to accommodate growth. Mating occurs in the spring and eggs are laid mostly in July; 5–20 eggs is the usual number in a clutch. The preferred site is a chamber in the middle of a mound of decaying vegetation (compost heaps are ideal); this provides warmth for egg development and humidity that prevents desiccation. The eggs are leathery, whitish and around 20–25mm across. They hatch a couple of months after being laid, the young snakes using an egg-tooth to tear their way out of confinement. In a state of dire distress, a Grass Snake will sometimes go limp and 'play dead', the effect enhanced by the production of a deeply unpleasant smell. OBSERVATION TIPS – Grass Snakes are easiest to observe in the spring when, newly emerged from hibernation, they are fond of sunbathing in exposed locations. In the summer months, females sometimes bask in the vicinity of vegetation mounds in which they have laid their eggs, occasionally on the mounds themselves. If you pick up a Grass Snake you do so at your peril, not because it is dangerous as such, but because it will produce quantities of foul-smelling and persistent faeces that will stain your hands and clothes.

swimming adult

sloughed skin

eggs

feigning death

GRASS SNAKE
ABOVE **adult, basking** RIGHT **juvenile**

SMOOTH SNAKE *Coronella austriaca* LENGTH 50–70cm

A graceful snake with vaguely viperine markings. The Smooth Snake has an extremely restricted distribution in the region and has acquired the status of a conservation emblem: its plight reflects that of the heathland habitat to which it is restricted. **ADULT** has a slender body, not dissimilar, in terms of overall proportions, to a Grass Snake. As its common name suggests, the unkeeled scales give the body of a Smooth Snake a particularly smooth feel. There is a distinct, rather rounded head, and the body tapers evenly along its length. The overall ground colour is variable but usually a shade of bluish grey or reddish brown. Along the length of the body are a staggered series of darkish spots that, in some individuals, are bold enough and sufficiently fused to create the impression of an Adder-like zigzag. The head is usually adorned with a distinct dark patch on the dorsal surface; sometimes the posterior margin has a reasonably well-defined V-shaped notch. Seen from the side, note the snub-nosed appearance and the dark eye stripe. A Smooth Snake has a rounded pupil in the eye and a golden iris (an Adder has vertical pupils and a red iris). **JUVENILE** is similar to an adult but with a darker head and darkish spots along the flanks. **VOICE** – Mainly silent but will hiss in distress. HABITAT AND STATUS – Although the Smooth Snake has probably only ever occurred in a fairly limited part of southern England, it was certainly much more widespread, say, a century ago than it is today. Of course, this is partly a reflection of the fact that heathland (the habitat to which it is restricted) was itself much more extensive in the past, but the quality of the habitat is important too: the Smooth Snake likes areas with a continuous history of cover by mature and bushy stands of Ling (*Calluna vulgaris*). Sadly, it has suffered from loss and fragmentation of its habitat through development for housing and afforestation. Fires (invariably started by people) that blight our heaths not only kill Smooth Snakes outright but also have a catastrophic effect upon habitat quality, thus reducing the likelihood of successful recolonisation taking place at a later date. Today, the Smooth Snake is entirely restricted to southern heathlands in the counties of Surrey, Hampshire and Dorset. Parts of the New Forest and the east Dorset heaths are its stronghold. HABITS AND NATURAL HISTORY – The Smooth Snake seems to spend much of its life in dense vegetation or underground in burrows. Although, like other reptiles, it likes to sunbathe in order to raise its body temperature, typically it seldom basks in the open as would an Adder. By contrast, it is likely to choose a spot where it can twine itself, at least partly, through the surrounding vegetation. Hibernation takes place underground and lasts from October to April. Following emergence, courtship and mating take place in the spring and gestation lasts several months. Smooth Snakes are ovoviviparous: the dozen or so young that are born are each constrained by a thin egg membrane from which they quickly break free. The diet of adult animals includes other reptiles (notably lizards, particularly Sand Lizards) as well as small mammals and nestling birds. Typically, prey is restrained by coils of the body while the snake negotiates swallowing the victim head first and alive. OBSERVATION TIPS – The Smooth Snake is undoubtedly the most difficult British reptile to observe in the wild, partly because of its rarity but also on account of its secretive habits. It is seldom seen above ground in the middle of the day (or at all in midsummer), and sunbathing is usually restricted to early mornings and late afternoons in spring and autumn. Smooth Snakes will often bask under sheets of corrugated iron on slightly overcast summer's days and can be discovered by turning these over. Bear in mind, however, that in many instances these man-made refuges will have been placed on heathlands by conservationists for the benefit of Smooth Snakes, not for human observers. Always return the corrugated iron to its original position and never handle a Smooth Snake if you find one – apart from anything else, the species is protected by law from disturbance.

adult

SMOOTH SNAKE
⌃ ABOVE **adult, basking** ⌄ BELOW **adult**

ADDER *Vipera berus* LENGTH 50–60CM (FEMALE), 45–55CM (MALE)

A plump and well-marked snake. The Adder is the only venomous reptile in the region. **ADULT** is rather variable in terms of the body ground colour, which can be reddish brown, greenish yellow, grey or creamy buff. However, almost all individuals are adorned with a striking, blackish zigzag line that runs the length of the dorsal surface of the body. At the anterior end, the dorsal zigzag culminates in something akin to an arrowhead, in front of which is a distinctive inverted 'V' marking on the head. In some parts of the species' range, so-called 'Black Adders' (melanic forms) are encountered on a regular basis. All Adders have a vertical pupil in the eye and a red iris. Seen in profile, the head is square-ended. Overall, females tend to have more stocky bodies than males. **JUVENILE** is considerably more slender than an adult and the ground colour is usually reddish brown. **VOICE** – Mainly silent but will hiss if distressed or agitated. HABITAT AND STATUS – The Adder is widespread across England, Wales and Scotland but its precise distribution is rather patchy. Today, it is effectively excluded from areas of intensive agriculture as well as urban locations; heaths, moors, open woodlands, rough, natural grassland and coastal dunes are its preferred haunts. An abundance of prey and natural cover, as well as a lack of human disturbance, are key factors in determining whether or not the species is present in a given area. Although the Adder is by no means rare (indeed it can be locally common), it has disappeared from many haunts where it occurred as recently as 50 years ago. Its increasingly fragmented distribution can only have adverse long-term implications for the species' future in the region. HABITS AND NATURAL HISTORY – Adders seem to spend more time basking and sunbathing than our other snakes and consequently they are encountered on a regular basis. Hibernation takes place mainly from October to March, although in northern parts of the region their appearance in spring may be delayed by up to a month compared to the south. Courtship and mating take place in the spring. In the presence of a female, rival males sometimes engage in ritual combat – the so-called 'dance of the Adders' – where, with bodies entwined and the front halves often raised from the ground, they engage in bouts of wrestling. The more powerful victor claims the female.

A female Adder gives birth to around a dozen or so young. At the moment of birth, they are still constrained by a thin membrane, but this is soon ruptured, liberating the baby snakes. From the moment they are born, Adders are venomous and armed with hollow, needle-like fangs with which the venom is delivered. Prey varies according to the size of the snake but small mammals are favoured by adults. The bite is administered in a lunging action: the mouth opens wide and the fangs are lowered so that the victim can be stabbed. The bite is over in a flash, after which the snake retreats. Usually the prey wanders off a short distance before it dies, and in due course the Adder follows, using its sensitive tongue to 'taste' the route of its prey. Satisfied that the victim is dead, the snake then swallows it whole, usually head first. OBSERVATION TIPS – Adders are easiest to observe in the early spring, shortly after they emerge from hibernation. They can sometimes even be found on sunny days in late February in southern districts, and it is not uncommon to see several individuals entwined, close to the entrance of their winter retreat. At this time of year Adders are relatively sluggish, but please do not mistake their lack of activity for docility: if they have the energy to leave the hibernaculum then they certainly will have the inclination to bite if provoked. When it comes to snake bites, provocation is the key word and you are most unlikely to get bitten unless you do something foolish – like try to pick one up. Biting a person is a means of defence for an Adder, not an act of aggression. In the unlikely event of a person being bitten, the consequences, while painful, are most unlikely to be mortal.

ADDER
⌃ ABOVE **adult, basking** ⌄ BELOW **adult**

LIZARDS Order *Squamata* – Family *Lacertidae*

WALL LIZARD *Podarcis muralis* LENGTH 14–17cm

female

Superficially similar to a Common Lizard but with a proportionately much longer tail. Most individuals have a brown ground colour, a variably complete dark vertebral stripe down the back, and incomplete dark stripes defining the upper and lower margins of the flanks; the flanks themselves are usually a richer brown than the dorsal surface. In many females this may be the extent of their markings, but some show a limited marbling of dark spots and bars on the back and tail, and white on the flanks. In most males, the dark and whitish marbling is much more extensive. In all individuals, the throat is whitish with variable dark marbling. Wall Lizards are native to Jersey but elsewhere in our region they have been introduced to a number of sites from mainland Europe. Probably the easiest colonies to observe are those found in coastal quarries on the Isle of Portland and on undercliffs on the Isle of Wight. In both locations the animals are fond of sunbathing on south-facing rocks. They hibernate, relatively briefly, from November to early March, and when active they feed mainly on insects.

GREEN LIZARD *Lacerta viridis* LENGTH 30–40cm

A robust and long-tailed lizard with a proportionately large head. An adult Green Lizard is stunningly colourful, with a mainly bright green ground colour. Females are variably adorned with dark spots on the back and flanks, while juveniles are mainly brown. The species is widespread in Europe and native to Jersey. Its occurrence elsewhere in our region is a result of introductions and colonies can be found on Guernsey and the Isle of Wight. Animals, released from captivity, are sometimes encountered in other locations. Favoured habitats include scrub-covered cliffs, dunes and heaths.

TURTLES Order *Chelonia* – Family *Dermochelyidae*

LEATHERBACK TURTLE *Dermochelys coriacea* LENGTH 1.5–2.5m; WEIGHT 500–900kg

A gigantic and unmistakable marine reptile. The body is protected by a distinctive dark shell that has longitudinal ridges along its length and which tapers to a point at the rear end. The head and huge front flippers (used for swimming) project from openings at the front of the shell and a pair of small flippers can be seen at the rear. Turtles are usually thought of as tropical animals with a dependence upon warm seas. With this in mind, it had been assumed that Leatherbacks seen in British and Irish waters were sick individuals carried here, passively, by the Gulf Stream. However, strange as it may seem, it now seems likely that some Leatherbacks actively migrate to the northeast Atlantic during the summer months to feed on jellyfish (almost the only thing they eat). In that sense, the species can be considered to be native to our region. Uniquely among living reptiles, they have the ability to generate body heat and this allows them to remain active in relatively cold seas. If you are extremely lucky you may encounter a Leatherback Turtle at sea. Sadly, most records in our region relate to individuals killed by trawlers or animals washed up on beaches; beached turtles are invariably either sick (often as a result of having swallowed plastic bags) or injured (by boats). If you do discover a beached animal, don't attempt to return it to the sea yourself – call a conservation or animal welfare organisation and leave it to the experts.

TERRAPINS Order *Chelonia* – Family *Emydidae*

RED-EARED TERRAPIN *Trachemys scripta elegans* LENGTH 25–30cm; WEIGHT UP TO 1kg

A well-marked and distinctive freshwater alien. The Red-eared Terrapin has a flattened, tortoise-like shell. The head and legs emerge from lateral openings and are, to a degree, retractable. The head and neck are adorned with yellow stripes and the red 'ear' is distinctive. The species is native to North America. It is a popular (initially) pet but in many instances it outgrows its welcome and, regrettably, people then release individuals into the wild without considering the consequences. In British ponds, Red-eared Terrapins have few natural enemies and can survive our winters quite happily. However, in turn they are voracious predators with appetites that expand as their own size increases. Native amphibians are quickly exterminated from ponds where terrapins have been liberated, and the terrapins' attentions then turn to fish and other larger quarry. Unsurprisingly, conservationists are keen to remove Red-eared Terrapins as soon as they are discovered living wild in our region. In practice, this is easier said than done because they are alert and wary animals. It goes without saying that you should NEVER contemplate liberating captive animals.

WALL LIZARD
◁ RIGHT male

GREEN LIZARD
▷ RIGHT adult

LEATHERBACK TURTLE
△ ABOVE adult swimming off the Cornish coast

RED-EARED TERRAPIN
▷ RIGHT adult

SMOOTH NEWT *Triturus vulgaris* TOTAL LENGTH 9–10cm

A widespread species that also goes by the name of Common Newt. During the breeding season, males are strikingly marked animals. At other times of year there is a risk of confusion with the Palmate Newt, especially with females and young individuals. **ADULT** has a ground colour of buffish brown with a whitish throat that is variably marked with dark spots. Females are adorned with relatively small black spots across the rest of the body; on occasions these coalesce to form lines that run the length of the body and continue onto the tail. In males, the dark markings on the body usually take the form of rather large, blotchy spots, which are usually more intense during the breeding season. At this time of year males also grow a striking crest that runs the length of the back and along the tail; dark patches and an undulating margin give the crest a wavy appearance. The male's belly is variably flushed with orange and adorned with dark spots. **JUVENILE** is similar to an adult female. **VOICE** – Silent. HABITAT AND STATUS – Like its cousins, the Smooth Newt is tied to water during the breeding season and so habitats that lack suitable pools will not support this species. Having said that, they are often found in relatively small water bodies, including ditches and garden ponds, and as a consequence the species is the most widespread newt in the region. Smooth Newts are unlikely to be found in flowing or acidic waters. Ponds that dry up in the occasional summer, or at least shrink, are ideal because they are unlikely to support fish populations: where fish do occur in larger and more permanent lakes, predation levels are likely to be too high for the newts to survive. Since a significant proportion of the species' year is spent on land, the terrestrial habitat that surrounds a breeding pond is important: open woodland, commons and mature gardens are all suitable. The Smooth Newt is widespread in England and Wales, although absent from, or least numerous in, the far west. It occurs throughout Ireland; in Scotland it is scarce in, or absent from, northern and upland districts.

HABITS AND NATURAL HISTORY – Generally speaking, most Smooth Newts spend November to February in a state of torpor, hidden away in a terrestrial retreat, under a stone or in a crevice or burrow in the ground. Come the spring, they migrate back to their favoured ponds and at this point males begin to acquire their breeding finery. The timing of their return to water depends upon the season and geographical location, but most ponds are fully occupied by early April. Courtship, an elaborate affair, culminates in the male depositing a spermatophore (a package containing sperm); with a little direction and encouragement from her partner, the female picks this up with her cloaca. Fertilisation complete, the female lays 200 or more eggs; each one is produced individually and wrapped, at least partially, in the leaf of a water plant. Smooth Newt tadpoles take 3–4 months to develop and in their latter stages they are rather uniformly pinkish buff with large feathery gills; they are almost impossible to distinguish from Palmate Newt tadpoles. Metamorphosis takes place mainly in late summer, at which point the juvenile newts leave the pond; most adults have left the water by early July. A few tadpoles fail to reach a sufficient stage of development for metamorphosis to occur that year and they remain at this immature stage until the following year; if, however, the pond dries up that summer, they are doomed to die. Smooth Newts are voracious predators.

Adults will eat freshwater crustaceans as well as frog and toad tadpoles; on land, their diet is presumed to comprise mainly invertebrates. OBSERVATION TIPS – Smooth Newts are easiest to observe in the breeding season and are relatively easy to catch by netting suitable freshwater pools. Courtship can be observed with the aid of a torch if you visit a breeding pool at dusk. At such times you can also witness the newt's almost insatiable appetite for tadpoles.

adult male spring

larva

egg

adult male on land

SMOOTH NEWT
ABOVE **adult male, spring** BELOW **adult female, spring**

PALMATE NEWT *Triturus helveticus* TOTAL LENGTH 8–9cm

J F M A M J J A S O N D

A widespread amphibian. As adults, Palmate Newts are the smallest of their kind in the region. Males are distinctive and easy to recognise in the breeding season, but less so at other times of year. Females are confusingly similar to female Smooth Newts at all times. **ADULT** of both sexes has a yellowish belly and a pinkish, unspotted throat throughout the year. A pale vertical stripe above the hind legs can usually be discerned. Breeding males develop diagnostic palmations between the toes on the hind feet and the tail terminates abruptly with a thin filament projecting at the tip. The body is olive-brown but variably marbled with dark markings; an orange-buff band extends along the length of the body and tail. At other times of the year,

larva

webs on the feet are absent or reduced in size, body colours and markings are less striking, and the tail filament and marginal crest are reduced or absent. However, the male retains a dark eye stripe and his rather flat-backed appearance. An adult female is rather uniformly yellowish brown. The unspotted, pink throat is the best feature for separation from a female Smooth Newt (where the throat is whitish and usually spotted). **JUVENILE** resembles an adult female. **VOICE** – Mainly silent.

HABITAT AND STATUS – The Palmate Newt is widespread and locally common in England, Wales and Scotland but entirely absent from Ireland. Although it is often found in the same ponds as its two relatives in the region, it is the newt species that you are most likely to encounter in acidic, nutrient-poor waters associated with heaths and moors. Hence it is the predominant (and often the only) newt species in upland and western districts. Relatively small ponds and pools are preferred by Palmate Newts for breeding; if the body of water in question is inclined to freeze solid occasionally in winter, or dry up in some summers, then this may favour the newts: fish (many species of which are major predators of newt tadpoles) will be unable to survive in the long term. Because adult Palmate Newts are to a large extent land animals between July and February, the quality of the terrestrial environment surrounding the breeding pool is obviously important. There must be plenty of cover, undisturbed crevices and other hideaways (used as daytime retreats in summer and more long-term refuges in cold winters), and plenty of invertebrate food.

egg

Whether the habitat is heathland, moor or scrub, so long as those criteria are met, and the breeding body of water is to their liking, then Palmate Newts will thrive. Unsurprisingly, the species is absent from areas of intensive agriculture. HABITS AND NATURAL HISTORY – Palmate Newts usually return to the breeding ponds in March and in some locations a few individuals may

hibernating adult

be present for much of the winter, if the weather is mild. Courtship, which takes place mainly in April and May, involves complex and rather elaborate dance-like manoeuvres on the part of the male, which culminate in the deposition of a spermatophore; after some cajoling, the female collects this and fertilisation takes place, her movements orchestrated by the male. Subsequently, she lays 200 or more eggs, each attached to (and sometimes wrapped in) the leaf of an aquatic plant. The tadpoles (essentially indistinguishable from those of the Smooth Newt) develop rapidly and breathe with the aid of feathery gills. Metamorphosis into miniature adults usually occurs by July or August. If the pond in question dries up then late developers will die; if it retains water then a small proportion of the tadpole population usually fails to metamorphose and stays in the larval state into the following year. Adult Palmate Newts eat a wide range of freshwater insects, crustaceans and molluscs while living in water, and presumably their terrestrial diet comprises a similar range of invertebrates. In spring, they are voracious predators of frog tadpoles. OBSERVATION TIPS – Palmate Newts are easily netted from suitable ponds and pools in spring, but disturbance should be kept to a minimum. For a less disruptive approach, simply sit quietly beside the water in question and watch. Before long you will be able to witness the elaborate courtship behaviour for yourself.

adult on land

PALMATE NEWT

⌃ ABOVE **adult male, spring**
⌃ LEFT **adult male, spring**
⌄ BELOW **adult female, spring**

GREAT CRESTED NEWT *Triturus cristatus* TOTAL LENGTH 14–16cm

An impressive newt and the largest of its kind in the region. During the breeding season, males in particular are unmistakable. **ADULT** has a mainly blackish-brown ground colour with a variable extent of dark spots and patches; typically, these are isolated and discrete along the back but more extensive and fused along the flanks and on the head. Note also that the body is adorned with numerous warts; those on the flanks are white-tipped. From the neck to the vent, the underparts are a striking orange-yellow colour, marked variably with distinct black spots; on the throat the pattern is often reversed, with smallish orange-yellow spots set against a black background. In the breeding season, the male acquires a large, jagged dorsal crest and a more undulating crest on the tail. A pale stripe runs along the centre of the tail. Outside the breeding season, the male resembles a female although a trace of the crest can usually be discerned. Even in the breeding season, an adult female lacks the male's crest and the body has a more uniformly dark ground colour. Note the yellowish-orange stripe that runs the length of the tail on its lower edge. **JUVENILE** resembles an adult female. **VOICE** – Silent.

HABITAT AND STATUS – As a breeding species, the Great Crested Newt is associated with ponds, typically ones that seldom, if ever, dry up completely in summer. Unsurprisingly, they seldom do well, or survive at all, in ponds where fish are present: predation levels, particularly of eggs and larvae, are too high. The species is widespread across lowland England and Wales, although its precise distribution reflects the patchy occurrence of suitable habitats. The water chemistry of breeding ponds is important and Great Crested Newts are unlikely to be found in acid, nutrient-poor waters. This explains the species' absence from, or scarcity in, upland and western regions. Several months of the year are spent on land and so the terrestrial environment that surrounds a breeding pond is clearly crucial for its survival. In addition to a rich invertebrate fauna (a source of food) there needs to be plenty of cover. Log piles and other undisturbed refuges are used as daytime retreats in summer and autumn (Great Crested Newts are mainly nocturnal), and for more extensive periods of torpor in cold winters. Although the species has declined in recent decades, it could still be described as very locally common. However, its ecological requirements are so precise, and its favoured habitats so vulnerable to destruction or degradation, that the Great Crested Newt has legal protection. Populations of this species in Britain are significant in European terms. HABITS AND NATURAL HISTORY – Great Crested Newts are often present in their breeding ponds from February to August, although occasionally some remain in the water for much of the year. Courtship begins soon after the bulk of the population has arrived in early spring. A sequence of ritual dance and display culminates in the male depositing a spermatophore, which is collected by the female. Fertilisation complete, she lays several hundred eggs, each one being individually wrapped in the leaf of a water plant. A mature Great Crested Newt larva is distinctive and easy to separate from those of its cousins: it is much bigger, and has much more robust proportions and extensive dark markings on its broad tail membrane. At all ages, Great Crested Newts are predators, their diet comprising invertebrates and the immature stages of other amphibians. OBSERVATION TIPS – Great Crested Newts are less easy to observe in the wild than their cousins, partly because they are most active after dark, and partly because a significant proportion of their time is spent at the bottom of their breeding pond. If you sit quietly beside a pond where they are known to occur, from time to time you will see one come to the surface to gulp air, diving to the depths with an audible 'plop'. If you visit a suitable pond in spring and after dark, with the aid of a torch you should be able to pick out animals moving through the shallows. Occasionally, Great Crested Newts are discovered hiding under logs near ponds. However, please do not go looking for them in such sites: they are sensitive to exposure and, besides which, their legal status means it is an offence to disturb them knowingly .

egg

breeding male

newly metamorphosed adult

larva

GREAT CRESTED NEWT
⌃ ABOVE **breeding male** ⌄ BELOW **female**

COMMON FROG *Rana temporaria* LENGTH 6–10cm

A widespread species throughout the region and probably our most familiar amphibian. The Common Frog is beloved of adult naturalists and children alike and is a welcome addition to gardens everywhere. **ADULT MALE** has smooth, moist skin. The ground colour is variable, but typically the upper parts are olive-yellow or greyish brown with variable amounts of dark blotching and spots. Darker red individuals are not uncommon in upland districts. The eye is relatively large and has a yellow iris with a dark, oval pupil. A dark mask runs back from the eye and overlies the eardrum. The underparts, including the throat, are usually pale greyish white with faint darker marbling. The legs are relatively short (compared to other frog species) and the hind feet have 5 webbed toes; there is a lumpy tubercle behind the shortest toe. During the breeding season, the male acquires a bluish throat and swollen nuptial pads on the innermost digits of the front feet; these are used for gripping the female when mating. **ADULT FEMALE** is similar to, but larger than, the male and has white granulations on the flanks that give the skin a coarse texture. **JUVENILE** animals, newly metamorphosed from tadpoles, resemble miniature adults but with proportionately larger heads. It usually takes 3 years before they reach adult size. **VOICE** – Males utter low-pitched croaking calls when courting in spring. HABITAT AND STATUS – Common Frogs are found in a wide range of habitats, the

common factors being the presence of still water, such as ponds and lakes, for breeding and nearby invertebrate-rich terrestrial habitats where they can feed during the summer months. Consequently, the species is found in most lowland habitats that harbour suitable bodies of water, and it even occurs on lower mountain slopes in Scotland. Common Frogs are found

throughout mainland Britain and Ireland and also occur on a few islands. HABITS AND NATURAL HISTORY – In mild winters, Common Frogs may not hibernate at all, but when conditions are harsh they usually enter a state of torpor either in the mud at the bottom of a pond or in a damp, terrestrial refuge. The breeding season starts early in the year. The precise timing depends upon the geographical location, so in the southwest courting frogs may be observed in January while in Scotland their appearance may be delayed until April. Typically, males appear first and there is intense competition for females as they arrive. Courtship complete, the male grasps the female with his front legs in a tight embrace called 'amplexus'. The mass of eggs is fertilised by the male as it is released by the female, and on contact with water the jelly coating surrounding each egg swells; the result is the familiar frogspawn. The pace of development of the spawn is influenced by water temperature, but typically tiny tadpoles hatch within a couple of weeks. Thereafter they grow rapidly, acquiring first their hind legs and then the front pair. Eventually, their

appearance changes, the body becoming more frog-like and the tail being resorbed into the body. Metamorphosis and emergence from the pond usually take place around 3 to 4 months after spawning. During the summer months, both adult frogs and newly metamorphosed young animals are usually found in waterside and marshy vegetation. They feed on a wide variety of invertebrates. In turn, they are consumed by numerous predators. Unsurprisingly, mortality in tadpoles is higher than in adult frogs. OBSERVATION TIPS – Common Frogs are easy to observe in spring, especially when courtship is in full swing. Although they will disappear beneath the surface of the water if disturbed, sit quietly and they will soon reappear. They are usually more of a challenge to find during the summer months, but following a heavy downpour of rain adults can sometimes be found moving through long grass.

J F M A M J J A S O N D

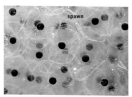
spawn

tadpole

froglet

COMMON FROG
⌃ ABOVE **adult**
⌄ BELOW **mating pair in 'amplexus'**

MARSH FROG *Rana ridibunda* LENGTH 11–13cm

A relatively large and impressive amphibian. As a result of introductions, the Marsh Frog has established several thriving colonies in southeast England. **ADULT** usually has rather uniformly green upper parts when full grown, and the body is covered to a variable extent with warts and dark spots; a few individuals show a hint of a pale vertebral stripe. The male's vocal sacs (seen when singing) are grey. Smaller specimens are rather olive-brown with variable dark markings, mainly towards the rear of the body and on the hind legs. At this stage, there is potential for confusion with a young Common Frog. However, in a young Marsh Frog the side of the snout is often flushed with bright green (to a variable extent) and the tympanum (the external ear membrane) is usually not surrounded by a dark brown patch, as it is in the Common Frog. **JUVENILE** has similar markings and coloration to a young adult. **VOICE** – Males utter a stuttering croak, roughly transcribed as *Whoa-aa-aa-aa*. HABITAT AND STATUS – As its common name hints, the Marsh Frog is always associated with aquatic habitats and it is more tied to water than its cousin, the Common Frog. It is tolerant of moderately brackish conditions and, typically, it is found on, or in, the water of its favoured drainage channels and pools throughout the year, seldom venturing onto dry land. Hibernation usually takes

froglet

place in mud at the bottom. The Marsh Frog is native to mainland Europe but its status in Britain is that of an introduced alien. Its first documented appearance in our region came in 1935 when a dozen individuals were liberated in a garden pond, on the edge of Walland Marsh in Kent. Within a few years both Walland and Romney Marshes had been colonised, and over the subsequent decades the species spread to many suitable areas of Sussex and Kent, sometimes with the assistance of humans. Within its restricted range in the region, the Marsh Frog is locally common. Nowadays, it is illegal to translocate it to new areas. HABITS AND NATURAL HISTORY – In spring, males sing, in chorus, at any time of the day and night. Females lay clumps of eggs that are protected by spawn and usually attached to submerged water plants. The tadpoles, which are marbled darkish olive-brown, develop rapidly and attain a length of around 6cm before they metamorphose in late summer or early autumn. Marsh Frogs are voracious predators and basically will eat, or attempt to consume, anything they can fit in their mouths. This includes other amphibians as well as invertebrates and small fish; cannibalism is not unknown. OBSERVATION TIPS – Marsh Frogs are relatively easy to see if you visit one of their known haunts (the Lewes Brooks in Sussex and Romney Marsh in Kent are strongholds). However, they are wary and alert, and, if you are not stealthy, all you are likely to see is a succession of animals plopping into the water in advance of your approach. With patience, however, you can usually creep up on one and, if you sit still, frogs that you inadvertently scared off will return to the surface after a few minutes. Imitating the call of a male Marsh Frog can sometimes trigger a responding chorus from nearby individuals.

MARSH FROG
⌃ ABOVE **adult** ⌄ BELOW **young animal**

POOL FROG *Rana lessonae* LENGTH 5–6.5cm

A relatively well-marked frog. The Pool Frog has a confused past and an uncertain future. **ADULT** is variable but usually has a greenish-brown ground colour on the back and legs; this is adorned with dark spots and patches of varying size, either side of a pale vertebral stripe. The flanks are usually yellowish green with dark spots. Compared to both Edible and Marsh Frogs, the hind legs are relatively short while the tubercle (lumpy outgrowth) on the inner toe of the hind foot is relatively larger. **JUVENILE** recalls a small adult but with less distinct dark markings. **VOICE** – Utters a duck-like quacking *ou-Whack*. HABITAT AND STATUS – The story of the Pool Frog in Britain is a sad one. Books about amphibians written as recently as 25 years ago barely gave it a passing mention. Then, the received wisdom was that it was just a variation on the Edible Frog theme and, like its cousin, an introduction to our region and hence not worthy of conservation. However, now it is recognised as a genuine species. Furthermore, although introductions may well have occurred to Britain, it appears that some populations in our region were genuinely native. Anecdotal evidence suggests that at one time it was probably widespread in the East Anglian fens; following widespread drainage, it became restricted to isolated pools. I use the past tense because, unfortunately, as the last millennium came to a close, so native Pool Frogs became extinct in our region. Regrettably, their passing went largely unlamented outside the herpetological world. There are plans to reintroduce the species to some of its former native haunts. Matters are confused by the fact that alien Pool Frogs undoubtedly persist alongside Edible Frogs at sites where past introductions (to garden ponds and the like) have occurred on an *ad hoc* basis (*see* below). HABITS AND NATURAL HISTORY – Pool Frogs are tied to water throughout the year. Courtship and mating take place in the spring and males sing loudly, inflating a pair of large, white vocal sacs on the sides of the head. Larval development and metamorphosis follow the lines of other frog species, but full-grown tadpoles are much larger than those of the Common Frog. OBSERVATION TIPS – Unless successful reintroduction of the Pool Frog occurs in the future, you are only likely to see it in Britain in a garden pond.

EDIBLE FROG *Rana × esculenta* LENGTH 7–9cm

A large and impressive introduced amphibian. **ADULT** is colourful and beautifully marked. The ground colour varies from green to yellowish brown, according to the individual, and invariably the upper parts are adorned with an intricate marbled pattern, or dark spots and blotches. A pale greenish vertebral stripe is usually present and often this is flanked by greenish- and buffish-brown longitudinal lines down the sides of the back. Compared to a Pool Frog the legs are relatively long. **JUVENILE** recalls a miniature adult but with less distinct and rather incomplete dark markings. **VOICE** – Males utter loud, croaking calls in spring. HABITAT AND STATUS – The Edible Frog is not native, but a few colonies occur in south and east England. All are the result of deliberate introductions and most are restricted to garden or ornamental ponds. Only relatively recently have genetic studies demonstrated that the Edible Frog is not a genuine species, as was once supposed: rather, it is a hybrid between Pool and Marsh Frogs. Species hybrids are not usually viable, so the fact that the Edible Frog is fertile has caused scientists to explore what actually constitutes a species. The genetic means by which Edible Frog populations remain viable is complex and beyond the scope of this book. However, with continued genetic input from pure Pool Frogs, Edible Frog colonies can persist indefinitely; this curious mixed species/hybrid coexistence occurs across mainland Europe. HABITS AND NATURAL HISTORY – The Edible Frog is tied to water throughout its life. Individuals are often seen basking on floating vegetation and the usual response to danger is to dive. Courtship and mating take place in late spring and larval development follows that seen in other frog species. At all stages, the Edible Frog is a voracious predator. OBSERVATION TIPS – You are only likely to see Edible Frogs in, or in the vicinity of, garden ponds where they have been introduced in the past.

froglet

adult

POOL FROG
⊘ ABOVE adult

EDIBLE FROG
⊘ BELOW adult

COMMON TOAD *Bufo bufo* LENGTH 7–9cm (FEMALE), 5–6cm (MALE)

A widespread and familiar amphibian and the commonest of its kind in the region. **ADULT** has rather uniformly coloured upper parts. The precise hue varies according to the individual and is influenced by the ambient light (Common Toads can lighten or darken their skin); olive-brown and greenish buff are fairly typical in animals observed in daylight. The skin is covered in toxin-containing warts. Note the red iris and the webbed hind feet. In early spring, prior to spawning, females in particular can look extremely plump. **JUVENILE** recalls a miniature adult with a proportionately large head. **VOICE** – Courting males utter a croaking call in spring. HABITAT AND STATUS – Common Toads are more terrestrial than most other amphibians and adults spend much of their lives on land.

They are found in a wide range of habitats, including woodland, scrub, grassland and moors. However, because they are still tied to water during the breeding season, most Common Toads are found within 2km or so of suitable breeding ponds. As a general rule, water bodies in which toads thrive tend to be larger and deeper than those that Common Frogs find optimal. The presence of fish does not deter Common Toads, the toxic skin of their tadpoles serving as a deterrent to predation. HABITS AND NATURAL HISTORY – The Common Toad is well known for mass migrations undertaken back to its spawning ponds; these movements take place early in the year, usually in February and March. Courtship, which happens in the water, is a vigorous, rough and tumble affair by any standards and can involve half a dozen or more males clambering over a single female in a writhing mass. The victorious male grips his partner in the posture known as '*amplexus*'; rough pads, which develop on the forefingers at this time of year, improve his grip. Spawn takes the form of long strings of jelly, containing a double row of eggs (although in stretched spawn it can look like a single row); it is entwined amongst aquatic plant stems. The developing tadpoles are uniformly blackish and they occasionally gather in conspicuous swarming masses at the surface. Adult Common Toads have usually vacated their breeding ponds by May. Newly metamorphosed youngsters leave the water mainly in August, although the speed of development and timing of departure are influenced by the prevailing weather. Common Toads are active predators, their diet including invertebrates as well as other amphibians. When on land, they are mainly nocturnal, hiding under a log or in a burrow during the hours of daylight. Particularly cold spells in winter are spent in a state of torpor in similar underground refuges. The typical gait consists of short hops, much more modest than those of a Common Frog. OBSERVATION TIPS – Common Toads are usually easy to observe at the start of their breeding season and their antics can be extremely entertaining, not to say comical. Although much activity takes place after dark (and can be viewed by torchlight), courting 'masses' of toads, and pairs in amplexus, can usually be found in the shallows in early March in broad daylight. At other times of year, using a torch, Common Toads can be found walking around on mild, damp nights. They can also be discovered in the daytime by turning over logs.

tadpole

spawn

tadpole with developed hind legs

adult

newly metamorphosed toadlet

COMMON TOAD
⊙ ABOVE **adult** ⊙ BELOW **courting mass**

NATTERJACK TOAD *Bufo calamita* LENGTH 6–7cm

A charming little amphibian. The Natterjack Toad is scarce and protected, and has an extremely restricted distribution in the region. **ADULT** is superficially similar to a small Common Toad but the pale yellowish vertebral stripe is diagnostic and allows certain identification. The upper parts are warty and the ground colour varies according to the individual, but yellowish brown or greenish brown are typical. The back is generally darker than the flanks and is marbled with dark spots; the underparts are creamy white. Note also the rather flattened body, the relatively short hind legs and the greenish-yellow iris in the eye (in the Common Toad the iris is orange). **JUVENILE** resembles a miniature adult but with a proportionately larger head. Note the diagnostic yellow stripe on the back, and the adornment of reddish warts. **VOICE** – During the breeding season, males utter a purring croak, often after dark. HABITAT AND STATUS – In Britain and Ireland, the Natterjack Toad is associated mainly with lowland heathlands, coastal dunes and, to a lesser degree, stabilised saltmarshes. On the face of it, these may appear to be dissimilar habitats but, from a structural point of view, they have factors in common. They are formed on free-draining soft – mainly sandy – soils (ideal for the toads to dig in) and support shallow, seasonally drying, ponds (like other amphibians, Natterjacks breed in water, but pools that dry up harbour fewer predators and competing species than permanent ones). Important locations for the species in our region include coastal dune systems in Norfolk and dunes and saltmarshes in northwest England. Natterjack Toads have disappeared from most of their former (heathland) haunts in southern England, mainly as a result of habitat destruction or degradation. However, reintroduction programmes, combined with correct habitat management, will hopefully reverse this trend. The species is also found in southwest Ireland, although a question mark hangs over its origins there. HABITS AND NATURAL HISTORY – Upon encountering a Natterjack Toad, the first thing you are likely to notice is the fact that it walks (rather than hops); despite a rather shuffling gait, it can achieve a commendable speed for such a small, squat animal. They also possess remarkable digging skills and, given a soft and yielding substrate, they can disappear from view within a matter of seconds. Natterjack Toads are mainly nocturnal and forage for invertebrates, insects and spiders being important in their diet. They spend the daylight hours holed up in a specially excavated burrow. Similar underground refuges are used for hibernation, which usually takes place from November to February. Water levels permitting, the breeding season extends mainly from April to June, although a thunderous summer downpour sometimes triggers a resurgence of activity. Males sing in chorus to attract females and spawning takes place while the pair is in amplexus. Spawn strings contain a single row of eggs and are laid among aquatic plants; tadpoles follow the usual stages of development seen in frogs and toads. A Natterjack tadpole's distasteful skin confers upon it a degree of protection from predators. OBSERVATION TIPS – It should always be borne in mind that the Natterjack Toad is protected by law and should not be disturbed. Having said that, it is relatively easy to encounter the species in the vicinity of breeding pools if you visit suitable locations in East Anglia and northwest England. At the height of the breeding season, males are sometimes vocal during the daytime in sunny weather. At other times of the year, the species is mainly nocturnal.

adult walking

spawn string

singing male

NATTERJACK TOAD
⌃ ABOVE adult ⌄ BELOW newly metamorphosed toadlet

FROGS Order *Anura* – Family *Ranidae*
EUROPEAN TREE FROG *Hyla arborea* LENGTH 4–5cm
A colourful and distinctive amphibian. The European Tree Frog is easily recognised by its bright green colour (although the precise hue can be modified to match its surroundings), the presence of suckers on the toes, and its predilection for living off the ground. The underparts are whitish and a dark stripe adorns the flanks. The species is widespread in Europe and occurs naturally as close to our region as the north coast of France. However, the European Tree Frog is not native to Britain and despite attempts in the past to introduce it, all known colonies have now died out. It continues to be kept in captivity (along with several other tree frog species) and escapes and deliberate releases are likely to occur in the future. The European Tree Frog favours well-vegetated wetlands.

AGILE FROG *Rana dalmatina* LENGTH 8–9cm
Although the Agile Frog is widespread across mainland Europe, in the region covered by this book it is restricted to the Channel Island of Jersey. Superficially it is very similar to the Common Frog, and one non-scientific way of distinguishing the two in our region is by distribution: the Agile Frog is the only *Rana* species that occurs on Jersey. Compared to its Common cousin, the hind legs are proportionately longer, the snout more pointed and the eardrum is closer to the eye. The body colour and markings are variable but broadly similar to most Common Frogs; the two species share similar habitat preferences. Were it not for the actions of conservationists, the Agile Frog's future on Jersey would be in jeopardy. Captive breeding maintains a reservoir of animals that underpins the dwindling population in the wild.

TOADS Order *Anura* – Family *Bufonidae*
AFRICAN CLAWED TOAD *Xenopus laevis* LENGTH 10–12cm
A bizarre-looking, flat-bodied amphibian, which, as its common name suggests, hails from southern Africa. The African Clawed Toad is a familiar laboratory animal and is occasionally kept as a pet; unsurprisingly, escapes from captivity and deliberate releases explain its presence in our region. The upper surface is usually yellowish brown and is adorned with numerous dark spots and blotches; organs that resemble suture stitches can be seen on the flanks. Note the beady eyes, which are located on the top of the head rather than the side. African Clawed Toads are exclusively aquatic animals. Various colonies have been established over the years in our region but only those in south Wales have persisted.

MIDWIFE TOAD *Alytes obstetricans* LENGTH 4–5cm
A rather small, short-legged and squat amphibian. The body is a rather uniform colour (usually greyish brown) on the upper parts and in this respect at least there is potential for confusion with a small Common Toad. However, note that the pupil in the eye is vertical in the Midwife Toad but horizontal in its Common cousin. Unusually among amphibians, courtship and mating occur on land and culminate in the male wrapping the string of eggs around the rear of his body and hind legs. The male carries the eggs around with him until it is time for the tadpoles to hatch, at which point he seeks out water. Midwife Toads are not native to Britain but several long-established colonies are present in the region.

AMERICAN BULLFROG *Bufo americana* LENGTH 15–20cm
By British and Irish standards this alien species is a huge amphibian. As its common name suggests, it comes from North America and it is commonly kept as an exotic pet. Unfortunately, captive animals put on weight rapidly and quickly outgrow their welcome. As a consequence, thoughtless owners not infrequently liberate individuals into the countryside without considering the implications of their actions. Because of its sheer size, even a lone Bullfrog will quickly exterminate native amphibians (and much other wildlife) from the pond where it is released. Consequently, conservationists are frequently obliged to catch and kill alien American Bullfrogs before they do too much damage.

EUROPEAN TREE FROG
⊙ ABOVE **adult**

AFRICAN CLAWED TOAD
⊙ ABOVE **adult**

AGILE FROG
⊙ ABOVE **adult**

MIDWIFE TOAD
⊙ ABOVE **adult**

AMERICAN BULLFROG
⊙ ABOVE **adult**

WILDLIFE-FRIENDLY GARDENS

There is a case for saying that conservation, like charity, begins at home, and what better way of putting this into practice than by creating a wildlife-friendly garden? Cynics may see it as merely a token gesture but the reality is that it can make a real difference, especially given the pressures on wildlife in the countryside at large. Of course, the range of species that can be encouraged is often limited and governed by the (usually) comparatively small space available.

Rather than focusing too exclusively on one particular group of animals (butterflies or birds, for example), try to think of the bigger picture and include plants, invertebrates and other forms of life in the

equation. As a result, wildlife generally will benefit, including any specific groups that you happen to be interested in, and you will end up with your own private nature reserve. However, for the purposes of this book, whose coverage is restricted to mammals, amphibians and reptiles, many of the specific suggestions relate to these groups. Because there are plenty of books on the subject, I have avoided covering gardening with birds in mind.

One approach is just to leave things alone and let nature take its course. And indeed, as a result, you are certain to end up with increased biodiversity, albeit in a setting that may come to resemble an impenetrable jungle rather than a garden. However, in most instances, gardeners want to

Most people are thrilled to discover that they are living with bats. Pipistrelles favour modern roof spaces while Brown Long-eared Bats (shown here) seem to prefer older properties.

enjoy the wildlife in an accessible way, so it is best to compromise and actually *garden* (that is, to encourage or remove certain things selectively) with wildlife in mind. In a sense this is no different from conventional gardening, except that the intention is to enhance the area for native wildlife species and not necessarily maximise floral display or vegetable production; of course, the two approaches are not altogether incompatible.

In order to create a wildlife-friendly environment you don't necessarily have to use the entire garden space. However, it is important not to use chemicals anywhere, or at the very least to avoid those designed to kill invertebrate 'pests' or plant 'weeds'. They are seldom as specific as manufacturers might have you believe and, besides which, many of the 'target' species can be thought of as actually beneficial, if wildlife in the broadest sense is considered. For example, insects such as aphids are food for all manner of predatory creatures; slugs and snails are eaten by shrews, hedgehogs and amphibians; and many so-called 'weed' plants are food for the caterpillars of a wide variety of moths. Of course, there are environmentally friendly ways in which some problem plant and animal species can be controlled. Generally speaking, however, it pays to redefine your gardening parameters and learn to live with, and tolerate, many of those plant diseases and insect infestations that do occur.

Hedgehogs will make significant inroads into your garden slug and snail populations, but they are quite partial to a saucer of bread and milk.

Many of the procedures for wildlife gardening are common sense but the following tips may be helpful:
- Create compost heaps and use the results as a natural soil improver.
- Never buy peat, quarried limestone pavement, or any other natural product that, when extracted on an industrial scale, damages the environment.
- If you need to get rid of twigs and branches then use a chipper and compost or mulch the results, in preference to lighting a bonfire. But if you do use the latter then check for Hedgehogs and other creatures before you ignite the pile.
- Plant native species wherever possible, especially when it comes to shrubs and hedges; just compare the number of native insects that feed on alien rhododendron (virtually zero) with native Hazel (hundreds).

○ Create 'neglected' corners as refuges for wildlife. Broken flowerpots can serve as daytime refuges for toads and old dustbin lids are ideal for Slow-worms and small mammals to hide under.

○ If you want to encourage butterflies and moths in particular, then research the food plants of their caterpillars and allow them to thrive, as well as providing nectar sources for the adults.

○ Before you rush to exterminate them, consider the valuable role played by wasps in the control of insects that you might otherwise think of as garden pests.

○ Consider extending your wildlife-friendly gardening approach to the house. Although the extent to which people are willing to go is limited (most find Brown Rats and mice to be unacceptable companions) always bear in mind that you may have bats in your loft or garage. Apart from anything else, there is now a legal obligation on home-owners to consider their well-being.

○ Create a pond for native wildlife if you have the space. Avoid stocking it with goldfish, or fish generally, since they will readily consume tadpoles and insect larvae. Remember to have plenty of terrestrial cover nearby because adult amphibians spend much of their lives on land. Occasionally, Common Frogs will spend some of the winter months at the bottom of the pond, taking up oxygen via their skins. If a layer of ice coats a small pond for any length of time there is a risk they will 'suffocate', for want of a better word. Try to keep the pond surface open to the air.

Leave refuges such as old dustbin lids in forgotten corners and you may encourage Slow-worms.

⊙ With the decline in small ponds in the countryside in general, those in gardens play a significant role in the survival of the Common Frog in many parts of the region.

ⓒ While domestic cats will certainly kill unwelcome garden visitors such as Rabbits and Brown Rats, you will never train them to avoid more desirable creatures selectively.

○ One of the best things you can do if you want to have a wildlife-friendly garden is not to have a cat, and to deter those belonging to neighbours. Really, there is almost no point in encouraging the likes of Slow-worms, frogs, small mammals and birds if you are going to allow access to the garden to cats: all you are doing then is providing them with a ready supply of things to kill, and in some cases, eat.

⊙ Like our other amphibians, Common Toads have to return to water to breed; garden ponds are important refuges in this context.

REPTILE WATCHING

British reptiles are always challenging animals to observe, partly because they are rather secretive but also owing to their habit of hibernating for a third of the year or more. However, understanding a little about their lives and biology can greatly improve chances of getting more than a fleeting glimpse of a disappearing tail.

Most of our reptile species emerge from hibernation and reappear onto the wildlife scene in March or April. Given that they rely on ambient heat (particularly directly from the sun), it is not surprising to find that they enjoy basking. And for the first few weeks after emergence from hibernation they are likely to spend several hours a day soaking up the sun's rays. In spring, it is usually easy to locate suitable sheltered, south-facing spots where Common Lizards or Adders like to bask. At this time of year, the reptiles are usually easier to approach than later in the season, when their elevated metabolism will mean they are far more active and inclined to avoid human encounters.

Like other British reptiles, Adders hibernate during the winter months. However, even as early as the beginning of March they will emerge from their winter dens to bask in the sunshine. It is not uncommon to see several animals entwined.

All our reptiles slough their skin on a regular basis. Given how secretive and wary some of our snakes are, the search for skins (which are usually sloughed intact) can be one of the best ways to discover their presence in a given area and, indeed, to gauge their population and size. This particular skin belonged to a 60cm-long Grass Snake.

To the litter-minded person it may seem like a strange concept, but reptile conservationists sometimes deliberately place sheets of corrugated plastic or iron, or roofing felt, in natural habitats to create refuges for reptiles. In other contexts, we would probably think of these objects as rubbish.

On dull days, and sometimes on days when the heat from the sun is too intense, some species – Slow-worms and Grass Snakes in particular – will seek refuge under natural fallen objects such as tree trunks, as well as man-made artefacts such as sheets of iron or even pieces of old carpet. With this in mind, herpetologists sometimes deliberately introduce foreign objects for the benefit of reptiles. If you have access to land that harbours reptiles, and you want to help and study them, you can always do this yourself. Do not undertake such a thing if there is a chance that the unwelcome attentions of other people will be attracted and, of course, you need to be mindful of the fine line you tread between benefiting reptiles and fly-tipping. It goes without saying that you need the permission of the landowner.

SEAL WATCHING

Although they are true marine mammals, seals are tied to the land in a manner not seen in cetaceans (whales and dolphins). Each day they bask out of water for extended periods of time and this give us, as terrestrial observers, the potential to get close to them. At some locations around Britain they are persecuted or, at the very least, actively discouraged, by those with commercial fishing interests; when this happens seals are understandably wary of people and difficult to observe. However, in places where this does not happen they are far more tolerant of being approached, and in a few sites where they are actively protected and encouraged they are positively indifferent to humans.

Probably the best-known and most organised seal-watching enterprises are those that visit Blakeney Point on the north Norfolk coast. A number of operators are involved and most embark in a coordinated fashion from Marston Quay, the departure times of trips dictated by the state of the tide. Although trippers' encounters with seals are restricted to just a few minutes, at their best the views of the seals are usually spectacularly close and the boats sometimes pass within a few metres of hauled-out animals. Both Common and Grey Seals are found around Blakeney, although the proportion of the two species varies throughout the year: typically, Greys are numerous in winter while Commons predominate in summer.

Probably the best location in our region for getting land-based views of seals is at Donna Nook on the Lincolnshire coast. In the lee of an RAF base, this national nature reserve supports large numbers of Grey Seals during the breeding season, mainly in autumn and early winter.

Elsewhere, hotspots for seal-watchers include the Farne Islands in Northumberland, where boat trips provide visitors with relatively close views of hauled-out Grey Seals. The encounters are relatively brief, however, because the trips are not specifically designed with seals in mind. Further north, many of the Orkney and Shetland islands have good seal populations (both species), and around the Pembrokeshire coast (and offshore islands) Grey Seals are relatively common and widespread too.

⊘ Boat trips around Blakeney in Norfolk provide visitors with some of the closest encounters with Grey Seals they are likely to get anywhere in the world.

⊘ In some locations, Grey Seals in particular are actively curious about human intruders into their domains.

WHALE BLOWS

Like all other mammals, whales and dolphins breathe air and have to come to the surface of the sea to replenish their oxygen supplies. When they exhale, larger cetacean species produce a conspicuous 'blow', sometimes referred to as a 'spout'. The blow is a cloud of condensed water vapour that is produced when the whale's warm breath comes into contact with cooler air. Blows can be used as a guide to whale identity. However, be warned they are not wholly reliable because blow height is difficult to judge at a distance, the blow varies throughout the duration of the exhalation, and it is influenced by wind speed and direction.

SPERM WHALE:
maximum height 5m

SEI WHALE:
maximum height 3m

HUMPBACK WHALE:
maximum height 3m

MINKE WHALE:
maximum height 1m

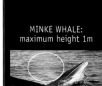

CETACEAN WATCHING

On the face of it, British and Irish seas, and the northeast Atlantic generally, are not the most promising of locations for the prospective cetacean watcher. Historically, the region was the first to suffer the depredations of the whaling industry, and exploitation during the 19th and 20th centuries was greater here than anywhere else in the world. As a consequence, numbers were decimated literally as well as figuratively. On top of that we have the weather to contend with: a combination of regular gales and the Atlantic swell mean that sea conditions are seldom ideal for observation.

Until comparatively recently, it is easy to understand why many people dismissed out of hand the prospect of seeing whales and dolphins on a regular basis in British and Irish waters. However, things have changed and today there is a very real prospect of being able to encounter these magnificent creatures for yourself and, in global terms at least, virtually on your doorstep. In part this is due to the fact that overall numbers of larger cetaceans are creeping up. But no small measure of thanks must go to the small band of British and Irish enthusiasts whose perseverance in the field has produced a better understanding of cetacean occurrence, distribution and habits in our region.

As a whale swims underwater, the force from its tail leaves a telltale 'fluke print' of calm sea at the surface.

FINS

As a whale or dolphin appears at the surface, the dorsal fin becomes visible and its size, particularly relative to the body as a whole, can be useful in identification.

| BLUE WHALE | FIN WHALE | MINKE WHALE | HUMPBACK WHALE |
| SPERM WHALE | KILLER WHALE | COMMON DOLPHIN | BOTTLENOSE DOLPHIN |

FIN WHALE:
maximum height 6m

BLUE WHALE: maximum height 10m

early stages of blow

A breaching Humpback Whale is a spectacular sight and one that will stay with the observer for the rest of his or her life.

Ferry-based whale watching is becoming increasingly popular, especially on routes that cross the Bay of Biscay from southern England.

Although land-based cetacean watching is a bit of a hit-and-miss affair, there are a few regions in Britain that are, to a degree, reliable hotspots. These include the following: west Cornwall and the Isles of Scilly (Common, Bottlenose, Atlantic White-sided and Risso's Dolphins, and Minke Whale); Hartland Point on the north Devon coast (Harbour Porpoise); the Moray Firth (Bottlenose Dolphin and Harbour Porpoise); Shetland and Orkney islands (Common Dolphin, Killer Whale and Long-finned Pilot Whale); the Hebrides (Minke Whale and Harbour Porpoise); the west and south coasts of Ireland (Bottlenose, Common and Risso's dolphins, and Fin and Minke Whales).

A few specific whale-watching companies operate around the British and Irish coasts, but an alternative boat-based option exists in the form of ferries. Services that cross the Irish Sea, between Cornwall and the Isles of Scilly, and which ply routes between mainland Scotland and the northern isles can be good. However, undoubtedly the most consistently reliable routes for cetacean spotting are those that operate between southern England and northern Spain. Indeed, specific whale-watching tours operate on the ferries at peak times. Do not expect the sort of close-up views that can be obtained elsewhere in the world: observations rely on chance encounters and tend to be fleeting and often distant. However, if you have never seen a whale or dolphin before, and are keen to see one in the northeast Atlantic, then such operations represent your best opportunity. (See p.220 for further details.)

Land-based observations of Minke Whales are the highlight of a visit to the Hebrides, although views are typically rather distant.

DEER WATCHING

In those parts of the region where they occur, our various deer species are typically the largest terrestrial mammals found living in the wild and, in many locations, they are among the most numerous. So, on the face of it, you might assume that observers stand a reasonable chance of getting good views of these animals. However, most deer are distinctly wary of people and spend much of the daylight hours in cover. Species the size of a Fallow Deer can be remarkably unobtrusive and even a small herd of these animals can blend in with its surroundings to a surprising degree. If you want to get more than a fleeting glimpse of a fleeing animal then knowledge of deer habits and behaviour can greatly improve your chances.

Deer have acute senses of smell, hearing and sight, the latter particularly honed when it comes to movement, so don't expect just to be able to walk up to them. In any case, unless you have approached from a downwind direction, and have been extremely stealthy, the chances are they will be aware of your presence even before they can see you.

One option is to sit yourself down in a concealed location (having taken into consideration wind direction, of course) before dawn, or in the late afternoon, perhaps at the margin of woodland from where deer are likely to emerge. Be sure not to break the horizon, or to move. Be warned, however, that in most parts of the country where deer are in any way numerous, people who want to shoot the deer rather than observe them will have the same idea. In some instances, observation from a car can be a suitable (and warmer) alternative, and it does allow you the luxury of being able to change location more easily – deer are less likely to be spooked by a moving car than a person on foot.

In relatively undisturbed areas of woodland, it is sometimes possible to get extremely good views of Roe Deer. Typically, the best opportunities are had in late winter and early spring when, in deciduous areas, there are no leaves on the trees. If you spot a deer, resist the temptation to stop and stare – this will simply alarm the animal and cause it to flee. But if you maintain your direction and speed, in many cases the deer will simply stare back at you and stay put. It goes without saying, if you want a close encounter with deer, then the worst thing you can do is take a dog with you. Even if it remains under control, the scent will be enough to instil panic in the deer.

In late winter and early spring, Roe Deer will often stand their ground and stare at human observers, so long as nothing is done to startle them.

When it comes to Red and Fallow Deer, you stand the best chance of getting good views of wild-living animals during the autumn rut. With both species, males announce their intentions with roaring calls that are audible from a considerable distance. Because the animals are distracted, observers can get surprisingly close – but don't try to get *too* close!

Seen as cheating by purists, a visit to a deer park can provide amazing views of these magnificent animals. One of the best-known sites is Richmond Park, on the fringes of London, where both Red (shown here) and Fallow Deer can be found; their numbers are managed by selective culling.

There can be few more impressive sights on the British and Irish wildlife scene than that of a rutting Red Deer stag.

BADGER WATCHING

The Badger is a distinctive and fascinating member of our mammal fauna. It is a sociable animal that lives in extended family groups, and Badger society is largely governed by complex patterns of behaviour and intriguing – to our eyes, often comical – social interactions. Almost all activity – at least that which takes place above ground – occurs after dark. However, by careful planning human observers can gain thrilling insights into their nocturnal behaviour by observing them at dusk.

Badgers are partial to peanuts and can sometimes be lured to feeding stations, well away from their setts, for close observation.

The first important point to make about Badger watching is that it should be undertaken only at sites where you have the landowner's permission. It is also vital that you, as an observer, should be able to approach and leave the site with a minimum of noise; apart from anything else, wilful disturbance of Badgers is an offence in law. You should also ensure that your presence and activities are not likely to attract unwelcome interest from people who might not have the best of intentions towards the Badgers. With this in mind, it is unfortunately important to emphasise that you should not assume that everyone else, landowners included, will share your enthusiasm for Badgers (*see* p.26). Sometimes, it may be best to leave the sett unwatched and keep other people in ignorance about the animals' presence.

Assuming you have fulfilled the above criteria, you need to survey the area during daylight. Do so from a distance with the aid of binoculars, however, to avoid disturbing the Badgers – they will undoubtedly hear and smell you if you go too close. You need to find a partially hidden spot, probably no closer than 25m to the sett entrance, that is not on one of the regularly Badger trails that radiate from the sett. You will also need to be able to approach silently so it is a good idea to sweep your approach route to remove rustling leaves and twigs that will snap.

An unwritten rule of Badger watching is that you should avoid disturbing the animals at all cost (you will see very little if you do). So you must arrive before they emerge, they should be unaware of your presence when they appear, and your departure should be delayed until after they have left to forage for food. Consequently, you should only consider Badger watching on evenings when the wind is in the right direction – in other words, blowing your scent *away* from the sett. If conditions are suitable, be in place at least an hour before sunset. Wear dark, soft clothing (not material that will rustle) and position yourself so that you can watch the comings and goings without moving.

Typically, if disturbance has been avoided then the Badgers will emerge about 20–30 minutes after sunset. They usually spend the next quarter of an hour or so interacting with one another, playing, and using nearby latrines. Thereafter, they usually amble off in search of food, and after this has happened (it is usually pitch-black by then) it is time for you to depart. Avoid using torches when you leave.

Keen Badger watchers sometimes build elevated viewing platforms, which have the advantages of offering a grandstand view and reducing the risk of human scent wafting over the sett. However, this option is only worth considering if the site is secure – both from the point of view of the Badgers, and in terms of vandalism.

A well-constructed viewing platform affords the Badger watcher a degree of comfort – sometimes even the luxury of a chair!

STUDYING AND HELPING BATS

Bats are essentially nocturnal mammals and typically lead unobtrusive lives during the hours of daylight. Consequently, many people are almost unaware of their existence in the British and Irish countryside and a surprising number of naturalists barely give them more than just a passing glance. That bats are difficult to watch, or at least to observe well, is not in doubt. However, there are ways in which the study of this fascinating group can be made more successful and rewarding, and an increased awareness of unique aspects of their biology and behaviour will only serve to increase their allure.

Sites chosen for roosting vary according to the species involved, but many favour locations such as hollow trees, caves, old mine shafts and the roofs and cellars of rural buildings. Many of the best locations are physically protected (for example, by metal grilles) against vandalism or disturbance, and

when visiting such locations you should never contribute to the bats' plight in any way (wilful disturbance of all bat species is an offence in law). However, it is possible to watch them in an unobtrusive manner when they emerge at dusk, and one of the best options is to lie on the ground so that the emerging bats are silhouetted against the night sky. Some species are more crepuscular than others and will take to the wing while a glimmer of light remains on the horizon.

Pipistrelles and other bats can sometimes be observed catching insects around outside lights, particularly if these are sited close to tree foliage.

Although many bat roosts are easily overlooked, species such as Noctule Bats sometimes inadvertently advertise their presence where their urine and faeces leave a stain around the entrance.

Bats feed on night-flying insects and so it is no surprise to discover that certain species – Common Pipistrelles and Brown Long-eared Bats in particular – often concentrate their attentions around outside lights, to which moths especially are attracted. Taking the principle one stage further, moth traps that use UV light sources are frequently excellent locations to watch feeding bats in action, often to the complete dismay of the lepidopterists to whom the traps belong.

Bats are remarkable in a number of ways, but their flying abilities, and particularly in pitch darkness, sets them apart. The latter skill depends upon their ability to echolocate – they emit high-pitched sounds that bounce off objects around them; the sounds are interpreted by the bat's brain to create a three-dimensional impression of the world around them. Bat echolocation sounds are, in the main, inaudible to the human ear, but so-called 'bat detectors' can be purchased and these modify the sounds so that we can hear them – typically, as a series of squelchy clicks. The frequency at which the sounds are uttered (this information is yielded by the detector) and the way in which they are delivered gives a clue to identity. Some species are easier to identify than others, but in many cases other factors have to be taken into consideration. And, if they are honest about it, even experienced users of bat detectors rely on educated guesswork to assign the caller's identity on many occasions.

Bat detectors give observers insights into the animals' behaviour and numbers. Certain identification of species is not always possible and experience counts for a lot.

Bats are under threat and need all the friends they can get these days. One thing that individuals can do is to make bat boxes for the animals to roost in. Use the plan shown here, and remember to use untreated wood in the construction. Although bat boxes can be placed on the side of a house (away from direct sun) it is more usual to fix them to trees. Site them well out of harm's way with the aid of a ladder; the greatest chances of occupancy come if three are sited close to one another on the east, north and west sides of

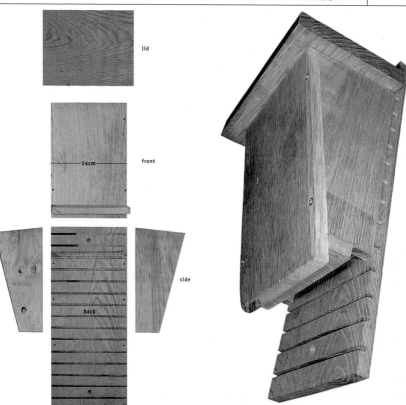

⊗ The component parts of a bat box, ready to assemble.

⊙ A finished bat box.

⊘ For optimum occupancy, place three bat boxes under the shade of the tree canopy, facing east, north and west.

the trunk. Because of the law, once in place, bat boxes can be inspected only by licensed bat workers.

In recognition of their plight, bats are protected by an array of British and European laws. Nowadays, not only are the animals themselves protected, but it is also an offence to disturb or destroy bat roosts, whether or not they are occupied. It is also illegal to attempt to remove bats from dwellings, without prior consultation from the relevant statutory nature conservation organisation, except where they have taken up residence in the living space of the home. In theory, offenders could face imprisonment or a fine of up to £5,000 per disturbed or killed bat. So if you see an offence being committed do not hesitate to report the matter to the police immediately. Perhaps more importantly, if you discover a new roosting site for bats then report its location to your local Wildlife Trust or bat conservation group.

STUDYING SMALL MAMMALS

The term 'small mammal' has no strict meaning in the biological sense, but most naturalists take it to be the loose collection that comprises our species of voles and mice (rodents) and shrews (insectivores). Members of the group lead rather unobtrusive lives and go largely unnoticed by most people but, nevertheless, in many parts of the region they are among the most numerous of all our mammals. Indeed, their numbers are such that they underpin the breeding success or otherwise of a wide range of mammalian and avian predators. So, their significance to British and Irish ecology alone makes them worthy of interest. Furthermore, their varied approaches to survival mean they are fascinating in their own right and with just a little bit of effort even the novice animal watcher can gain insights into their brief lives.

For much of the time, our small mammals are rather secretive, mainly nocturnal, or both, which makes them hard to observe. Shrews, which for the most part forage in dense undergrowth, are a particular challenge. However, people with good hearing can sometimes detect their shrill calls and a bat detector can come in handy in this respect too. Of our three mainland species, the Water Shrew is the one you are most likely (perhaps *least unlikely* is a better way of putting it) to encounter during the daylight hours, particularly if you sit quietly beside an unpolluted stream or watercress bed.

Ⓐ Field Vole nests and tunnels can sometimes be discovered by turning over fallen planks of wood lying in grassy areas.

Ⓒ Wood Mice, and some other small mammals, can sometimes be tempted out of cover by baiting a spot with nuts and sunflower seeds. Indeed, they will often forage beneath bird tables, after dark, picking up fallen scraps.

A more hands-on approach to studying small mammals involves live-trapping, and a range of proprietary makes and models is available on the market. Probably the most familiar is the metal Longworth trap, which comprises a tunnel and trapdoor that lead to a chamber in which bedding (dry grass) and food bait can be placed. A similar principle applies in the case of clear plastic trip-traps; although these are much cheaper than Longworths, they are less robust and on a couple of occasions I have known Yellow-necked Mice to nibble their way out in the space of a few hours.

A Longworth trap set for small mammals.

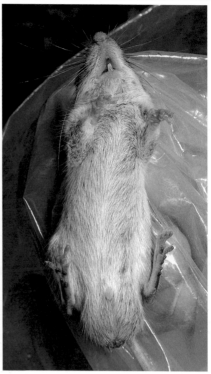

Because you will have no idea of the contents of a tripped Longworth trap, the best option is to open and empty it inside a large, clear plastic bag.

If you want to take a close look at a small mammal, to decide on its identity or gender perhaps, then either place it in a clear tank or, if you are in the field, 'scruff' it by holding the skin on the back of the neck. However, this potentially harmful procedure should only be undertaken by, or under the supervision of, an experienced small-mammal handler.

Regardless of which option is chosen, the idea is to place the trap in, or close to, a small mammal run so that passing animals are lured inside by the prospect of food. Once trapped, the food is eaten by the captured mammal and the bedding can be used to make a temporary nest for warmth. If you take these precautions, almost all captured animals will survive quite happily until their release. However, the occasional mortality will undoubtedly occur from time to time so, if you are unwilling to accept this risk, do not get involved with small-mammal trapping.

Before you site your small-mammal traps, be sure to number them and make a list and sketch map of where they are being placed. Ideally, tie a piece of coloured string onto a twig in the vicinity of each trap to make finding them easy – you will be amazed how easy it is to misplace them. Trapping should never be undertaken if there is the slightest risk of them being disturbed or vandalised by other people.

Generally speaking, the target species for small-mammal trapping are mice and voles, and as a consequence the typical food bait would comprise a segment of apple and some wild birdseed. On occasions, however, shrews will wander in and become trapped. Bear in mind that it is illegal to trap shrews intentionally (without a licence), but if you feel there is any risk of accidental entrapment then a small portion – say, half a teaspoon – of cat food is an essential addition to the contents of the trap; in desperation most shrews will eat this to avoid starvation while in the trap. However, despite this, shrews quickly die without proper sustenance, and so, in locations where shrews are known to occur, traps should not be deployed unless they can be checked every few hours. It is a good idea to site the traps where their entrances are visible from a distance; in this way you will not need to disturb the trap to discover whether or not the door has been tripped.

DORMOUSE CONSERVATION

Among our small mammals, naturalists have singled out the Hazel Dormouse for special attention and its image is frequently used as an icon for nature conservation. In part, it generates so much interest because it is genuinely scarce and endangered. Furthermore, it has such precise habitat requirements that, in many parts of its range, the long-term survival of the species depends to a large extent on the actions of humans. But the Dormouse's ability to strike an emotional chord in people cannot be denied. In part, the animal's vulnerability, as a hibernating animal, has instant appeal but perhaps more than anything else, it is because it is just plain 'cute'.

You are most unlikely ever to come across a Dormouse by chance. Because they never willingly cross open ground, they are seldom, if ever, caught in conventionally sited small-mammal traps. Which is just

⊘ Few can resist the appeal of the Dormouse's large, beady eyes.

as well because the species is protected by the law. Ironically, however, although it is extremely difficult to observe in nature, it is probably the easiest of all our small mammals to help and study, and specially constructed Dormouse boxes are a great aid.

A Dormouse box resembles a conventional bird box in many respects, except that the entrance hole faces the trunk of the tree or shrub to which it is attached instead of being open to the elements. Baffles ensure that there is a narrow gap between the back of the box and the trunk, the intention being to allow Dormice to enter but to discourage birds; however, this avian deterrent does not always work.

Before you undertake a Dormouse box scheme, it is important to determine whether the species really is present in the woodland you have in mind. So search for evidence in the form of stripped honeysuckle bark (used for nests), cut honeysuckle flowers (a source of nectar) and

⊘ If you are keen to monitor Dormouse populations, and use a box scheme as part of this, then it is a relatively straightforward matter to obtain training and subsequently a licence to handle the animals. Contact the Mammal Society or PTES for further details (see p.220 for contact details).

☾ During the summer months, Dormice spend the hours of daylight in a state of torpor and, under licence, this is when researchers choose to study them.

⊙ The component parts of a dormouse box, ready to assemble.

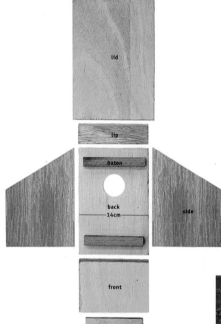

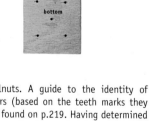

⊙ A completed Dormouse box.

⊙ The ideal location for the box is in a mature coppiced clump of Hazel. First of all, fix a wire loop to a nail in the main trunk, then slip the box through the loop and secure it with another nail.

nibbled hazelnuts. A guide to the identity of rodent nibblers (based on the teeth marks they leave) can be found on p.219. Having determined that there is good evidence for the presence of Dormice it is time to build a few boxes, and a flat plan design is shown above; the component parts can be joined together easily using screws.

Most animals will have emerged from hibernation by May and so it is a good idea to have the box in place by early April. Although a few Dormice will occupy boxes soon after their emergence from hibernation, typically the main occupancy occurs in the summer months and females often build maternity nests inside and give birth to their young. Unless you have a Dormouse licence, resist the urge to examine the boxes at this time of year because, apart from the disturbance you may cause, it is illegal to disrupt the animal's lives knowingly.

LARGE SKULLS, BONES AND ANTLERS   APPROX. SCALE: 15% LIFESIZE

Although a few people may find the sight of skulls rather off-putting, for most naturalists they are a fascinating part of animal biology. Being so robust and well constructed, mammal skulls in particular usually remain intact long after the death of an animal. Similarly, larger bones and antlers (the latter, where they are not eaten by the deer themselves) persist. Consequently, they are frequently discovered in the countryside and, in some cases, they can provide us with useful insights into the presence of certain species.

COMMON PORPOISE LENGTH 25cm

GREY SEAL LENGTH 24cm

HORSE LENGTH 50cm

GREEN TURTLE LENGTH 18cm
(SIMILAR TO LEATHERBACK TURTLE)

COW LENGTH 42cm

SHEEP LENGTH 23cm

MUNTJAC LENGTH 14cm

ROE DEER
SKULL LENGTH 20cm
ANTLER LENGTH 20cm

DEER ANTLERS
① APPROX. SCALE: 20% LIFESIZE

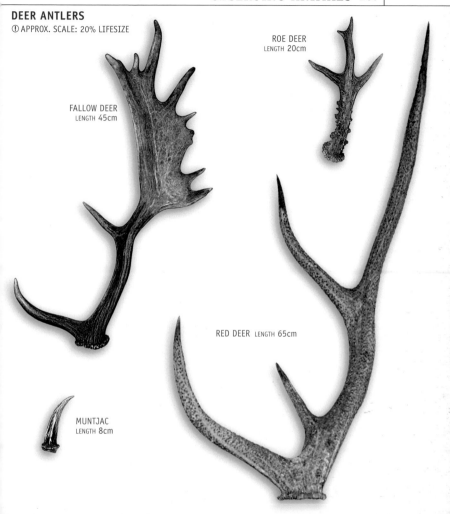

ROE DEER
LENGTH 20cm

FALLOW DEER
LENGTH 45cm

RED DEER LENGTH 65cm

MUNTJAC
LENGTH 8cm

MARINE FINDS
Once in a while large cetaceans, such as this Sperm Whale, are washed up on our shores. They present a wonderful, if rather smelly, opportunity for the naturalist to examine these animals at close quarters.

Despite the ravages of wave action and sea water, the bony remains of whales often persist for quite some time on the seashore. This Minke Whale vertebra would be a particular prize for the beachcomber.

This curious object is the vertebral disc of a dolphin. Sadly, with the rise in cetacean numbers killed by the fishing industry, such finds are becoming increasingly common.

MEDIUM-SIZED SKULLS APPROX. SCALE: 45% LIFESIZE

Study the structure and dentition of the following medium-sized animal skulls and you will gain an insight into the animals' habits and lifestyles. Pronounced canine teeth and molar and premolar teeth with cutting edges are indicative, in most cases, of a carnivorous diet and exclusively predatory habits; being an omnivore, the Badger is an exception to this rule. With lagomorphs and rodents, which have a mainly herbivorous diet, look for the striking incisor teeth at the front, and the gap between these and the grinding teeth at the back of the mouth.

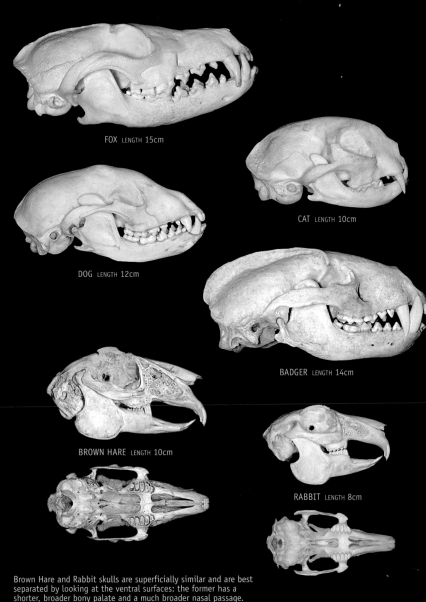

FOX LENGTH 15cm

CAT LENGTH 10cm

DOG LENGTH 12cm

BADGER LENGTH 14cm

BROWN HARE LENGTH 10cm

RABBIT LENGTH 8cm

Brown Hare and Rabbit skulls are superficially similar and are best separated by looking at the ventral surfaces: the former has a shorter, broader bony palate and a much broader nasal passage.

SMALL SKULLS APPROX. SCALE: 80% LIFESIZE

Despite their small size and rather delicate construction, the skulls of small mammals are occasionally found intact. As with larger animals, their dentition and overall structure provide clues about the diet and lifestyle of the previous owner. In many cases, their appearance is unique enough to allow certain identification to take place even in the absence of other evidence.

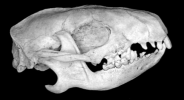

HEDGEHOG LENGTH 5.6cm

COMMON SHREW LENGTH 2cm

LESSER WHITE-TOOTHED SHREW LENGTH 1.6cm

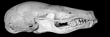

MOLE LENGTH 3.2cm

POLECAT LENGTH 6.5cm

WEASEL LENGTH 3.2cm

MINK LENGTH 6cm

STOAT LENGTH 5cm

GREY SQUIRREL LENGTH 6cm

BROWN RAT LENGTH 5cm

SHORT-TAILED VOLE LENGTH 2.2cm

OWL PELLETS

Small mammals are extremely important in the diets of many predators. In the case of mammalian predators, such as Foxes and Weasels, the prey is, to a degree, dissected and chewed before it is swallowed. The digestive process completes the process so that, except to an expert eye, what comes out the other end is largely unrecognisable in terms of its dietary constituents. However, in the case of avian predators, notably owls, a different process is involved. Voles and mice are swallowed whole, the bodies are then partially broken down in the crop, and the indigestible remains (mainly fur and bones) are regurgitated in the form of pellets. These accumulate at favoured roost sites and can be collected by naturalists for further investigation. Because the bones remain largely intact, it is usually possible to determine the identity and number of prey animals involved. It is not hard to imagine how such information can be a valuable aid when studying the relationship between predators and prey.

Having collected a pellet, the best approach is to soak it in warm water to which a couple of drops of washing-up liquid have been added. If anyone is feeling squeamish at this point it is worth remembering that owl pellets, unlike mammalian droppings, are virtually odour-free and their contents relatively inert. After half an hour or so, you will be able to tease the pellet apart; in fact it will probably have fallen apart of its own accord. With tweezers, gently remove the bones that appear and allow them to dry before closer examination.

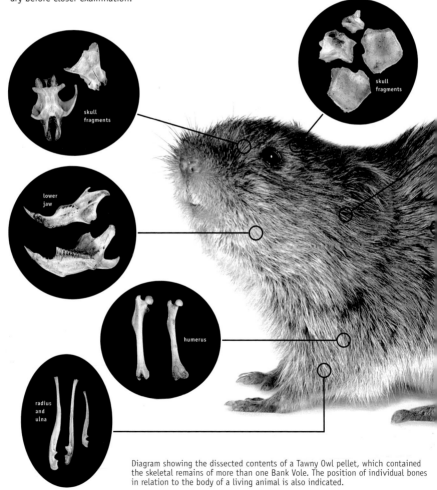

skull fragments

skull fragments

lower jaw

humerus

radius and ulna

Diagram showing the dissected contents of a Tawny Owl pellet, which contained the skeletal remains of more than one Bank Vole. The position of individual bones in relation to the body of a living animal is also indicated.

Like other avian pellets, that of a Tawny Owl contains the indigestible remains of prey animals in compacted form.

Tawny Owls rely almost exclusively on small mammals for food.

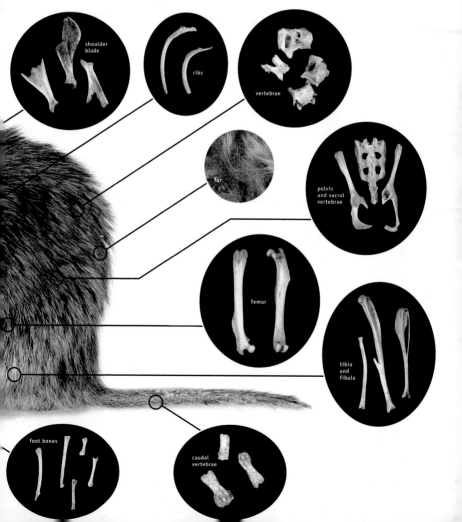

shoulder blade

ribs

vertebrae

fur

pelvis and sacral vertebrae

femur

tibia and fibula

foot bones

caudal vertebrae

RODENT TEETH AND SKULLS   APPROX. SCALE: LIFESIZE

If you examine owl pellets on a regular basis you will soon amass a large collection of small rodent bones. Those from the limbs or backbone usually require an expert eye to assign species identity with any degree of certainty. With skulls though it is a different matter, as each species possesses unique characters, the dentition of the grinding teeth (molars and premolars) being key among them. These features remain obvious despite the fact that, after a skull has been through an owl's crop, it is often in fragments. Armed with the knowledge of what to look for, almost anyone will be able to identify a mystery rodent skull using nothing more sophisticated than a hand-lens.

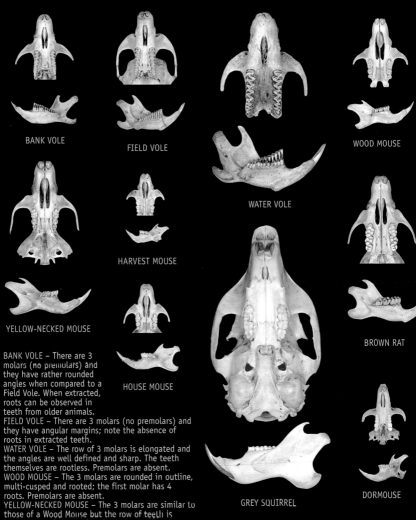

BANK VOLE

FIELD VOLE

WOOD MOUSE

WATER VOLE

HARVEST MOUSE

YELLOW-NECKED MOUSE

BROWN RAT

HOUSE MOUSE

DORMOUSE

GREY SQUIRREL

BANK VOLE – There are 3 molars (no premolars) and they have rather rounded angles when compared to a Field Vole. When extracted, roots can be observed in teeth from older animals.
FIELD VOLE – There are 3 molars (no premolars) and they have angular margins; note the absence of roots in extracted teeth.
WATER VOLE – The row of 3 molars is elongated and the angles are well defined and sharp. The teeth themselves are rootless. Premolars are absent.
WOOD MOUSE – The 3 molars are rounded in outline, multi-cusped and rooted; the first molar has 4 roots. Premolars are absent.
YELLOW-NECKED MOUSE – The 3 molars are similar to those of a Wood Mouse but the row of teeth is longer. Premolars are absent.
HARVEST MOUSE – The 3 molars are small, with a rounded outline. The first molar has 5 roots. Premolars are absent.
DORMOUSE – There are 3 molars and 1 premolar; all are unique (by rodent standards) in appearance, having a smooth surface that looks as though it has been polished with a grindstone. Note the transverse, not irregular, lines.
HOUSE MOUSE – The molars are rounded and broadly similar to those of other mice species. However, the third molar is proportionately much smaller than its neighbours, and the first molar has 3 roots. Premolars are absent.
BROWN RAT – There are 3 molars, all rather rounded in outline; premolars are absent.
GREY SQUIRREL – There are 3 molars and 1 premolar, all of which are rooted.

HARVEST MOUSE
LENGTH 3MM

WOOD MOUSE
LENGTH 4MM

YELLOW-NECKED MOUSE
LENGTH 5MM

HOUSE MOUSE
LENGTH 4MM

FIELD VOLE
LENGTH 6MM

BANK VOLE
LENGTH 6MM

WATER VOLE
LENGTH 10MM

DORMOUSE
LENGTH 4MM

APPROX. SCALE:
3.5× LIFESIZE

BROWN RAT
LENGTH 7MM

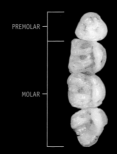

PREMOLAR

MOLAR

GREY SQUIRREL
LENGTH 10MM

⊘ For the sake of clarity, the grinding teeth isolated from the upper right jaws of our native small rodents are shown here side by side. Note that in the Grey Squirrel and Dormouse, these grinding teeth comprise 1 premolar (the top tooth in their respective illustrations) plus 3 premolars. In all the other rodent species shown here, premolars are absent and the grinding teeth comprise just 3 molars. The teeth are shown to scale, on the assumption that they come from adult animals. It must be borne in mind that the age of any given rodent will have a bearing on its size and hence the size of its teeth.

◇ A rodent's incisor teeth grow throughout its life. The exposed cutting edge may appear relatively short but by removing one of this Grey Squirrel's incisors from its socket (easily done in most rodents) its true extent is revealed.

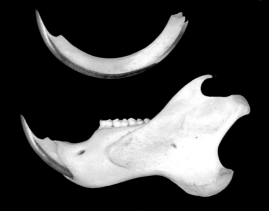

MAMMAL DROPPINGS

The study of mammal faeces is, understandably, not an area that attracts armies of enthusiastic naturalists and there's no getting away from the fact that, at times, it can be distinctly unpleasant. However, mammal dropping can provide a valuable insight into the diet of many animals and, more importantly, their size, shape and colour are often unique enough to allow accurate identification to be made of the species that produced them. As such, they are valuable tools in the modern naturalist's armoury.

With many species, the study of droppings is simply one of many that can be used in the context of surveys. However, in the case of some secretive and rare animals, the search for droppings can represent the only realistic prospect of detecting their presence in a given area. On occasions, they can be valuable quantitative tools when it comes to surveying, particularly since some animals deposit droppings in conspicuous locations as a means of defining their territorial boundaries. Although fascinating, the study of droppings does have unpleasant connotations and the reality is that it is sometimes a smelly occupation. So, be thankful that this is not a scratch-and-sniff book!

DEER DROPPINGS

Wander through woodland or across open country and sooner or later you are likely to come across droppings produced by one or more of our deer species. However, to confuse matters, a number other ruminant animals (some of which are domesticated) produce droppings that are broadly similar. The following samples are some of the most frequently encountered. But it is important to bear in mind, on the principle of 'you are what you eat', that diet can have a striking effect on the appearance of droppings. As a result, in the space available, it is impossible to be entirely comprehensive.

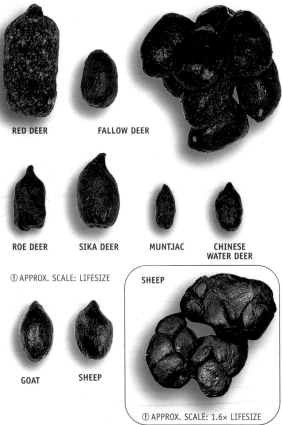

RED DEER   **FALLOW DEER**

ROE DEER   **SIKA DEER**   **MUNTJAC**   **CHINESE WATER DEER**

ⓘ APPROX. SCALE: LIFESIZE

SHEEP

GOAT   **SHEEP**

ⓘ APPROX. SCALE: 1.6× LIFESIZE

RED DEER LENGTH 30mm – Usually rather cylindrical, but pointed at one end, producing a somewhat acorn-like appearance.
FALLOW DEER LENGTH 16mm – Often rather ovoid in shape, but variably pointed at one end and indented at the other.
FALLOW DEER HEIGHT 40mm – Depending on the diet at the time, sometimes the individual droppings stick together in a clump.
ROE DEER LENGTH 17mm – Rather cylindrical in overall shape but distinctly pointed at one end and indented at the other. Usually scattered on the ground.
SIKA DEER LENGTH 20mm – Typically rather ovoid in shape but indented at one end and pointed at the other, the point often curving over.
MUNTJAC LENGTH 12mm – Small and cylindrical in shape, pointed at one end and indented at the other.
CHINESE WATER DEER LENGTH 13mm – Usually ovoid in overall shape but pointed at one end and slightly indented at the other.
GOAT LENGTH 16mm – Rather ovoid in shape but often slightly pointed at one end.
SHEEP LENGTH 16mm – Usually ovoid to spherical in shape but usually pointed at one end.
SHEEP – Depending on diet, sometimes individual droppings stick together to form a clump.

OTHER DROPPINGS

The droppings of some small to medium-sized mammals disintegrate rapidly, or are produced in locations where they are unlikely to be discovered. However, with many species they are encountered on a regular basis and, indeed, some are likely to be on prominent display.

A. RABBIT LENGTH 12mm – Spherical and fibrous. Often deposited on bare, conspicuous patches of ground as territorial markers.

B. BROWN HARE LENGTH 15mm – Spherical and fibrous. Often deposited in piles in favoured feeding areas.

C. MOUNTAIN HARE LENGTH 14mm – Spherical and fibrous. Often deposited in piles.

D. BROWN RAT LENGTH 18mm – Ovoid, but usually distinctly pointed at one end.

E. GREY SQUIRREL LENGTH 18mm– Ovoid and fibrous. Fresh droppings sometimes appear slightly greenish.

F. HOUSE MOUSE LENGTH 3mm – Small, irregularly cylindrical to ovoid, and friable. Often deposited in small piles.

G. WOOD MOUSE LENGTH 5mm – Irregularly ovoid to cylindrical.

H. YELLOW-NECKED MOUSE LENGTH 6mm – Irregularly ovoid to cylindrical. Larger than those of Wood Mouse.

I. FIELD VOLE LENGTH 4mm – Irregularly cylindrical to sausage-shaped. Often deposited in piles beside runways. Fresh droppings often appear greenish.

J. BANK VOLE LENGTH 5mm – Irregularly cylindrical to sausage-shaped.

K. WATER VOLE LENGTH 12mm – Cylindrical to sausage-shaped. Deposited in piles, at waterside locations, as territorial markers.

L. COMMON PIPISTRELLE LENGTH 4mm – Small, friable and superficially similar to mouse droppings. Insect remains are often visible.

M. HEDGEHOG LENGTH 40mm – Irregularly cylindrical to sausage-shaped. Often contain beetle wing-cases and other insect remains.

N. PINE MARTEN LENGTH 100mm – Cylindrical, tapering and pointed at the ends. Typically deposited in prominent spots as territorial markers.

O. MINK LENGTH 70mm – Cylindrical, tapering and pointed at the ends. Typically deposited in prominent spots (e.g. on rocks beside water) as territorial markers. Smell is unpleasant, pungent and slightly rancid. By comparison, Otter droppings (often found in similar locations) are sweet, almost pleasant-smelling; they are extremely friable and disintegrate quickly. See p.136.

P. STOAT LENGTH 120mm – Cylindrical and tapering, with twisted points at the ends. Prey remains (fur and bone fragments) are often visible.

Q. WEASEL LENGTH 50mm – Cylindrical and tapering, with twisted points at the ends. Prey remains (fur and bone fragments) often visible.

R. FOX LENGTH 60mm – Cylindrical, tapering at both ends and superficially dog-like. However, prey remains (e.g. fur, feathers and bone fragments) are often visible. Usually deposited in conspicuous places (such as on a grass tussock) as territorial markers. Fresh droppings are usually dark and have a pungent 'foxy' smell; they bleach with age.

S. DOG LENGTH 120mm – Cylindrical, tapering at the ends and often appearing almost segmented. Fresh droppings are accompanied by a deeply unpleasant smell. Size depends on breed of dog. Often deposited in piles beside, or on, tracks and paths.

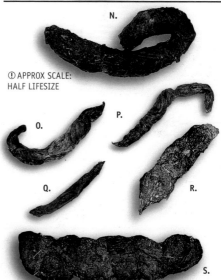

① APPROX. SCALE: LIFESIZE

① APPROX SCALE: HALF LIFESIZE

On occasions, the droppings of certain bird species, such as this Pheasant, can have rather mammalian qualities.

TRACKS, TRAILS AND SIGNS

It is amazing how much information can be gleaned about the mammals present in our countryside simply by looking for tracks, trails and signs. At the basic level, in the case of the larger animals, it is usually possible to determine the identity of the animal that made the track. But in addition, other signs of life, such as hair, are sometimes left behind and in some cases traits of animal behaviour are indicated by the clues they leave.

⊙ Badger hair sometimes gets snagged in barbed wire or on bramble sprays. The hairs are pale at the base and tip, but dark in the middle.

⊙ Heavy falls of snow provide an excellent opportunity for the naturalist to gain an insight into the activities of otherwise shy or nocturnal species. The tracks shown here were made by a Rabbit.

⊙ So-called rutting rings, formed in this case by a Roe Deer chasing prospective mates around a fixed point, are a conspicuous sign of the species' presence in an area of woodland.

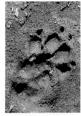

Soft mud and sand is usually the best medium for the formation and preservation of good-quality tracks. The soil needs to be damp, of course, but not water-logged. Unsurprisingly, the autumn and winter months usually offer the best opportunities for finding tracks.

ⓘ APPROX SCALE: 30% LIFESIZE

ⓒ **DOG** LENGTH DEPENDENT ON BREED
One of the most commonly encountered tracks on land to which the public and their pets have access. Track size depends upon breed of dog. Note the 4 toes and the presence of visible claw marks in clean prints.

ⓒ **CAT** LENGTH 3cm
Prints are rounded in overall appearance with 4 toes. Because the claws are retractable, no marks are visible.

ⓒ **RABBIT** LENGTH 3cm
Tracks are characterised by long prints left by the hind feet and smaller, rounded ones formed by front feet; these often appear on top of one another in slow-moving animals

FOX LENGTH 4.5cm
Tracks are more oval than those of a dog. Note the 4 toes and presence of claw marks. Typically, tracks follow a straight line.

BADGER LENGTH 6cm
Prints are broad with 5 toes and conspicuous claw marks.

SIKA LENGTH 5.5cm
Similar to Fallow Deer but typically broader.

FALLOW DEER LENGTH 5.5cm
Relatively narrow slots that are usually more or less parallel to one another.

RED DEER LENGTH 8cm
Slots are relatively long and often splay outwards towards the tip.

ⓒ **ROE DEER** LENGTH 4cm
Rather dainty tracks, which comprise slots that are broad-based but distinctly pointed at the tip.

ⓓ **MUNTJAC** LENGTH 2cm
Tiny prints with slots that are proportionately narrower than in Roe Deer.

SHEEP LENGTH 4cm
Track could be confused with those of medium-sized deer. Depending on the speed of movement of the animal, the tips are sometimes slightly splayed.

GOAT LENGTH 4cm
Tracks are relatively narrow, the slots often touching at the base but cloven at the tip.

HORSE LENGTH 15cm
The imprint of an unshod horse or pony is almost unmistakable given the unique shape of the single toe on which the animal stands.

COW LENGTH 15cm
Usually unmistakable on account of the size. Note that the 2 slots usually abut one another.

ⓘ APPROX SCALE: 20% LIFESIZE

NESTS AND HOMES

Although some of our larger terrestrial mammals do not use homes or refuges in the accepted sense, many medium-sized and small mammals do. In some species, an underground setting is favoured – an excavated tunnel perhaps – and whether any bedding or a special nest is employed depends upon the species involved. Being subterranean, however, these are seldom discovered. However, three species of rodents do construct nests that are found on a regular basis in the countryside and each is unique enough for certain identification to made (*see* the illustrations below).

Ⓒ The refuge used by an Otter is called a holt. The entrance to its riverside home is often made more obvious by the presence of a mud-slide running from the burrow mouth to the water's edge.

⊙ A Harvest Mouse nest is a miraculous construction of grass stems and leaves, not much bigger than a tennis ball. It is woven among the swaying stems of grassland vegetation and, being sited off the ground, this means that it goes undetected by many terrestrial predators.

⊙ The winter nest of a Dormouse is usually located underground, often among the tangle of roots at the base of a tree. It is constructed from dry leaves, woven grass stems and stripped honeysuckle bark.

⊙ The summer nest of a Dormouse is typically constructed in a tangle of Honeysuckle, and stripped bark from this climbing plant is the main component of the nest itself. The nests are surprisingly difficult to spot and often only become visible once the leaves have fallen from the trees in early winter. By this time, the Dormice will have moved elsewhere to hibernate.

A Grey Squirrel's nest is called a drey and is often sited in the fork of a branch, high in the tree canopy. It is relatively large, the outer layers being made of twined twigs and stems; fresh greenery is often visible.

NIBBLED NUTS AND OTHER SIGNS

The sizes of their mouths, and the structure of their skulls and teeth, influence the ways in which different rodent species tackle the task of nibbling and gnawing. In many instances, their teeth leave conspicuous marks on the remains of their food and sometimes these are easy to discern with the naked eye.

Many tree and shrub species serve as sources of food for rodents but one in particular – the Hazel – stands out because of the importance of its nut in the diet of many woodland species. Five rodent species eagerly gnaw open the hazelnut's hard case to extract its nutritious contents. Each leaves telltale and diagnostic marks on the nut's empty shell (*see* below). These can be discerned with comparative ease using a hand-lens and this line of study is a useful tool for those interested in woodland mammals. Of course, it is most significant in the detection of the rare and endangered Dormouse, which, arguably, leaves the neatest and most perfect of hole in a nibbled nut (*see* p.67).

Dormice will begin to tackle hazelnuts while they are still green and not yet fully ripe.

When hazelnuts turn a rich brown, they are fully ripe and feasted upon by woodland rodents.

⊝ Bank Voles enlarge the initial hole they have gnawed in the nut with their noses inside the shell. As a result, their lower incisors leave a series of tooth marks on the sloping inner cut; the outside of the shell usually remains relatively unscathed.

⊝ A Wood Mouse will gnaw at the hole it has made in the nut with its nose outside. As a result, the lower incisors are inside the hole as it gnaws and they leave teeth marks on the inner slope; the mouse's upper incisors create scratch marks on the outside of the shell.

⊝ Yellow-necked Mice open hazelnuts in a similar fashion to Wood Mice, and leave similar marks.

ⓒ Inexperienced Grey Squirrels often shatter the hazelnut shell in an attempt to gain entry, leaving a jagged cut margin.

⊙ An experienced Grey Squirrel will usually crack the nut neatly in half, leaving just a small nick at the top of one of the shell halves where it began to prise the nut open with its incisors.

⊛ ⓒ Having created a hole in the nut, a Dormouse will use its incisors to chisel around the hole, in a circular fashion, to enlarge it. The result is an inner edge that is almost entirely smooth and, rather than sloping at an acute angle to the surface of the shell, the angle is usually 90 degrees or more.

FURTHER READING

Beebee, T.J.C., and Griffiths, R.A. (2000). *The New Naturalist (87) Amphibians and Reptiles*. Collins.

Corbet, G.B., and Harris, S. (eds) (1991). *The Handbook of British Mammals*, 3rd edn. Blackwell Science Ltd.

Harrison Matthews, L. (1952). *The New Naturalist (21) Mammals in the British Isles*. Collins.

Harrison Matthews, L. (1982). *The New Naturalist (68) Mammals in the British Isles*. Collins.

MacDonald, D.W., and Barrett, P. (1993). *Field Guide to Mammals of Britain and Europe*. Harper-Collins.

MacDonald, D.W., and Tattersall, F. (2001). *Britain's Mammals: The Challenge for Conservation*. Peoples' Trust for Endangered Species.

Sterry, P.R. (1997). *Complete British Wildlife*. HarperCollins.

USEFUL WEBSITES AND TELEPHONE NUMBERS

Bat Conservation Trust www.bats.org.uk

Biscay Dolphin Research Programme www.biscay-dolphin.org.uk

Bramley Frith Environmental Education Centre www.bramleyfrith.co.uk

British Herpetological Society www.thebhs.org

British Wildlife www.britishwildlife.com

Cetacean Research and Rescue Unit www.crru.org.uk

Company of Whales www.companyofwhales.co.uk, for whale-watching tours

English Nature www.english-nature.org.uk

Herpetological Conservation Trust www.herpconstrust.org.uk

Irish Whale and Dolphin Group www.iwdg.ie

Jersey Zoo www.durrellwildlife.org

Mammal Society www.mammal.org.uk

Mammals Trust UK www.mtuk.org

Marine Conservation Society www.mcsuk.org

National Federation of Badger Groups www.nfbg.org.uk

National Photographers Limited www.naturephotographers.co.uk

National Strandings Hotline 020 7942 5155

Nature Photographers Ltd, www.naturephotographers.co.uk

ORCA (Organisation Cetacea) www.orcaweb.org.uk

People's Trust for Endangered Species www.ptes.org

RSPCA www.rspca.org.uk

Shannon Dolphin and Wildlife Foundation www.shannondolphins.ie

Turtle Code www.euroturtle.org/turtlecode

UK Turtle Database www.strandings.com

Vincent Wildlife Trust www.vwt.org.uk

Whale and Dolphin Conservation Society www.wdcs.org.uk

Wildlife Conservation Research Unit (WILDCRU) www.wildcru.org

Wildlife Trusts www.wildlifetrusts.org